ESSAYS

ON

ENGLISH LITERATURE

E. Scherer

From a photograph by G. Camus

Sampson Low & C? Ltd.   Heliog Lemercier & C? Paris.

ESSAYS

ON

ENGLISH LITERATURE

BY

EDMOND SCHERER

TRANSLATED BY

GEORGE SAINTSBURY

Essay Index Reprint Series

 BOOKS FOR LIBRARIES PRESS
FREEPORT, NEW YORK

First Published 1891
Reprinted 1972

Library of Congress Cataloging in Publication Data

Scherer, Edmond Henri Adolphe, 1815-1889.
    Essays on English literature.

    (Essay index reprint series)
    Reprint of the 1891 ed.
    Selected from the author's Études sur la littérature
contemporaine, and placed in the order in which they
occur in those volumes.
    CONTENTS: George Eliot-"Silas Marner".--John Stuart
Mill.--Shakespeare. [etc.]
    1. English literature--Addresses, essays, lectures.
I. Title.
PR99.S4 1972   820.9   70-39072
ISBN 0-8369-2719-2

PRINTED IN THE UNITED STATES OF AMERICA
BY
NEW WORLD BOOK MANUFACTURING CO., INC.
HALLANDALE, FLORIDA 33009

PREFACE

WHEN I was asked by Mr. Stuart Reid—to whom M. Scherer himself had some years ago indicated the essays in which he would like to be presented to the English public—whether I would undertake the present book, I was pleased with the commission for three reasons, two private and one public. In the first place, translation, though there has been some dispute as to its effect on the reader, is most undoubtedly good for the soul of the translator, especially if he be a critic by profession. Nothing creates, and nothing maintains, that sense of difference as between language and language, which is one of the most important points in criticism, so well as the effort to transfer the effect of one into the other. In the second place it had so happened that M. Scherer, not very long before his own death, had written at some length a criticism of a work of my own, which I think I may describe at once naturally and sufficiently by saying that it did not strike my perhaps prej-

udiced eyes as the happiest instance of his critical
powers. Now I should certainly have preferred
that M: Scherer should praise me. "Every fellow,"
as we know, "likes a hand."   And I do not know
that I can plead guilty to the charge of being
pigeon-livered and lacking gall.   But I had understood, years before, the differences in point of
view, in taste, and so forth, which not only made it
impossible for M. Scherer to sympathize with my
criticism of the literature of his own language,
but made it even possible for him, a most accurate
and conscientious critic, to some extent to misrep-
resent it.   *Tout comprendre* (as we also know) *c'est
tout pardonner*.   And consequently I was very glad
to have an opportunity of raising a little pile of
coals of fire on M. Scherer's defunct head; an
occupation as interesting to the man of humor as
it is creditable in the eyes of the philosopher and
the divine.

But neither of these reasons would have induced
me to undertake a task which, however useful it
may be as an exercise and agreeable as a *revanche*,
is much more troublesome than original composition, if I had not also thought that such well-
nourished and robust criticism as M. Scherer's is

particularly suited for English reading at the present day. This criticism is not faultless, and I have in the introduction thought it the best compliment I could pay to point out its faults as well as to acknowledge its merits. But these merits are such as particularly suit our present condition. There is a real interest, if not always an interest according to knowledge, in literature among us. The way in which almost anybody who will speak as one having authority on literary questions is followed, the audience given to lecturers on the subject, even the somewhat comical institution of Societies, and such like crutches for cripples, are evidences of the fact. But the interest is too often divorced from thorough knowledge —seems, indeed, sometimes as if it would try to occupy the place of knowledge — and the authoritative exponents are not always careful so to qualify themselves as to make up for the shortcomings of their disciples. Dogmatism without reading at the back of it, æsthetic eccentricities without reading at the back of them, are not exactly unknown among the critics of to-day in England. Now for such things, M. Scherer's criticism is a very powerful corrective. When Mr.

Matthew Arnold praised it, I think he was a little
bribed, as we are all apt to be, by the fact that
it was so different in form and style from his own
that the two, to a certain extent, set off and set
out each other. But that it needs no illegitimate
or at least adventitious advantage of this kind the
examples which follow will show; and I hope
that the introductory essay will at least not interfere with the presentment. When M. Scherer was
approached by Mr. Reid on the subject, he said,
I am told, "Why should I pour my little pailful
into the ocean of English literature?" The meta-
phor was modest but not exact. I think it will be
found that the "pail" was rather used in drawing,
from no common depths, samples of that literature
to be analyzed with no common science.

It may be well to say that the essays are here
taken from the volumes of M. Scherer's "Études
sur la Littérature Contemporaine," and are placed
in the order in which they occur in those volumes, references to the original being given in the
contents. That they are sometimes dated, and
sometimes not, is in strict observance of the
author's own practice. His notes are given without any indication; my own, which I have made as

few as possible, are bracketed and signed "*Trans.*"
I should, perhaps, add that I have exercised a
certain discretion in inserting or omitting passages from his authors which M. Scherer gave
sometimes in the original, sometimes translated.
They appear wherever they are necessary for the
comprehension of the text; where they are merely
illustrative or exemplary I have economized space
by omitting them. Sometimes M. Scherer allowed
himself a certain liberty of compression or paraphrase, and in such cases I have generally restored
the original or omitted the citation, inasmuch as
a literal retranslation could serve no purpose for
English readers. But once or twice, where I could
not hit on the exact passage cited, I have so
retranslated. I have only to add that I have stuck
as close to my original as was possible. M. Scherer,
though writing strong, correct, and dignified
French, very seldom "sacrificed to the Graces"—
an aged phrase which has, I think, a new, a special,
and a rather humorous application to critical fine-
writing — and it was therefore deemed to be, not
only unnecessary, but in bad taste to trick or
frounce him in English. Nor have I endeavored
entirely to obliterate the Gallic forms and flavors

of the original. Unless I am mistaken, a translator, though he should never write what is not the language into which he is translating, should, in such a case as this, aim at conveying to those who *ex hypothesi* cannot read the language from which he translates some gust of its own savor.

CONTENTS

INTRODUCTION

THE life of Edmond Scherer, who was born in April of the Waterloo year and died in March 1889, was a pretty long one, and it was, as regards occupations and interests, rather curiously divided into two widely separated parts. During about thirty years — from the age of fifteen to the age of forty-five — almost all M. Scherer's thoughts and studies were directed to theology : first of all in the mood of boyish doubt, then for many years in that of fervent faith, then in that of rationalizing but still confident criticism, and lastly in' an active and rather painful polemic on what may be called offensive-defensive lines in regard to his own complete though gradual abandonment of definite theological belief. After these jars ceased thirty other years were occupied in literary and political journalism, and (after the war of 1870) in active participation in politics. The first period left an ineffaceable impression on the last, but the last period cannot be said to have been in any respect prophesied by the first. And I do not think it superfluous or uncritical to observe that, excellent judge as M. Scherer was of literature, and, in the main, acute and sensible as were his views on politics, criticism,

both literary and political, was to him something
of a *pis aller*. It was only when he was driven
from his theological studies that he resorted to
these others — to speak fancifully, they were a
sort of reverse cloister to which he turned weary
of things divine, as others have sought the real
cloister weary of things worldly. And though he
certainly never indulged in, and has, I think in one
of the very essays here translated, spoken scorn-
fully of, the habit of whining over lost faith, a
kind of nostalgia of his first loves and first studies
always clung to him. We can trace the theologian
within the publicist, the preacher underneath the
historian of so unexpected a hero as "Tyran le
Blanc," and the critic of Fromentin or of Baudelaire.

The remarkable knowledge of English literature
and the English language which the contents of
this book display did not come to M. Scherer by
accident, nor can it be said to have been merely
the result of deliberate and personal fancy. He
was on his father's side descended from a Swiss
family which had been settled in France for about
a century, but his mother was an Englishwoman.
Moreover, when he was about sixteen, and was, as
became a schoolboy of sixteen in 1831, inclined to
Deism, self-destruction, and general despair, he
was sent to England to board with a certain Rev.
Thomas Loader at Monmouth. M. Gréard's [1] per-

[1] Every writer on M. Scherer must acknowledge indebtedness
to M. Octave Gréard's *Edmond Scherer* (Paris, 1890).

haps pardonable ignorance of English ecclesiastical
matters makes his account of this sojourn rather
vague, but it seems most probable (I have no
positive information) that the "Rev." Mr. Loader
belonged to some Dissenting sect. However this
may be, it is certain that he not only kept his
pupil hard at work, but induced in him a fervent
and, notwithstanding the final catastrophe, a solidly
founded piety. When Edmond returned to Paris
he studied law to please his family and philosophy
to please himself. But he was resolved to become
a pastor, and in his twenty-first year he obtained
permission to study theology at Strasburg. He
took his degrees, married early, and was ordained in
April 1840, being then a pronounced and thorough
believer in "l'autorité de la Bible et de la Croix."
He tarried, however, for several years longer in
Strasburg, and he does not seem to have undertaken any directly pastoral work, though he
preached and wrote hymns with much unction.
In 1845, I think, he was appointed to a professor-
ship in the École Libre de Théologie at Geneva and
embarked, still in full confidence, on a course of
teaching designed to establish and defend a sort of
orthodox Protestanism, not admitting any ecclesiastical tradition, but solely founded on the Bible.
I have neither room nor desire to trace at length
what followed, nor does it concern us much. I
need only say that the result was what it was, to
any person having some tincture of theological

study and some knowledge of human nature, certain
to be in the case of a restless and inquiring spirit,
impatient of compromise, rejecting *ab initio* the
idea of the Church as the supernaturally appointed
depository of supernatural truth, and, indeed, insisting generally that the supernatural shall allow
itself to be treated as if it were not supernatural.
By degrees Scherer's theology grew more and more
"free," less and less orthodox.   But the "complete
theological shipwreck," as he has called it himself
in another case, was not reached in less than fifteen
years; and it was not till 1860 or 1861 that he
made, as M. Gréard says, his "profession de foi
hegélienne," in which I should myself see less of
Hegelianism positive than of anti-supernaturalism
negative.   For the rest of his life M. Scherer clung,
indeed, to the Hegelian doctrine of the relativity of
all things, and carried on a truceless war with the
Ding an sich.   But he had nothing in his nature of
the transcendentalism with which Hegel himself
was still penetrated, and which unites him to the
great succession of critical Pantheists.   I am not
here reviewing him from the philosophical standpoint, though it might be interesting to do so.   The
important thing for us is to remember that we
have in the literary critic whom we are to survey a
naufragé, a man who has distinctly taken refuge
in another employment from the employment to
which he had at first given himself.   Unless this is
remembered many points in M. Scherer's attitude,

both to politics and to literature — his two interests
thenceforward — will remain dark to us, while if
it be remembered these things will, I think, become
reasonably plain.

To return to the course of M. Scherer's life, the
last thirty years, or nearly so, give us Paris for
scene, and literature and politics for subjects. The
"Revue des deux Mondes" was not shut to M.
Scherer, but almost the whole of his work in both
departments was given to the "Temps," then under
the direction of M. Nefftzer, who was akin to him
in race and general sentiments. The character of
this paper was very mainly formed and settled by
M. Scherer's collaboration. He was a very active
journalist, though he was not, I believe, obliged
to write in order to live; and it may very likely be
that his literary activity was spurred as well by
some domestic troubles (of which we hear dimly)
as by the necessity of making good the lost ideals.
He had, as it were, at once summed up and said
good-bye to his interest in religious subjects proper
in his "Mélanges d'Histoire Réligieuse." Later he
contributed (I believe in English, which he wrote
excellently) to the "Daily News" on French politics.
This matter, which again would interest me very
much, again does not concern us directly here. He
began as a moderate and rational opponent of the
Empire. Against this he carried on a war at once
vigorous and free from the mere *fronde* to which
men of purely French blood are so liable, and

which not uncommonly ends in such lamentable things as the fate of his friend Prévost Paradol. But in politics, as previously in religion, M. Scherer exhibited certain weaknesses, for preservation from which those who have escaped them should rather thank their good fortune than their merits. During the war he was called upon to play a most difficult part, and played it in a manner which cannot be too much admired, especially when we remember that he was a literary recluse, fifty-five years old, and with very little experience of business. He, who never feared anything, was the last man likely to be a *pantouflard*, and to contemplate the agony of France from the safe seclusion of Geneva or London. But it could scarcely have been anticipated that he would take up and discharge to admiration the hard and hateful duty of administering the affairs of Versailles (his place of residence) during the German occupation. He seems to have done this necessary and odious work with the most admirable good sense and fortitude, standing between his countrymen and the invaders and being proof alike against the unreasonable sensitiveness of the former and the inconsiderate roughness of the latter. Such work is not always rewarded, but it speaks much for M. Scherer's townsmen and the inhabitants of the department of Seine-et-Oise generally that when the peace came they at once selected him to represent them.

He very soon became a life Senator and retained
the position till his death. He was a member of the
Centre — rather of the Centre Gauche than otherwise, but still centrical. And yet at the same time,
though universal suffrage is simply the be-all and
end-all of the Government which he supported, and
of which, in a way, he formed part, he grew more
and more disgusted with it. Almost at the opening of his literary career, in an article here translated, he had — rather hastily, I think — given his
own case away by declaring the logical necessity of
this arrangement. But he had at the same time
manifested a strong objection to its practical
results. The acknowledgment weakened as time
went on and the objections strengthened till but
a very few years ago he published some positive
jeremiads on the subject; yet he always declared
himself a Republican. Here, too, we may observe
some peculiarities which will be of service to us
in our investigation proper — the investigation to
which we must now turn — of M. Scherer's position
as a literary critic. As we noted that his theological studies and his relinquishment of them had
given a color to his work and impressed on it, what
he would himself call "preoccupations"— a tendency
to subordinate form to matter, a distinct inclination to the heresy of *enseignement,* and a certain
tone of bitterness — so it is observable that his
political disillusions reacted on his literary judgments. He could not believe in progress, and he

would not believe in reaction, so that if it were
worth while a parcel of the most curiously contradictory judgments on all subjects in which these
two things are concerned might be produced from
him.

We must now go back a little, and imagine him
a man of forty-five, setting out in the year 1860,
or thereabouts, on his career of literary critic.   He
had for thirty years been an omnivorous student,
though not in every direction.   Readers of him
must have observed (what M. Gréard, I think,
admits) that either his knowledge of or his inclination to classical and mediæval literature was
somewhat lacking in width and depth.   He is said
to have studied scholastic philosophy, but I do
not see many signs of it, and I should imagine
that it must have been exclusively from the theological side.   Even the earlier Renaissance appears
to have had few attractions for him, and it is only
from the seventeenth century onward that he is
really at home with literature.   He knew — a very
rare thing with Frenchmen even now, and much
rarer then — English and German, the literatures
and the languages, very nearly as well as he knew
French, and was even more thoroughly at home
with them.   I have sometimes thought, perhaps
wickedly, that his declaration of love for Racine
and some other specially French authors, though
no doubt quite honest (M. Scherer was nothing if
not honest), had a certain unconscious touch of

affiche in it. But he knew French literature of
the last three centuries thoroughly, and he had a
most pure and correct taste in it, while his familiarity with the other literatures gave him that
power of comparison which Frenchmen have so
frequently lacked. His knowledge was extremely
exact and his acuteness (where he did not go
wrong for reasons presently to be mentioned, in
which case he never came right) was extraordinary. Above all, he had the healthy mania of
always trying to bring his critical conclusions
under some general law: he was never satisfied
with informing the world that he liked this, and
did not like that. He never (at any rate in important cases) concluded from his ignorance to
someone else's knowledge, and, above all, and first
of all, he never made criticism an occasion for
cracking epigrams or unfurling fine writing. It is
impossible to read a criticism of M. Scherer's, even
when one most disagrees with it, without being
informed, exercised, "breathed," as our fathers
would have said. It may not be amusing, it may
be irritating; you may think that you could upset
it beautifully; but if you know enough about the
subject yourself to be able to see knowledge where
it exists you never can pronounce it unimportant.
And there is so much criticism which crackles to
deafening with epigram, which blazes to dazzling
with epithet, which amuses even while irritating,
and which yet is, alack! absolutely unimportant.

The drawbacks of M. Scherer's criticism were
summed up not long ago in a really brilliant *mot*
by a writer of the new French school, for whom,
on the whole, M. Scherer had a much greater admiration than I have myself, and who was in many
respects in sympathy with him. "Il ne jugeait
pas les écrits," says M. Edouard Rod, "avec son
intelligence; il les jugeait avec son caractère." I
am not at all fond of critical fireworks, but this is
not a firework, it is a lamp. Intelligence adapts
itself, character does not; intelligence is charitable, character is apt to be a little Pharisaic;
intelligence has no prejudice, character has much.
It was probably to some extent because he did not
take to literary criticism till so late in life that
M. Scherer manifested the *raideur* with which he
has often been charged; it was no doubt also
partly because of those vicissitudes and experi-
ences of soul which have been briefly noticed.
But there must have been in it much of personal
idiosyncrasy. We hear early of the "effet pénible
et angoissant que font sur cet aimable Scherer-les
nouvelles connaissances," and the amiable lady
who wrote this had cause to know it. She had
gone to meet him when he came on a preaching
errand and found him "un jeune homme d'un
abord glacial" who got into the carriage "sans
répondre à mon accueil" (this, we may trust, was
not set down to the *tenue britannique* with which
he was also credited). Many years afterwards

most friendly critics have expressed their regret
that Scherer did not mix more with younger men
of letters.   One of the few unpublished personal
stories I have ever heard of him was to the effect
that a very few years ago, when he was in a London drawing-room, a fellow guest came up to the
host and said, "Who is that Scotch clergyman?"
All his life, except to a few very intimate friends,
he seems to have been more imposing than attractive, and the same may be said of his criticism.
M. Rod, who is, as I have said, a witness above
suspicion, records and deplores the small practical
effect which this criticism had, and the kind of
resentment with which it was received.   One very
amiable and accomplished French man of letters
spoke of his *fiel Protestant*.   I remember a legend
set afloat by someone of the opposite school that
a practical joker once went round to the book-
sellers saying that he was a collector of *second* editions, and wished for copies of M. Scherer's
"Études" in that state, which nobody could give
him.   It is certain that these "Études," though
containing by far the most valuable corpus of
criticism which France has produced since Sainte-
Beuve's "Causeries," and superior, if bulk, range,
and value be taken together, to anything to be
found in English literature for many years past,
have never been widely popular.   Probably the
sale of the whole nine volumes has not equalled
that of a single one of some of the collections of

clever froth which, in M. Scherer's own latter
days and since, have caught the taste of Frenchmen and of those Englishmen who think that to
admire the latest French thing is to be *dans le
mouvement*, and not to admire that thing is to be
out of it.

As our chief business is with M. Scherer's essays
in English literature, it may be well to go through
the essays here translated before resuming their
author's critical position in general. Some of them
are already well known in England by the eulogies
of Mr. Matthew Arnold; all deserve, I think, to
be very well known indeed. Their excellence
increases as they go on both in writing and in
matter. But they are all good, and what may be
especially praised in them is the admirable critical
summaries — much resembling those of Jeffrey, a
critic who had many points of contact with M.
Scherer — of different periods of English literature.

The apparent disproportion of the space given to
George Eliot is, now that the essays are collected,
likely to strike most people, especially since the
somewhat extravagant estimate of the author of
"Adam Bede" which was common some years ago
among "thoughtful" Englishmen and foreigners
has subsided, as, indeed, is usual in such cases, to
a point perhaps almost as far below the just level
as the excess was above it. It is the very last
secret of criticism, the degree which few critics
reach, to be as independent of the charms of

novelty as of those of antiquity, and to look at
things new and things old from the combined
standpoint which things old and new together give.
But it must always be counted to M. Scherer that
in the later essays — that on "Deronda" and the
final one on the "Biography" — he retracted not
a little, or, to speak more justly, readjusted to
sounder standards, a good deal of the rather effu-
sive and uncritical laudation of the paper which
opens this volume.   It was, indeed, impossible
that he should not somewhat overvalue a writer
whose mental history was in so many respects
identical with his own, and whose final standpoint
(though he has indicated the interval very subtly
and accurately in the last essay) was so near
his.   The weak point in both, (and this, naturally
enough, he has *not* indicated), was an insufficient
devotion to the great god Nonsense, whether in his
Avatar of Frivolity or in his Avatar of Passion.
They could neither of them conjugate the verb
desipere; the delights of hearing the chimes at
midnight in the full metaphorical sense were shut off
from them; they had no fine madness.   They were
both (it is needless to say it in George Eliot's
case to an English audience, but it may be con-
fidently affirmed of M. Scherer also) susceptible
enough to certain kinds of wit and to certain kinds
of humor; while one of them, as we know, could
create both humor and wit of those kinds.   But
M. Scherer has wonderingly commented on the

unlucid interval of this susceptibility in which George Eliot wrote "Daniel Deronda," and he has shown a similar eclipse in his own case in the blind ferocity with which he attacked Baudelaire. Yet this very community of defects, as of qualities, constitutes, of course, a security for mutual understanding, and it is nearly impossible that any better criticism of George Eliot — from the sympathetic side, yet not idolatrous — shall be written than that contained in this volume. There is much to add, no doubt, from the unfavorable side, but that can be easily done.

The second essay — that on Mill — is particularly interesting, because it was written at a time and from a point of view which are not recoverable except by a *tour de force* of critical translation of one's self into other circumstances. There was no reason, political, religious, or, to a certain extent, philosophical (for M. Scherer's Hegelianism always had a touch of Scoto-French experience-doctrine in it), why author and critic should not be in touch with each other. But, little of a Mill-ite as I am myself, I should say that M. Scherer is, if anything, rather less than more just to Mill. It would be curious if, as I half think, this falling short of justice is due to the fact that Mill had never gone through M. Scherer's own soul-history, while George Eliot had. But it must also be remembered that at this time the future Senator was only beginning his purely political studies. He came much nearer afterwards to some views of Mill's which he here seems but half to relish.

Of the two Shakespeare essays the first is beyond all question the weaker, though they must have been written very much at the same time, considerable as is the gap which it pleased M. Scherer to set between them in the order of republication. It is fair, however, to observe that it is in some sense a preliminary dissertation, a sort of getting over of the facts and history of the subject before tackling the strictly critical work. The second, the "peg" of which is the Shakespearophobia of the excellent Herr Rümelin, is one of the best examples of M. Scherer's critical grasp. Its survey of the successive attitudes of German Shakespeare-criticism may be vulnerable in parts — it is the way of these surveys to be so and therefore, tempting as they are, both for display of skill and for the pleasure there is in doing them, some critics are rather shy of the indulgence. But this is one of the best of the kind — full of knowledge easily borne and well digested, and written with a *maestria* which never becomes ostentation or virtuosity. In ends, indeed, with a sort of false note, or, rather, an equivocal use of terms. To make Goethe, while inferior to Shakespeare on the whole, superior to him in universality may seem at first sight, in the literal sense, preposterous. But a moment's thought will show that M. Scherer was using "universal" in a special sense, was referring, not to nature, but to the encyclopædia. In the main no man has ever been sounder on Shakespeare than he, and that is the *articulus stantis aut cadentis criticismi.*

The sixth volume of the "Études" (we have spoken of the essay on "Daniel Deronda," which, though much later in date than those of which we are going to speak, appeared in volume form earlier) is peculiarly rich in papers on English subjects. Here is the remarkable paper, written many years before, on M. Taine's "History"; here that just discussed on "Shakespeare and Criticism"; here the famous "Milton," famous not merely by Mr. Arnold's praise of it, but, with the possible exception of that on Wordsworth, as the chief example of M. Scherer's power in our own subjects; here the less valuable but interesting paper on "Sterne." With the subject of this last it might at first seem as if M. Scherer could have been in but imperfect sympathy; and I am not prepared to deny that a desire to give a helping hand to a young and very promising man of letters — a member of the group of Swiss-French Protestant men of letters, of which Vinet, M. Scherer himself, the Monods, and others were pillars — may have had something to do with the selection of it. But Sterne, who loved the French nation, has always had an attraction for them, the causes of which it would not be difficult to work out, and a passage on humor here, though oddly prefaced, is one

of the best things in this volume. The other
two essays are of the very first quality. It can
scarcely be said that M. Scherer has not done
justice to M. Taine; but nowhere have the two
great faults of a book which, brilliant as it is, is
almost more faulty than brilliant — its false air
of method and its *tapage* — been more severely
handled. Indeed, M. Scherer, who, whatever the
faults of his own criticism, rarely saw things quite
out of focus or rendered them quite out of drawing,
could not but be scandalized at the prevalence of
these two eccentricities in M. Taine's work. As
for the "Milton" it is difficult to admire it too
much. Inevitably, M. Scherer is too severe on
Milton's theological views and assumes divers
things which he would have been hard put to
prove against an active and well-armed antagonist.
Inevitably, likewise, he is too lenient to Milton's
character, which seems to have had a great many
points of contact with his own. As a criticism "of
art" on "Paradise Lost" (it touches other matters
only incidentally) it is nearly impeccable. The
ineradicable differences of national taste may come
in a little, and may make us think that, for instance, the poetic magnificence of the Sin and
Death passage should have saved it from M.
Scherer's condemnation. But these are details,
and of the merest. As a whole, I should include
the essay in any collection of the best dozen or
sixteen critical exercises of the last half-century

in Europe. Enthusiasm, old and new (for it is impossible in reading it to forget the time when M. Scherer himself saw, as they say, eye to eye with Milton in religious matters), has aroused in the critic a more glowing style than his usual sober medium, and though once or twice this is a little too "purple," the best examples of it are admirable.

The seventh volume also is pretty rich in our material. The appearance of Lord Beaconsfield's "Endymion," the death of Mr. Carlyle, and the publication of Mr. Matthew Arnold's "Selections from Wordsworth" gave M. Scherer within a very few months opportunities of speaking on English literature, and he took them to his and our very great advantage. The paper on Wordsworth is the longest of his English, and one of the longest of all his essays, and I do not know that he has anywhere examined a subject more thoroughly or with greater gusto. Here, again, the attraction of personal sympathy is manifest. Wordsworth, like Milton, was both in literary and in moral character thoroughly congenial to M. Scherer. He might from his later standpoint smile at the religious views of both as childish, but he had gone through them, and in Wordsworth's case there was, with all his orthodoxy, also a sort of vague undogmatic theosophy which appealed directly to the critic. Wordsworth's seriousness, his austerity, his perpetual regard to conduct, were sure to conciliate M. Scherer; and though

the latter as a Frenchman could not but deplore
the poet's lack of sense of the ridiculous, he was
probably more than consoled by his lack of frivolity and by his total freedom from disorderly passion. Indeed, if M. Scherer had been a poet (he
had in his youth, like most critics, considerable
poetical velleities), and if instead of a French
Protestant he had been an Anglican, I really do
not know that it would have taken much more to
make him a Wordsworth. But as it was there
could be none of the jealousy which often arises
between likes, and none of the want of sympathy
which is commoner still between unlikes. Everything made for righteousness and for unction combined in the criticism, and the combination duly
appears in it. It is interesting also for its *obiter
dicta* on Mr. Arnold, and on the poetic succession
in England during this century — another of M.
Scherer's admirable surveys. This is, perhaps, not
the place to say much on the sympathy between
Mr. Arnold and M. Scherer, and it must be confessed that, as we should expect, the French critic
is not quite sound upon Keats. It is, on the whole,
rather wonderful that he does him as much justice
as he actually does. Yet here also we find more
than one of those notes of purely personal or
national dissonance which no transcendence of
critical talent can ever wholly reconcile, which perhaps none can ever even thoroughly comprehend.
M. Scherer says that Lamartine is "plus tragique,

plus sublime, plus grand " than Wordsworth, and
he produces these two lines as an example : —

> Adore ici le Dieu qu'adorait Pythagore,
> Prête avec lui l'oreille aux célestes concerts.

I have myself been upbraided with setting French
poetry too high; I have thoroughly subdued my
" German paste "; I honestly think that the reading of millions of lines of French verse has attuned
my ear to any possible cadence of it from the
Chanson de Roland to *Parallèlement*. But if there
is anything in this distich comparable to such
Wordsworthian passages as M. Scherer quotes, if
it is not a mere school exercise beside the great ode
or the *Tintern Abbey*, I consent to be written down
as other than a two-legged creature. Here, however, we come once more to the *mysterium*, the
" This is this to me and that to thee " beyond
which no criticism c.n get.

In the next essay, the necrology on Carlyle, we
find M. Scherer in part, though by no means
wholly, in his worse vein as a critic, in a vein not
otherwise obvious to the reader of this volume
merely, and less disastrous even here than in
regard to some French authors, but still characteristic and not favorably characteristic. Not only
the date and circumstance of the essay, but probably also a real growth of critical faculty kept him
from bluntly dismissing Carlyle, as he had done
twenty years before, with the words " insupport-

able jargon," and there are excellent things in the
paper, short as it is. But we feel at once that
there is a thorough antagonism between author and
critic, and that the critic has not taken too much
pains to neutralize it. If there was one thing
which M. Scherer hated more than anything else it
was the bizarre. I am afraid that I excited his indignation by describing him in the book which
he criticised so unfavorably as "an untrustworthy
judge of what is not commonplace," and I can see
now that the words are susceptible of a disobliging
interpretation which I had not myself attached to
them. I did not mean by them that M. Scherer
liked the commonplace, much less that he was
commonplace himself; but that anything distinctly
out of the commonplace, anything bizarre, *outré*,
fantastic, extravagant, *baroque*, and so forth, excited in him a sort of prejudice and mistrust which
deprived him for the time of his better critical
faculty. He could pardon a good deal of affectation if it was unassuming and urbane; he could
even in this same essay make that astonishing
selection of Mr. Arnold as "not affected," as "having the courage to remain simple and sincere."
But he simply hated ostentatious paradox, neolo-
gism, oddity of style and thought — in fact, almost
everything that was characteristic of the form, and
much that was characteristic of the matter of Carlyle. This dislike had shown itself twenty years
earlier in the unadvised speaking with the lips of

his first essay on George Eliot; it showed itself
four years later in his last on her. It gathers
itself up here a little softened, as I have said, in
form by the occasion, but still evident in fact.

One is surprised, on the contrary, by the tolerance which M. Scherer shows to a very different
writer in the article on "Endymion." We might
have expected that Lord Beaconsfield's literature
and his politics alike would be Anathema Maran-
atha to M. Scherer, and that Mr. Gladstone would
in his political, if not in his literary, capacity be a
man after M. Scherer's own heart. Can it be that
the rigid orthodoxy of the Liberal and the pre-
sumed freethinking of the Tory had anything to
do with the critic's judgment? Perhaps it was the
spectacle, always dear to French eyes, of a mere
man of letters, a mere gentleman of the press, forc-
ing himself, with a minimum of assistance from
birth, education, wealth, or friendship, to the very
topmost height, which allured him. I know not:
but the fact remains that his judgment on Mr.
Gladstone is anything but enthusiastic, and on
Lord Beaconsfield is positively lenient. That he
does not speak very highly of "Endymion" itself
is not surprising. I know very enthusiastic admirers of Lord Beaconsfield who are equally unkind
to it.

And so we come to the last essay of all, that on
Mr. Cross's life of George Eliot, which has been
already discussed, and of which we need say no

more than that it is not merely an excellent appre-
ciation and summary of the subject, but full of
side lights on the author himself. It exhibits in
particular that kind of Nihilism — of Nihilism not
exasperated or aggressive, but blank, hopeless, and
with even a point of bitterness piercing through
the even surface of its would-be Stoicism — which
distinguished M. Scherer's later years and later
writings. Even George Eliot is a little too positive, a little too credulous, for him, and he twitches
that nymph's last garment of childish faith off
with a rather icy gravity and apparently without
the slightest pleasure.

Here, however, we return to a subject which, if
not exactly taboo, and, indeed, to some extent
necessary to be touched upon, is not our main concern. It will be better to finish with a general
summary of the main characteristics of M. Scherer's
literary criticism. They are well and favorably,
though not quite exhaustively, illustrated in these
essays on English writers, in which his French
friends sometimes thought that he showed an undue
partiality — a kind of xenomania. In the much
larger body of his work on French and other subjects, we shall find nothing to alter, though something to supplement and fill out, the estimate
which may be formed from these only. In contra-
distinction to those of his friend and eulogist, Mr.
Arnold, his estimates never neglected the historic
element, and I cannot but think that this gave him

a decided advantage.   We all know, of course, what Mr. Arnold meant by his decryings of the historic estimate; and we know also that they were compatible in his own case with much fine criticism and more delightful writing.   They were also exceedingly convenient as justifying the somewhat eclectic character of Mr. Arnold's critical philosophy, as enabling him to skip periods, authors, literatures, that he did not care about, and as fortifying him in those secure and extremely one-sided generalizations which he executed with such an incomparable mixture of audacity and grace.   To put the thing bluntly and briefly, too many parts of Mr. Arnold's stately pleasure domes of æsthetic elegance would go down in half an hour's battering from the historic estimate, and he showed wisdom in ruling that estimate out.   M. Scherer, on the other hand, did not want to build stately pleasure domes; he never wanted, at least knowingly, to do anything but comprehend; and he saw the immense advantage in comprehension which the historical approach gives.   Never abusing, never, indeed, accepting without grave modifications the product-of-the-circumstances theory, he always attended to circumstances, to origins, to the filiation of work and of talent in the great literary pedigree.

He had, on the other hand, or fancied that he had, a rather singular repugnance to another great engine of criticism, the comparative method.   I say "fancied that he had," for, as a matter of fact, he sometimes uses it; but he seems to me to have confused two different kinds of comparison — the one a kind as bastard and as mischievous as possible, the other the secret of all really lasting and satisfactory critical judgment. The comparison which says, " What! *you* like *that?* *I* like *this,*" and justifies its dislike of That because it does not possess the characteristics of This, is as idle, as uncritical, as mischievous, as M. Scherer or anyone else pleases. But the comparison which takes This and That, puts them together, notes what This has and That lacks, observes how This excels That in one way, and That excels This in the other, appears to me to be, on the contrary, the one method by which you can get at really luminous results. These results will be not, as the private impressions even of culture are often, mere will-o'-the-wisps, or, as *a priori* and positive theories are, lights too remote and casting too long shadows to be safely used, but honest hand-lanterns which will lead you about the labyrinth of the world's literature with as few chances as possible of losing your way. I think that M. Scherer did use these lanterns, though he affected to despise them; and I think that the careful reader of the following pages will find traces of the use pretty frequently.

For the rest, that reader will certainly find here many other things which belong to good — to the best — criticism. It was out of M. Scherer's way in the present essays to indulge in many of those interesting discussions on the more abstract and general points which he has handled elsewhere, as, for instance, in his capital discussion of the interest and value of translations of poetry. Excellent English scholar as he was, he had too keen a sense of the fitness of things to descend into verbal criticism, of which he was a great master, as witness another capital essay of his on "La Déformation de la Langue Française," an essay which has been sometimes echoed as to English by those who do not or will not see that in this respect the genius of the two tongues is diametrically opposed. He could not, of course, in this bare dozen of essays show anything like the range of literary knowledge and literary interest displayed in the entire collection of probably a dozen dozen, which has still to be reinforced with his volumes on Diderot, on Grimm, and others. But if he misses some opportunities he avoids some snares. I have spoken of his greatest critical blunder, the unsparing damnation of Baudelaire, not merely because of his faults, which are great, but in spite of his merits, which are greater. He was not likely, on any English writer, to fall into the queer wrongheadedness of his attack on Molière. If his attitude towards Carlyle shows something of the same mistake as his attitude towards Diderot, the half-score pages which he has devoted to the one did not admit anything like the development of the error which was possible in the volume given to the other.

And here, as in all his work, the reader will find
certain qualities which are more rare than they
ought to be, or would seem at first sight likely to
be, among critics, that is to say, among persons who
deliberately set themselves to work to judge the
writings of others, and who publish their judgments.
The first and foremost of these qualities is an ample
preparation of study. The "facetious and rejoicing
ignorance," as another great critic has said, which
takes for granted, first, that in this business an
ounce of mother-wit is worth more than a pound of
clergy, and, secondly, that so much more than an
ounce of mother-wit has fallen to its own lot that
it could dispense with clergy altogether, was not in
M. Scherer's way; indeed, he hated few things so
much. In the second place, without giving himself any airs of *sacerdoce*, he knew very well, and
always acted on the principle, that to make an
avowedly critical study a mere stalking horse for
shooting random shots of pleasantry, a mere em-
broidery frame for elaborating patches of fine
writing, is a gross offence against art and a gross
dereliction of literary duty. If he was less proof
against prejudices of various kinds, he at least
never consciously and deliberately indulged them;
and if his favorite principle, that a work of art
must have a philosophy, be wrong in itself, and
goes perilously near to the teaching heresy, he at
least never admitted this latter, and did not intend
that his own maxim should involve it. He has

been charged with lack of charm, and you certainly do not read him merely for the sake of his style; but you have the compensatory advantage that he himself never writes merely for the sake of it. "Il avait," says M. Gréard, "des exaltations de satisfaction intellectuelle quand il arrivait à se prouver l'insuffisance des explications communes." This is not an exceedingly cheerful business, nor do I by any means contend that it is the whole duty of critical man. But it is an elementary part of that duty, and M. Scherer himself, Nihilist as he sometimes seems to be, had in literature too many and too ardent likes and dislikes to make his pursuance of it a mere process of dull destruction. The perfect critic, if he ever exists, will possess in about equal parts the intimate grasp, the universal range, the everlasting tolerance of Sainte-Beuve, the literary grace and girlish charm of Mr. Arnold, the intuition of Hazlitt, the sympathy of Lamb, and, lastly, a certain quality, or set of qualities, which confer solid and manly augmentative power, not hesitating if necessary at dissolving analysis. But this last quality will be of as much importance to him as any of the others, and in surveying the list of his intellectual ancestors he will see few if any better representatives of it than Edmond Scherer.

ESSAYS ON ENGLISH LITERATURE

I

GEORGE ELIOT[1]

THERE are perhaps not a few of my readers who
have never heard the name of George Eliot: and
yet George Eliot is the first novelist of England.
Her works are regarded there as so many literary
events, and her talent, far from exhausting itself,
seems to show greater variety and greater vigor in
each new production.

There is a curious contrast between the general
manliness of English manners and the strain of
affectation which may often be remarked in them.
We are equally struck, as we survey our neighbors,
by the strong individuality of some of them and by
the pretentious childishness of others. Every kind
of affectation is to be found on the other side of
the Channel — the soldier's and the sportsman's,
that of the dandy and that of the man who is

---

[1] *Silas Marner, the Weaver of Raveloe.* [See introduction on
this essay. It is important, for numerous allusions in it, to
remember that it was written in 1861. — *Trans.*]

"used up," the affectation of fashion and the affectation of Liberty Hall. One man has climbed every peak in the Alps, another has hunted in the Sahara. Here you meet girls who have travelled in India by themselves, and they will be the lionesses of the season till Major So-and-So comes to exhibit the rifle with which he "dropped" so many Neapolitans in the Sicilian campaign. This kind of thing has slipped even into religion. Dissent is not becoming; but Puseyism is as *comme-il-faut* as possible. I know ladies who, having lived at Rome, have embraced Catholicism, and who make a display of their confessor and their oratory: I know others who pique themselves on being freethinkers, and stand up for "Essays and Reviews."

It will easily be understood that the region of the arts has not escaped this invasion of deliberate singularity. It was an English sculptor who conceived the idea of tinting his statues, and it was England that saw the birth of præ-Raphaelitism, that grotesque compound of Byzantine naïveté and poetry after the fashion of M. Courbet. As for English literature, it is with that as with a handsome woman who tries to hide the traces of age by the artifices of the toilet. Writers set before themselves only one aim; their business is to revive jaded senses. Style, arrangement, everything, testifies to the desire of striking heavy blows. The reader's mind must be kept in a perpetual state of expectation and surprise. Hence comes the study

of singularity, the study which engenders pretentiousness, the pretentiousness which leads to charlatanism. Eccentricity has become a means of
attracting customers, and even the most eloquent,
even the profoundest, are not free from calculation.
There is deliberation, scheme, set purpose, in the
cunningly balanced antitheses of Macaulay, in the
artistic paradoxes of Ruskin, in the intolerable
jargon of Carlyle; but there is most of all in the
English novel.

Consequently English novelists, despite their
great talent, make me constantly think of Cali-
fornian miners in quest of some productive vein.
They are not obedient to a vocation. They are
prospecting for mannerism and for success. All
roads which lead to that end are good. We have
the fashionable novel and the theological novel, the
didactic novel and the "fast" novel, the imitation
of Sterne and the imitation of Smollett, Dickens's
reforming mania and Kingsley's heroic clergyman.
There is indeed no lack of verve in this literature,
nor could we wish for less fertility and variety of
resource. What we could wish for is merely a little
less study of effect, a little more simplicity and
sanity.

I suspect that the weariness produced by so
many attempts at refining counted for much in the
success of the "Scenes of Clerical Life," George
Eliot's first work, and in that of "Adam Bede,"
which is still her masterpiece. Readers passed

from the heated atmosphere of an opera-house to
the freshness of a country morning, and experienced in the presence of this inspiration, at once
deep and simple, an unaccustomed kind of pleasure.
It was felt that the author had told her tale after
the manner of the old bards, without listening to
her own voice, without self-consciousness, and as it
were yielding to the Muse who presides over immortal creations. What a joy for those who possessed taste and soul to find, at last, an artist who
was thoroughly sincere! What a beneficent impression was experienced at the sight of this virgin
genius, in the presence of this masterly execution,
which knew nothing of the tricks of the studio,
nothing of the devices of behind the scenes!

It must be owned, too, that mere curiosity helped
the success of these works; for it was soon seen
that the name they bore was a pseudónym. It was
asked what was the writer's sex. Not a few of the
authors in vogue had the honor of having attributed
to them a book which certainly none of them was
capable of writing. There were guesses and coun-
ter-guesses in the columns of the newspapers. One
critic — a French critic, it is true — had just with
elaborate induction proved that the author of
"Adam Bede" must be a man, and what is more
an English clergyman, when the veil was rent.
The enchanter was an enchantress — Miss Evans
by name. But there was something that doubled
the mystery at the very moment when it seemed

to vanish. Miss Evans was by no means utterly unknown in the literary world. She had worked on a very serious periodical, the "Westminster Review." She had written theological articles in it. A translation of Strauss's celebrated work on the Life of Jesus was hers. What a mixture of contradictions and surprises! It was not enough to have to acknowledge a woman as the first novelist of England; more than that, this woman combined faculties which had never been associated in the memory of man. She was at once a savant and a poet. There was in her the critic who analyzes and the artist who creates. Nay, the pen which had interpreted Strauss — the most pitiless adversary of Christian tradition that the world has produced — this very pen had just drawn the charming portrait of Dinah, and had put on the lips of this young Methodist girl the inspired discourse at Hayslope and the touching prayer in the prison.

It is impossible to read "Adam Bede" without thinking of "Jane Eyre," and yet there are no points of likeness between these two works save the mystery in which they were at first wrapped, and the sex of the authors to whom we owe them. Miss Brontë's novel has more dash, more vigor, more eloquence; and I am not sure whether there is anything to be found in Miss Evans's work equal to Jane Eyre's flight when, after leaving Rochester's house, she wanders at random, the victim of a conflict of feelings dominated by the inexorable

authority of duty.   But here Miss Brontë's superiority ceases.   She soon betrays her want of experience.   She flies to melodramatic devices; her creations have more strength than truth; and, in short,
what remains of her book after a second reading is
no great thing.   It is quite otherwise with Miss
Evans; in her novels everything is simple, mature,
finished, and it is scarcely possible to re-read them
without discovering fresh beauties.

Besides, after "Jane Eyre" Charlotte Brontë
merely repeated herself; while her rival has as yet
given no sign of exhaustion.   I have mentioned
the surprises which George Eliot sprang on the
public, but the public had not yet come to the end
of them.   After recovering from the excitement
caused by so great a merit and so great a success,
readers (who are soon tired of admiration) said to
themselves that it was their turn.   "Let us wait
and see," said they, "what her next work will be
like."   The next work was not long delayed.
"The Mill on the Floss" appeared a year after
"Adam Bede," and the most fastidious criticism
was obliged to acknowledge that, if there was a
little less finish in the new-comer, the power and
talent which it showed were not less.   Yet another
year — less than a year — has passed away, and
"Silas Marner" comes to show in its turn that the
author, among the other secrets of genius, possesses
that of fecundity.

"Silas Marner" is a story of village life.   The

hero is a poor weaver, pious of heart and ingenious of mind. But in his inner being an unjust sentence has destroyed faith in the order of Providence. He gives himself up thenceforth to the material cares of life, becomes a miser, heaps up his gains, and sets his affections on the contemplation of his hoard. The hoard is stolen, and Silas falls into a kind of brute despair, from which he is rescued by the interest with which a little girl inspires him. Her mother has died of want at his door, and he has been the first to be called to assist her. He takes charge of the child, nurses her, brings her up, and is himself born again to happiness in thus once more finding some good to do and some one to love. As great as the gloom of the solitary days, when the weaver drudged for the sake of hoarding, is the brightness of the old man's last years in the company of his adopted daughter. It is a second youth, a new life, the solution of all the painful problems which had formerly weighed this human soul down into the dust.

Every novel is a mixture of three elements — character, dialogue, and action. The action in a work of fiction is a factor which is at once capital and subordinate. On the one hand, there is no interest in a story where the plot is weak; on the other, we have seen memorable examples in which, though the action may have been conducted with consummate skill, the story has yet not taken rank as literature. It may amuse, it may be popular, and yet at the end of a year or two it will be nothing but a memory.

The real stuff of the novel lies in the characters; but at the same time the character-drawing is effected by the dialogue. A great change in this respect has passed over the literary kind of which we speak. Formerly the novelist contented himself with analysis; he was privileged to read the souls of his personages, and it was his business to tell us what he found there. Nowadays (Walter Scott was the chief author of this innovation), it is the business of each personage to express his own feelings, and the dialogue by means of which the personages make themselves known has become the capital part, and in some sort the whole, of the novel. The modern novel is a drama; description holds the place of scenery, narrative gives a clue to the *mise-en-scène;* but it is the talk which constitutes the main substance and texture of the work.

Now George Eliot's talent excellently suits the requirements of the style which we have just described. In her books the action is always ingeniously simple, equidistant from the commonplaces of fiction and from the affectation of romantic invention. Still it is in character-drawing that our author's superiority is especially manifest. Here we find the precision of outline, the truth of color, the infinite variety, the sustained individuality, the moral unity which mark alike the works of Nature and those of genius. What

wonderful creations are Dinah and Hetty, Maggie
and Silas, old Lisbeth and the Dodson family!
Every one of George Eliot's personages, however subordinate the part, however passing the appearance,
has a special physiognomy and characteristic style of
speaking. But this brings us back to the dialogue.

I have said that in the novels of our day it is the
business of the dialogue to set forth the characters,
so that two different gifts — the talent for creating a
character, and that of making it speak — are now
indispensable the one to the other. And yet these
two talents are quite distinct. It is possible to outline a character which is both original and true
without succeeding in putting in its mouth interesting and natural language. On the other hand, dialogue in itself either pointed and ingenious, or lofty
and profound, may lack that secret unity which,
properly speaking, constitutes character. The writings of Dickens exemplify what I mean. That
clever novelist excels at modelling a laughable or a
repulsive physiognomy, at fixing the mask on a lay
figure costumed with equal oddity, and then at
lending to the hero who is thus built up some grotesque catchword, some humorous repartee which,
thrown in among scenes of great variety, produces
a sort of debased comedy. The beings thus created
are striking; you know them when you see them;
but they are not alive; they have not the consistency of an individuality which remains faithful to
itself, while ceaselessly revealed under new aspects.

It is quite otherwise with George Eliot's books.
Here the personages are not only infinitely various,
they are not only each provided with a language
proper to itself, but this language is always at once
alike and different, suitable to the character it expresses, and animated by the unexpectedness which
springs from the particular situation.   More than
this, the writer has sown broadcast all over her
work the salt of the best kind of pleasantry.   Not
one of her rustics, of her artisans, of her lower
middle-class folk — not an old maid or a child in
her pages — but has a special naïve originality, a
special humor, jovial or sly, and a special and delightful cast of drollery.   I do not think that any
novelist has strewed over his work wit so abundant
or so varied, so fruitful in surprises, so full of sallies.
Mrs. Poyser in " Adam Bede," is in this respect one
of the most extraordinary creations of prose fiction.
The reader must imagine a good-tempered farmer's
wife, speaking much at every occasion and to every
comer, who says nothing without seasoning the
speech with some piquant phrase, who is ready
with a repartee for every one, whose inexhaustible
verve is independent of catchwords, whose good
sayings have all the raciness and the strongly
marked character of popular proverbs.   Mrs. Poyser is of the right lineage of Sancho Panza.

For the rest, is it a paradox to say that dialogue
and character, invention and description, the wit
that amuses and the imagination that charms, all

these elements of the novel, all these gifts of genius, are but secondary ? and that, if work which is to last cannot do without them, it is still not they that make the work immortal? I leave out of count the circulating library subscriber, for he is incapable of tasting George Eliot; I speak of the reader who reads a second time, who reflects upon and who relishes what he reads. What he consciously or unconsciously seeks in a novel, what attracts or repels him in it, is, if we follow it home, the philosophy which is expressed there. It is philosophy with which a novel can least dispense. If there is no philosophy, there is no meaning; and if there is no meaning, what have we to do with it ? Man is so made that he seeks for himself everywhere. In nature he hunts a mystery which is merely his own, in history he questions his own destiny. Art, in order to interest him, must talk of himself. Novels themselves are nothing to us if they are not an interpretation of the world and of life. Now George Eliot's work is full of the lessons which the work of the great artist always contains. The author, it is true, has drawn hardly anything but ordinary life ; her favorite heroes are children, artisans, laborers — her favorite subjects the absurdities of middle-class life, the prejudices of small towns, or the superstitions of the country. But underneath these externally prosaic existences the writer makes us behold the eternal tragedy of the human heart. We meet once more the failures of will, the calculations of egotism, pride, coquetry, hatred, love — all our passions and all our foibles, all our littlenesses and all our errors. Nor is this all: something rises from these creations; there emanates from them, as it were, a perfume of wisdom; there drops from them, as it were, a lesson of experience. George Eliot looks at men's faults with so much sympathy, mixed with so much elevation; the condemnation she passes on evil is tempered with so much toleration and intelligence; the smile on her face is so near tears; she is so clear-eyed and so resigned; she has our weaknesses so well by heart; she has suffered so much and lived so much — that it is impossible to read her pages without feeling ourselves won by this lofty charity. We are at once moved and calmed; it seems that she has enlarged our ideas of the world and of God. We feel as we shut the book that we are more at peace with ourselves, calmer in face of the problems of destiny.

II[1]

JOHN STUART MILL

M. Dupont White is among the small number of writers who still treat politics as a science, and we owe to him both original and translated work on this science. He has courageously grappled in his books with the questions which touched the destinies of France nearest — that is to say, the relations between the individual and the State, between liberty and centralization. He has brought to the settlement of these questions views which are his own, and which are supported by the study of facts and by ingenious reasoning. His whole work is instructive, paradoxical, stimulative of contradiction. Nor has M. Dupont White deserved less well of the French public in making known to it the political writings of one of the most eminent thinkers of contemporary England, Mr. John Stuart Mill. Mr. Mill's book on "Representative Government" is an important work on a great subject: the principles, namely, and the conditions of government in democratic States. It is on this book that I wish to discourse to my readers to-day; but

[1] *Representative Government.* By J. Stuart Mill. Translated and preceded by an introduction by Dupont White. 1862.

it will not be useless to begin by pointing out what
the author's other works are, what are their distinguishing tendencies, and what place they hold in
the intellectual movement of our time.

Mr. Mill's mind and his views have been developed under the action of several successive influences. Our author began with Bentham; he passed
later under the sway of Auguste Comte, nor did he
finally escape the fascinations of the French Socialist
systems. His father (well known by his "History
of British India" and by divers philosophical and
political works) was one of Bentham's most devoted disciples. Our author was brought up in the
lap of the Utilitarian school, and he began his career
as a publicist under the eyes of its founder. But
the utilitarian doctrines have both their sources
and their issues in a definite group of ideas; and
these ideas are exactly those which found their expression in Positive philosophy. When he passed
from the school of Bentham to that of Comte, Mr.
Mill did not change his direction. He merely followed the course of utilitarian ideas to the point
where they debouch and lose themselves in a
vaster system. The Positive philosophy, if I am
not mistaken, has done little more than mark the
tendency of all modern science to become "positive"
— that is to say, to exclude everything which lies
outside of experience. Comte gave formal expression to the eagerness of our time to free itself from
metaphysical ideas. He assigned to this movement

its place in the evolution of the human mind. This
is all he did, but this is itself a service rendered to
thought. To connect facts, to unite ideas, to lay
down a law is to make science advance; and this
is why the name of Comte has henceforward its
place in the history of philosophy.

It is worth noticing that the Positive doctrine
has been more successful among our neighbors than
among ourselves. In France it hardly numbers,
among strictly orthodox disciples, more than one
name[1] which has other titles to distinction. It
is not so in England. Comte's formless volumes
have been there abridged by the elegant pen of
Miss Martineau. More than one periodical — the
"Leader," the "Westminster Review"— has served
as an organ of the party ideas. Several men of
ability or of learning have constituted themselves
its interpreters. Mr. Mill has written the Positivist "Logic." The work of Mr. Lewes on the History of Philosophy, that of Mr. Buckle on the Philosophy of History, are connected with the same
school. Even political Positivism has found in Mr.
Congreve a disciple enthusiastic enough and naïf
enough to request his countrymen to give up India
and Gibraltar. ·The teachings of Comte have everywhere taken root in the country of Locke, as though
in their native soil: and if the English have sometimes done us the honor of regarding Mr. Mill as
possessed of specially French qualities, we might

[1] [That of M. Littré, no doubt. — *Trans.*]

almost make them a present of the founder of the
school as one of themselves.[1] It is customary to
set the two nations against each other as totally
opposite: ought we not to modify such a judgment
when we see France adopting Locke and Reid, and
England returning the compliment by borrowing
the books of M. Cousin[2] and the ideas of M. Comte?

Mr. Mill's first great work was his "Logic," which
appeared in 1843. This is an exposition of the
essential principles of the Positive philosophy, and
it is easily to be understood how this philosophy
reduces itself to logic. Positivism is philosophy
minus metaphysics — that is to say, philosophy
minus philosophy, purely formal, wholly method-
ical. Nor do I know in the history of ideas a
closer connection than that which binds Mill's
teaching to the teaching of his predecessors of the
English school. From the moment when sensation
becomes the sole source of our knowledge, it is
clear that phenomena are the only objects of it,
and that the phenomenon itself is only an individual or, as they say, subjective impression.
From this to Hume and to Berkeley there is but
a step. If we know nothing of things but the
impression produced on us, we can neither know
nor affirm anything of things considered in them-

[1] [For this kind present I fear Englishmen will not be duly
thankful; at least I am not. — *Trans.*]

[2] [If this is an innuendo against Sir W. Hamilton and his
school, it is not quite worthy of M. Scherer. But he was at this
time in the ardor of Hegelian " conversion."— *Trans.*]

selves — not even their real existence. Such is the ground on which our author takes his stand. The aim of his book is to eliminate from science the transcendent element — that is to say, everything which lies beyond experience. If we take his word, a thing is but a bundle of attributes, and essence is but a word. "Cause" in the same way is but the constant succession of two phenomena: "law" itself has no necessity, and is only a probability founded on the frequent repetition of facts. Thus the Infinite, the Absolute, everything that is universal and necessary, vanishes from nature and from science. There remains nothing but man and his perceptions, but facts and their relations. I make not the least pretence of refuting Mr. Mill's system: I prefer simply to seek in it for indications of the tendency of his mind. Besides, to tell the truth, I do not think it possible to refute phenomenalism: the task would be self-contradictory. If a man confines himself to the regions of personal impression, you never can persuade him that there is anything further, for the very conditions of his knowledge oppose themselves thereto, and the man cannot go out of himself to penetrate the nature of things. It is impossible for him to see them otherwise than as they appear, or to assure himself that this appearance is not their whole contents. At the most one can but remind him that the partisans of Positivism do not take into account all the elements of the problem as it states

itself in human consciousness. It is true that our
senses do not attain to anything in the object save
attributes : but it is equally certain that we have a
notion of some substance distinct from these attributes — that we cannot get rid of this notion, and
that the very word "attribute" implies it. So is
it, too, with Cause. We cannot actually take hold
of anything but the sequence of two phenomena.
Yet in using the word "cause" we mean something much more than that — we mean that one of
the facts is contained in the other, and that they
are inseparable by thought. And, lastly, it is true
that when we see phenomena accomplishing themselves in a constantly uniform manner, we know
really but one thing — that the sequence has not
as yet failed. But it is equally true that we have
an invincible belief in the eternal constancy, the
absolute validity of the rule. Thus our judgments
carry into things a datum which is not furnished
by experience — one of which we cannot consequently say that it is supplied by reality, but
which is none the less inherent in our minds, and
of which we are absolutely unable to get rid. This
is what Kant comprehended so admirably and what
he tried to explain: and this is why Positivism,
which does not see it or does not take account of it,
falls short of philosophy proper.

Five years after his " Logic," Mr. Mill published
a not less monumental work on Political Economy,
in which he attacked every question, and showed

on all points at once a profound knowledge of all
theories, and that independence of mind which
enslaves itself to none. Yet this work, which in
England has ranked the author by the side of Adam
Smith and of Ricardo, had less originality than
thoroughness. The author showed more sense and
information than freshness : and gave us an encyclopædia of the science rather than a system of his
own. It differed in this respect from the " Logic ":
and if it could not but increase the repute of the
author by showing all the extent of his study and
his qualifications, it was certain also to arouse less
surprise and start fewer discussions.

The newest part of the book was that in which
Mr. Mill enlarged his subject by including in it
some political problems. After treating matters
purely economical under the three heads of Production, Distribution, and Exchange, the author sets
forth certain considerations on the progress of
society and the influence of government. In this
last part he examines the possible and desirable
limits of the action of the State. And it is here
that we find, amid the most jealous fears on the
subject of centralization and the encroachments of
power, and in company with the expression of the
most enlightened love for liberty, certain assertions
which seem contrary to these principles, and which
have not failed to cause some astonishment. Our
author, while handling State intervention, comes
across the various systems of Socialism, or, to

speak more exactly, Communism, since the question is of a state of things in which collective is to take the place·of individual property.   Mr. Mill calls a halt at this subject and discusses it.   Nay, he does more, he declares that, if the choice between Communism and the suffering and injustice which private property involves at the present time were necessary, it could not be doubtful.   Indeed he is not quite sure that Communism is not the best form, and the final form, of society.   And so, as I have said, the influence of yet another French school has added itself in Mr. Mill's case to the influence which Auguste Comte had already exercised over him.

There is a real analogy between these two doctrines as well as between both and our author's cast of mind.   He is as a thinker bold rather than profound :   he possesses ingenuity, sagacity, precision, but no great suppleness.   With all his cleverness in analyzing and expounding, discussing and surveying a subject at its origins, and in pursuing its applications with all his logical and investigating strength, he is lacking in the gift of original creation, and even in that of intuitive perception.   He fails in *finesse.*   He does not entirely understand anything but what is measured and numbered. Imponderable elements, spiritual influences, escape him.   He ignores the play of passion, the part borne by moral forces.   In short, look at Mr. Mill from what side you like, and you will always recognize the Positive philosopher.

This should make it clear how he was of necessity exposed to the blandishments of which I have spoken, for Socialist theories naturally serve as the politics 'of Positivism; and there is a kinship between the two systems. We must take good care, moreover, to recognize that in itself, and as a mere theory, Communism is invulnerable. The society which it offers us is perfectly organized, regular, logical, symmetrical. It has but one fault, and that is that it is ideal, or, in other words, impossible. It does not take man as he is, with his foibles, his tendencies, his caprices. It sees in him only a fixed quantity, a product, a machine. And for this same reason it takes no account of his needs of development and of liberty. I know, of course, that there are very liberal Communists; but I cannot help thinking that they are so only by virtue of a contradiction. *Laissez-faire* has no real place in their conception of society.

Now Mr. Mill must needs have fallen more easily than another into this contradiction. There are indeed two men in him. There is the systematic thinker, and the Englishman accustomed to the exercise of liberty and the enjoyment of the advantages resulting from it. There is the *savant* for whom individual and society both are the results of certain forces, the action of certain machinery; and there is the manly spirit which cannot endure the placing of fetters on independence of opinion. There is the Benthamite who looks at institutions from the point of view of utility (that is to say, as a result or quotient), the "scientist" who contemplates the fated laws followed by humanity; and there. is the citizen who has learnt to esteem these same institutions in accordance with their influence on the development of man and the formation of character.

This last aim is that which dominates in the little book "On Liberty," while both are found in the volume on "Representative Government." I cannot here dwell on the elder of these two works, but I must express my admiration of the inspiration under which it was written. Nowhere is there to be read a more eloquent defence of the rights of individualism, a more generous protest against the tyranny of governments, and still more against that of custom and opinion. It is in this religious respect for the liberty of all, this tolerance for every idea, this confidence in the final results of the struggle, that we recognize true Liberalism. The author's notions have not always equal solidity, but his instincts are always lofty. We see on every page the man whose own independence has set him at odds with prejudice. "Despotism itself does not produce its worst effects so long as individuality subsists by its side; and everything that crushes individuality is despotism by whatever name it is called, and with whatever disguise it adorns itself." These words of the author might serve as a motto for the volume.

In his work on "Representative Government," Mr. Mill begins by determining what the end of all government is. It is a double end. A government has functions, it exists for the management of interests, and it ought to manage them as well as possible; but it must at the same time contribute to the people's moral progress, and help to raise the national character. This last task is, indeed, the more important of the two; and if it could be separated from the other, it would have to be attended to first. Who has not heard the benefits of a wise despotism extolled among ourselves? Who has not heard set against the inconveniences of free governments the superior manner in which absolute governments accomplish the material part of their task, the success with which they make war, the secrecy with which they negotiate, the swiftness with which they hurry on public works? This is the talk that we are condemned to listen to every day; and the answer, alas! is but too easy. The machine works admirably, but it is only a machine. And what good is the greatness of a State if society goes from bad to worse? What good is administrative perfection if this perfection is compatible with the moral degradation of the people?

Moreover, Mr. Mill is by no means disposed to allow to absolute power the privilege of discharging the special functions of government. Self-government has in his eyes two advantages, not merely that of accustoming citizens to the exercise of civic virtues, but also that of assuring the well-being of the people by a thorough control. For no one is ignorant that rights and interests are never better secured than when those interested in them are responsible for their defence.

So, then, popular government is that which best attains the divers ends of governing. Yet it can only be directly exercised in very small States, such as the Greek republics, or certain Swiss cantons, where the whole assembly of the people can find room in the market-place. In our great modern States it is unworkable. Hence came a device, familiar to us, but unknown to antiquity — the device by which the people delegates its powers to deputies, by which the nation governs itself through representatives elected for that purpose.

Yet we must not deceive ourselves as to the aptitudes of representative government. Bring the numbers of a chamber of deputies as low as you will, it will always be unfit for the direct management of public affairs. It cannot administer, it cannot even, in Mr. Mill's judgment, draft the laws which it discusses. Its business is to be not so much a government as the check and overseer of a government. Its principal function, in our author's phrase, is to be a committee of grievances and a congress of opinion.

Nor does Mr. Mill deceive himself any the more as to the conditions which are indispensable to the establishment and the prosperity of the government of which we speak. That it may work, the people must have at once an independence which cannot endure tyranny, and a respect for law without which all free governments end by succumbing to disorder. There must be in the nation neither the ambition of command, which urges the individual to enterprises against the liberty of his fellow-citizens, nor the reluctance to obey which cannot bring itself to yield to the yoke of law. I hasten to add that in my opinion the benefits of representative government are so great that it remains the best — I will go further, the only one desirable — even when the national character seems least to endure it. The school of liberty is liberty itself.

If we pass from general considerations on representative government to the application of them, we shall meet, first of all, two capital questions to which Mr. Mill has the merit of having invited our utmost attention. I refer to the distribution of the suffrage among the electors, and the distribution of votes among the deputies to be elected.

Mr. Mill is a partisan of universal suffrage. Without exactly relying on the abstract rights of man, he regards as false and dangerous all arbitrary limitation applied to the exercise of civic functions. In a full-grown and civilized nation there should be no pariahs. The only exclusions which he proposes are drawn from the nature of the duty to be fulfilled. Thus he would have the electors possess elementary instruction; and universal education in his view ought to precede universal suffrage. He is also of opinion that only the man who pays a certain proportion of taxes can be admitted to the nomination of an assembly by which taxes will be voted. On the other hand, our author demands the extension of electoral rights to women — the difference of sex in such a matter seems to him to weigh no more than difference in height or different-colored hair. Mr. Mill does not seem to have reflected that from the woman-voter to the woman-candidate there is but a step, or rather that there is not even that. However, these are things not to be argued about; for the question becomes too delicate. But was I not thoroughly right in saying above that Mr. Mill is lacking in *finesse* ?

I prefer, I must say, another notion of our author's on the suffrage — a notion which he has worked out under the title of the "plural vote." When the institution of universal suffrage is subjected to unprejudiced examination, objections of incontestable gravity present themselves; for universal suffrage reposes first of all on a right, and if France has adopted it, it is, no doubt, a result of that care for natural right which forms one of the features of our national spirit. Enamoured of simple ideas, and especially of the ideas of equality and of justice, we thought that the generic character of mankind is its predominating feature, that one man is literally as good as another: that the fundamental likeness outweighs all differences in talent, in culture, and in social position. We thought so; and this led us to equal and universal suffrage.

The argument would be as invulnerable as it is simple if the suffrage were merely a right. Now it certainly is this; but it is also a trust. When he gives his vote to a representative the elector takes an influential part in public affairs. Now from this point of view, which is that of personal qualification, it is clear that equality no longer exists. One human being, as a general thesis, may be the equal of another man; the ignorant of the learned, the vicious of the virtuous, the negro of the white, the woman of her husband. We may, on the strength of an ideal principle, abstract all differences so as to leave nothing but the identity of species remaining. But so soon as there is any function to discharge, we shall be obliged to put these abstractions on one side and inquire into capacity; and as soon as capacity comes to the fore, all the natural inequalities which had been held so cheap will reappear.

How are we to get out of this difficulty? How reconcile the rights which are equal and the capacities which are not? This is the true statement of the problem, and I do not think anyone can deny that it is a pressing one, or that the future of democracy is directly concerned in it.

The solution which Mr. Mill proposes has the advantage of simplicity. Starting from the distinc-

tion we have just drawn, we may thus express it.
Rights being equal, each citizen shall have a vote;
but capacities being at the same time unequal, one
elector may have more votes than another. As to
the way of settling the number to which each is
entitled, we must lay stress on the nature of their
occupations, and on the social distinctions which
carry with them, or suppose, superior intelligence
and information. Thus, if a workman has one
vote, his master will have two, and the practitioner
of a liberal profession three. The important thing
is that the proportion shall be clearly enough
founded on facts to be accepted by the public conscience. Such is the system which Mr. Mill calls
the plural vote. He is not afraid to add that, with
this organization of voting excluded, universal suffrage may perhaps be preferable to other forms of
government; but that it remains false in principle,
and that the evils by which it is accompanied will
always get the better of its advantages.

The criticism is just, and the remedy is ingenious. We have still to discover whether it is prac-
ticable. Universal suffrage is not only, as I have
said, a right and a trust: it is something more, or
(if anyone likes) something less; in plain words, it
is a *pis-aller*. It has its roots in the principle of
equality; but the force with which it thrusts itself
on modern societies comes still more perhaps from
the difficulty experienced by the mind in finding a
middle term between the narrowest oligarchy and

the most unbridled democracy. Electoral qualifications, wherever they exist, have a tendency to be lowered; and they seem likely to be abolished everywhere for want of a sufficient *raison d'être.* Nobody can deny that the Haves have more at stake in the commonweal than the Have-nots; nor can anyone deny that distinctions of fortune do, in a general way, correspond to differences of education and intelligence. But at the same time it is impossible to settle exactly the relations between these differences and political capacity. This is what helps to make classification odious by making it arbitrary. Now I ask myself whether it would not be the same with Mr. Mill's plan. Theoretically irreproachable, specious in general appearance, it could hardly fail to meet with difficulties in execution. Public opinion might no doubt acquiesce in giving more votes to a Marshal of France, a judge of the Court of Appeal, or a member of the Institute, than to an ordinary person — even in giving more to a master than to a man. But the system could not be applied as a whole. The different categories could not be drawn up without the reappearance of the struggles of the principle of equality against distinctions which do not rest with sufficient evidence on the nature of things.

The system set forth by Mr. Mill is, however, none the less worthy of attention. If the need of organizing universal suffrage is ever felt, it is assuredly in this direction that the solution of a singularly thorny problem must be sought. The plural vote seems at all events preferable to the expedient of indirect election, and the reader will find in the work under notice some very just remarks on the faults of this latter kind of suffrage.

The second question raised by representative government and suffrage-organization is that of the manner of electing. Nor let anyone think that nothing but a mere working detail is here at stake. Now or never we may say that the way of doing the thing is more important than the doing of it. " Two very different ideas," says Mr. Mill excellently, "are usually confounded under the name democracy. The pure idea of democracy, according to its definition, is the government of the whole people by the whole people equally represented. Democracy as commonly conceived and hitherto practised is the government of the whole people by a mere majority of the people exclusively represented. The former is synonymous with the equality of all citizens; in the second (strangely confounded with it) is a government of privilege in favor of the numerical majority, who alone possess practically any voice in the State. This is the inevitable consequence of the manner in which votes are now taken, to the complete disfranchisement of minorities."

And further: — " In a representative body the minority must of course be overruled: and in an equal democracy the majority of the people, through

their representatives, will out-vote and prevail over
the minority and their representatives. But does it
follow that the minority should have no representatives at all ? Because the majority ought to prevail, must the majority have all the votes, the
minority none ? The injustice and the violation
of principle," adds our author, "are not less fla-
grant because it is a minority which suffers from
them. For there is not equal suffrage where each
individual does not count for as much as any other
single individual in the community."

I shall also quote the following reflection, which
adds the last touch to the full picture of the
danger which democracy should try to avert: —
"The great difficulty of democratic government has
hitherto seemed to be how to provide in a democratic society what circumstances have hitherto
provided in all societies which have maintained
themselves ahead of others — a social support — a
point d'appui for individual resistance to the tendencies of the ruling power, a protection and a
rallying point for the opinions and the interests
which the ascendent public opinion views with dis-
favor. For want of such a *point d'appui*, ancient
societies, and all but a few modern ones, either fell
into dissolution or became stationary (which means
slow deterioration) because of the exclusive pre-
dominance of a part only of the conditions of social
and mental well-being."

There is but one means of curing these vices of

democracy, which is to organize minorities. But how are we to set about doing this? Here our author adopts and warmly defends a plan proposed in 1829 by Mr. Hare,[1] the chief features of which I may sum up as follows : —

(1) Representation is no longer linked to a town, an *arrondissement*, or any territorial circumscription. It ceases to be local. All the deputies are elected by votes collected throughout the country. Every representative represents all the citizens who at any place have voted for him ; in other words, the people votes by *scrutin de liste* and for candidates who stand for the whole nation.

(2) Each elector's voting-ticket is a graduated list, on which the candidates he chooses figure in the order of his preference for them.

(3) Each elector shares in the nomination of one candidate only; but if the candidate he has put first fails, his second vote, his third, and so on may rank for another.

(4) The number of votes necessary to seat a

---

[1] [It was not quite so early, I think (1829 is either a slip of memory or a misprint for 1859). M. Scherer is not entirely just to the plan of Mr. Hare, who died recently, with less public notice than might have been expected. His scheme, which was favored by many able men of all political parties, had, as far as general elections go, perhaps only the drawback of *apparent* complexity. A party list cannot be more dangerous to electoral independence than a single party candidate : and M. Scherer does not seem to have realized that no party could possibly be over-represented except by falsification of the tickets. — *Trans.*]

deputy is determined by the number of voters divided by that of the seats to be filled. However, that no votes may be lost, those which are obtained by any candidate over and above the necessary proportion are no longer set to his credit, and are on each ticket carried to the credit of the candidate who comes next.

(5) The complete examination of the votes lodged thus supplies a list from which are taken the number of members required to make up the chamber of representatives.

I must refer the reader for more details to Mr. Mill, who himself refers to Mr. Hare's own book. But I confess that I feel some surprise at the eager welcome with which our author greets these proposals, for the objections they arouse are evident. Thus one does not see how the desired number of representatives can be assured, unless each ticket bears a number of names equal to the total number of deputies — which in the case of a large assembly would lead us straight to the absurd. Besides, if the number of names to be inscribed were reduced to a much smaller figure — fifty, thirty, even twenty — it would be impossible for the electors, especially those of the lower classes, to know the titles and deserts of so great a number of candidates. They would therefore be driven, in order to fill up their tickets, to follow party directions; and this brings us to a still more serious objection. Mr. Hare's plan would not prevent the country from splitting up into several great parties, as happens in the United States; nor would it prevent these parties from drawing up lists, and from getting them adopted by their adherents. Far from attaining the end it proposes, I incline to think that the project in question would give to party a still more powerful organization, and would thus tend to diminish instead of to increase the actual part played by minorities. In this discussion, as in many others, Mr. Mill's merit will be seen to lie less in having solved the problem than in having stated it — stated it, I may add, with the clearness of a thought which is always exact, of a logic which is always rigorous.

It is no small advantage to survey a subject under the conduct of a guide who knows its byways, who is acquainted with what has been said on every point, who has perfect information and direction ready for the reader, who presents questions under all their aspects, who discusses them with sagacity and good faith, who brings to the argument no prejudice and no passion. Led by such a guide, we feel ourselves advancing with a steadier step; and we find that we have explored not a few scantily known regions. True, there is something higher, something more precious still. There are writers who have the eye of the diviner; who surprise us by unforeseen discoveries and striking remarks; who unite originality with exactness, depth with sagacity, genius with talent. These men we meet, few and far between in history; and they mark eras in the annals of the human mind. Mr. Mill, doubtless, is not of this number, but he ranks immediately below them, among those who, taking to be their province the whole knowledge of a period, and carrying into it complete probity of criticism, themselves shed on many points an unexpected illumination.

III

SHAKESPEARE[1]

MOST of the books written on Shakespeare belong to one or other of two classes: they are either panegyrics which do not tell us much that is new, or commentaries which are certainly useful, but which do not suffice for the understanding of the poet. There is no reader of the great dramatist who must not have wished to have at hand some substantive work in which he might find information on the life of Shakespeare, on the date and order of his pieces, on the condition in which they have been preserved, on the interpretation which has been put upon them, and on the distinctive characteristics of their writer's genius. Such a book would make use of the labors of scholars without losing itself in detail, and would endeavor to please men of taste without plunging into vague æsthetic speculation. But I am wrong in speaking of this desire as if nothing had been done to satisfy it. Long ago M. Mézières conceived the plan of such a book as that whose programme I have been

---

[1] *Prédécesseurs et contemporains de Shakspeare. Shakspeare, ses œuvres et ses critiques. Contemporains et successeurs de Shakspeare.* **Par A.** Mézières. 2 édition. 3 vols.

sketching, and carried it out with much erudition and much taste. His volume on Shakespeare is certainly the best hand-book that one can recommend to readers who wish to devote to the English poet that serious study to which alone he yields the whole secret of his power. Moreover, M. Mézières has not confined himself to this. As soon as he had resolved to introduce precision of historical information in handling his subject, it became impossible for him to omit the surroundings of Shakespeare — that is to say, the models imitated by the poet, the influence he exercised, and, in short, the whole of the literary and social conditions amongst which he was produced, and amongst which we must place him once more, if we wish really to comprehend him. This is what M. Mézières very clearly saw, and this is what gives so much value to his volumes on the predecessors and contemporaries of Shakespeare — the completest history that we have of the English theatre up to the seventeenth century.

It is exactly 250 years since Shakespeare died; and he thus belongs to an age of full historical light. Nor was he one of those whose merit is unrecognized till long after their own day. His contemporaries did homage to his genius, and the well-known verses of Milton are enough to show what place the great dramatist held in the estimation of the next age. And yet we know next to nothing of the life of this extraordinary man. Most of the items which compose his traditional biography, such as the poaching affair which forced him to quit his native town and his humble occupations in London, before he trod the boards, rest, I say, on no foundation of evidence. The history of his work in drama is to a great extent conjectural. It has even been doubted whether he was a Protestant or a Catholic. The rather uncertain information which we have in regard to him reduces itself to what follows. Shakespeare belonged to a middle-class family, in easy circumstances, and was born at Stratford-on-Avon, in April, 1564. He was married at the age of eighteen, and was only twenty-two when he left his wife and children at Stratford to go and seek his fortune in London. There he joined a troup of actors, of whom Burbage was manager, and was not long in distinguishing himself, if not as an actor, as a dramatist. He cultivated other styles of poetry at the same time: published "Venus and Adonis" in 1593, and "Lucrece" in 1594. He made money by the theatre. We find him buying a house and lands at Stratford, which he liked to re-visit, and whither he finally retired about 1604, at the age of forty. But if he left the actual theatre, he did not renounce the dramatic art, and many of his works are posterior to the date I have just mentioned. He died on April 23, 1616, in the same year as Cervantes, twenty-four years after the author of the "Essays," and twenty years before the production of the "Cid." These dates indicate sufficiently the stage of formation of Shakespeare's language, which is a kind of English less archaic than the French of Montaigne is to us, and yet less finally settled than is that of Corneille. The authenticity of the famous portrait known as the Chandos Shakespeare, and now belonging to the London National [Portrait] Gallery, is not certain enough for us to flatter ourselves with the idea that we know the poet's features. His direct descendants have long been extinct. He left two married daughters, who in their turn had issue : but these children died childless.

The strangest thing in Shakespeare's life is the indifference which he seems to have felt in regard to his reputation as a dramatist. He published his poems and his sonnets with the greatest care ; and yet he neither himself caused any of his plays to be printed nor left his heirs any directions to that effect. It might seem that in writing them he had no other care than for theatrical success and its contingent profits. And it must not be supposed that this indifference was common to all the dramatic writers of the time. Ben Jonson, for his part, took as much pains in correcting his work as in composing it. But what complicates the problem still further, is that Shakespeare's plays were in his lifetime eagerly sought after by readers. The proof of this is that some fifteen of them were printed and re-printed then and there, though without his connivance or acknowledgment, and in the

most incorrect fashion. They were, in fact, simple
piracies intended to satisfy the public curiosity anyhow. Indeed, there were published under the poet's
name plays that were not his; and Shakespeare did
not interfere in any way with these publications. He
died: and it was not till seven years after his death,
in 1623, that a collection of his dramatic works at
last appeared. This collection announced itself as
printed from the originals; but nothing could be less
well founded than this assertion, as the errors of all
sorts with which the volume swarms show. The
editors had simply followed the earlier editions, and
where these failed them, they had used copies made
for the purposes of the theatre.

It will, after this, be understood that the study
of Shakespeare meets, as a first difficulty, with the
absence of a sufficiently correct and authentic text.
There are numerous passages where we have simply
the choice of readings equally doubtful, just as
happens in the study of Greek and Latin authors.
It is true that the comparison of variants, as they
are called, is sometimes curious or instructive.
There is one work especially in which by this means
we can catch the poet's genius, as it were, in the
act and fact of creation: and this is "Hamlet." We
have an edition of this play in which it is hard not
to recognize the first draft of the author's thought.
Polonius is called Corambis. The progress of the
piece is not that which was adopted later; and
towards the end a scene between the Queen and

Horatio has disappeared. Still, though the early version contains some fine lines which have vanished in the latter, it gives, in a curiously abridged and imperfect form, the most celebrated passages of the drama, such as Hamlet's soliloquy and that of the King on prayer. In the same way we possess rehandlings of "Romeo and Juliet." It is clear that Shakespeare went back on his works, that he elaborated and perfected them.

No one will begin the study of Shakespeare without inquiring what is the order of succession in his pieces. We feel a desire to know what were his first attempts, at what epoch of his life he produced his masterpieces, and whether his genius maintained itself to the last. Fortunately these questions are not so insoluble as they might be supposed to be, considering the obscurity in which the author's life is still plunged. Information of various kinds comes to help us here, and we may regard the chronology of Shakespeare's theatre as fairly settled. The poet began by reshaping for acting purposes plays already existing and of unknown authorship. Such was the origin of "Titus Andronicus," of "Pericles," and of the three parts of "Henry VI." These pieces thus but half belong to Shakespeare, and it is impossible nowadays to determine what part he had in them. The second period of his dramatic life begins about 1594, when he was thirty years old. It was then that he wrote the plays drawn from the history of

England, and most of his comedies. His final period lasted from 1600 to his death, and saw the birth of his greatest work — the four great dramas "Hamlet," "Othello," "Macbeth," and "Lear"; the Roman tragedies; and those delightful romantic comedies "Cymbeline," "The Winter's Tale," and "The Tempest." It is taken as agreed that Shakespeare continued to write for the stage even after he had left London and returned to Stratford, and that "The Tempest" was the last of his works, and a kind of farewell to the art which he had made illustrious.

A farewell to art : we might let this expression pass, on the understanding that it is merely to be taken as figurative. But some have gone further, and have tried to find in "The Tempest" an actual adieu addressed by Shakespeare to the public, or, as it has been said elsewhere, the dramatic testament of the poet, the epilogue of his work and of his life. M. Mézières has lent to this hypothesis the authority of his excellent wit, and quite recently M. Montégut,[1] the subtlest and most ingenious of our critics, has reproduced it with a fulness of confidence which may cause some misapprehension as to the strength of the arguments he uses. It is indeed by no means the first time that the spectacle of Shakespeare, given up as a prey to contradictory interpreters, has been seen. All have made him out

---

[1] [M. Emile Montégut, still (1891) alive, and still deserving the description of him which M. Scherer gives. — *Trans.*]

as being on their own side; all have sought and have found in him just what they wanted. It has been thought to exalt him by attributing to him all sorts of profound intentions; and Herr Gervinus has made of him a moralist exclusively concerned with delivering lectures to society. The attempt is truly unlucky. For never did any genius give itself up to art with a more supreme indifference to anything but art itself. In Shakespeare's eyes, as he himself has told us, the drama is simply a mirror held up to Nature, in which Nature reflects herself under her most diverse aspects. Indeed the impersonality of our poet's theatre is so great that it is impossible to draw from it the least information as to his ideas, his passions, his character. But if Herr Gervinus has failed to perceive this capital feature of Shakespeare's work, what are we to say of M. Rio,[1] who regards it as thick-sown throughout with allusions to the events of the time and the special situation of the poet ? M. Rio has a thesis : for him Shakespeare is a Catholic, who is obliged to hide his faith, and who makes up for it by slipping into his scenes as many orthodox allusions as he can. " Julius Cæsar" becomes a glorification of Essex's plot; "Measure for Measure" is intended to rehabilitate

---

[1] [Rio, one of the Montalembert-Lacordaire group of Neo-Catholics, was a very amiable person, and something of an authority on Christian art, but not a man of much mental power. Any folly, however, that he may have committed in interpreting Shakespeare has long been eclipsed and outstripped. — *Trans.*]

the ascetic ideal of cloistered virginity; "Othello" had been a crusader — all evident proofs of the author's secret sympathies. But M. Rio should have explained to us how a writer so attached as Shakespeare to a prescribed form of worship has brought himself in "Romeo and Juliet" to talk of an "evening mass." However, it is fair to recognize that M. Rio has but exaggerated a proceeding employed by many others, both before and after him. It is a received doctrine that the vestal of whom Oberon speaks in "A Midsummer Night's Dream" (Act ii. scene 2) is no other than Queen Elizabeth, as if the very context of the passage did not show that the chaste Phœbe is referred to.[1] The learned Warburton went further still when, in the same passage, he applied to the marriage of Mary Stuart with the King of France's son the image of the siren on a dolphin's back. But let us return to M. Montégut. His hypothesis on "The Tempest" has not more solidity than those which I have just mentioned. It will not stand a moment's examination. It shatters itself at once against literary feeling and against the facts; and M. Montégut does not even seem to have formed a clear conception of what he wanted to prove. Shake-

---

[1] [Disinclined as I am to the school of comment which M. Scherer is denouncing, I cannot go with him here. There is certainly no reference to the chaste Phœbe: M. Scherer has misinterpreted the "watery moon," and the reference to Elizabeth is of the highest probability. — *Trans.*]

speare, in his view, has in "The Tempest" taken
leave of the public on the eve of his retirement —
it is his farewell to the stage. Now what are we
to understand by this? That the poet was on the
point of quitting London to return to his native
town? But he had already resumed his residence
at Stratford for some seven or eight years. That he
was unwilling to write any more for the stage, out
of fear of not keeping up to his own standard?
What! Shakespeare feel fears of this kind at forty-
seven or forty-eight, in the vigor of his age, at the
very moment when he had finished "The Tempest,"
one of his masterpieces? Indeed, it is enough, in
order to refute such suppositions, to state them in
the terms in which they appear. Who can believe
that Sycorax is literary barbarism; that Caliban
stands for the poet Marlowe; that the history of
the Enchanted Isle is, "stroke for stroke," the history of the English stage — in a word, that the
whole piece is a "synthetic allegory" in which
Shakespeare sums up his work; a picture of what
he has undertaken and executed "in the poetical
solitude of his life"? Nor is this all. If you venture to suggest that the dramatic interest of the
work allies itself but ill with allegoric intentions,
if you risk the remark that the poet may very well,
after all, have obeyed the simple inspirations of his
creative fancy, the critic replies that "these pre-
tended rights of poetic fancy are among the most
idle notions of our time." This, at any rate, is

intelligible enough : it means that the poet is only a teacher, and art only a veil for instruction.

M. Mézières has discussed the genius of Shakespeare very well, seeking what constitutes the true greatness of the poet, and not conceiving himself bound to share either the concern of German criticism for system, or the superstitious reverence of the critics of England. What makes Shakespeare's greatness is his equal excellence in every portion of his art — in style, in character, and in dramatic invention. No one has ever been more skilful in the playwright's craft. The interest begins at the first scene ; it never slackens, and you cannot possibly put down the book before finishing it. This does not mean that the action is always single. " King John " is the chronicle of an entire reign. There are two pieces in " King Lear," the story of the King and that of Edgar; but the reader is carried along by the rapidity with which one event follows another. Hence it is that Shakespeare's pieces are so effective on the stage; they were intended for it, and it is as acted plays that we must judge them. They are often played in Germany, and always applauded by the public. They might succeed better still if the conditions of representation had not changed so much in the last century. We demand to-day a kind of scenic illusion to which Shakespeare's theatre does not lend itself. The action shifts too often; you have to represent battles, castles, ramparts. The fifth act of " Julius

Cæsar" sets before us all the vicissitudes of the battle of Philippi; the fifth act of "Richard the Third" shows us the two rivals encamped and asleep, so near each other that the ghosts are able to speak to each of them by turns. There is no modern stage management which can overcome such difficulties. Thus it would appear that Shakespeare is destined to be played less and less; but the playwright's cleverness which he displays is not more wasted for that. From it comes the life, the incomparable activity, with which his pieces are endowed, and which is felt in the reading no less than in the representation.

If there is no drama without action, neither is there any without character. It may be that the creation of character is the highest function of art. There is nothing which more resembles divine power than the exploit by which the poet evokes from the depths of his imagination personages who have never lived, but who thenceforward live forever, and who will take a place in our memories, in our affections, in the realities of our world, exactly as if they had been formed by the hand of the Most High. And if a single creation of this kind suffices to immortalize a writer, what shall we say of a poet who, like Shakespeare, has drawn crowds of characters, all different, all alive, uniting the most distinct physiognomy and the intensest reality to the highest quality of idealism and poetry? The English dramatist is in nothing so marvellous

as in this. He is the magician who can give life
to anything by his wand; or rather, he is Nature
herself, capricious, prodigal, always new, always
full of surprises and of profundity. His personages are not what are called heroes; there is no
posing in them; there is no abstraction; the idea
has become incarnate, and develops itself as a
whole, with all the logic of passion, with all the
spontaneity of life. The only thing which can be
brought against the author is at times a too sharp
change — one, so to speak, effected on the stage —
in the sentiments of his characters. Aufidius, for
example, passes too quickly from hatred to sorrow
when he sees Coriolanus fall; and in "Richard
III." Anne accepts with too great ease the ring of
the man on whom she has just spit in contempt;
while Elizabeth is too quick in giving her daughter
to the man who has just massacred her sons. This
is certainly turning the corner too sharply, and
there is a want of truth in it.

I think that something of the same kind may be
said of Shakespeare's style. The language which
he puts in the mouths of his characters is not
always appropriate — is sometimes far from being
appropriate — to the circumstances, even to the
characters themselves. The poet delights too much
in the expression for itself and its own sake. He
dwells on it, he lingers over it, he plays with
equivalents and synonyms. Menenius thus com-
plains of the change which has occurred in Corio-

lanus's humor: — "The tartness of his face sours ripe grapes: when he walks he moves like an engine, and the ground shrinks before his treading: he is able to pierce a corselet with his eye: talks like a knell, and his hum is a battery. He sits in his state as a thing made for Alexander. What he bids be done is finished with his bidding. He wants nothing of a god but eternity and a heaven to throne in" — I take this quotation at random to exemplify what I mean. The form in this poet sometimes overruns in this fashion; the expression is redundant and out of proportion to the situation. This remark applies still better to the conceits and the word-plays which Shakespeare, without troubling himself about the occasion, puts in everybody's mouth. The most pathetic speeches are not free from them. It is not that the author is not conscious of the incongruity of these quips.

> Do sick men play so nicely with their names?

asks Richard III. of the Duke of Lancaster, and it is certain that his last works have much fewer of these blots than his first. But if there is sometimes ill-placed wit in our poet, what verve is there in this wit, what gayety, what exuberance! With what freedom and caprice does fancy develop itself! How well (to employ an expression of Madame de Staël's) do excess and license of talent suit this unbounded invention! And we must also say at once that this wit is but one of Shakespeare's

qualities. He possesses imagination and feeling
in at least equal measure. He has felt everything,
has understood everything. No man has lived
more, has observed more, has better reproduced
the outward world. And yet he is at the same
time the most lyrical of poets; he expresses in
finished form, in inimitable poetry, all the emotions of the heart. He says things as no one else
says them, in a manner at once strange and striking. He has unbelievable depths, subtlenesses of
intuition as unbelievable. There rises from his
writings a kind of emanation of supreme wisdom;
and it seems that their very discords melt into
some transcendent harmony. Shakespeare has
enlarged the domain of the mind, and, take him
all in all, I do not believe that any man has added
more than he has to the patrimony of mankind.

IV

DANIEL DERONDA [1]

FACILITATING communications does no good. We
are still as far from England as if she were at the
Antipodes. The differences which part us have
their origin in race, in historical development, in
religion ; and they betray themselves every moment
in the spirit which animates institutions, governs
manners, and presides over literature. English literature in particular, lending itself to what may be
called a verification of fact, daily gives us palpable
proofs of the extent to which England is still a
foreign country to us. Which of us has any notion
of the intellectual activity that occupies our neighbors ? Who has even a superficial knowledge — a
knowledge even of the names — of the schools of
poetry which follow each other on the other side
of the Channel, and divide the interest and the
admiration of the public there ? But the most
striking example, in my eyes, of the ignorance of
the concerns of English literature in which we live
is as follows. There lives in England to-day, in the
full vigor of her talent, a woman-writer inferior to
no one of the sex, except Madame de Staël, in

[1] By George Eliot. 1876. 4 vols.

depth, brilliancy, and flexibility of genius. This lady has published half a dozen novels, each one of which is a masterpiece. Every work that comes from her pen becomes at once the event of the day, holds the attention of the nation, is the subject of all talk, sets all critics at defiance, interests the thinker almost as much as it delights the artist and strikes the fancy of the man of the world. Well, this writer is almost unknown in France; the translations of some of her books which have been risked have found no public; her name is lacking in the "Dictionnaire des Contemporains," and when our reviews have spoken of Mrs. Lewes,[1] it has been oftenest in the most superficially superior manner, and with absolute incompetence to judge.

Miss Evans, now Mrs. Lewes, who has published the whole of her imaginative work under the pseudonym of George Eliot, was born about 1820. Up to the age of thirty-six she had only employed her talents and knowledge in publications dealing with philosophy and theology; at this epoch she sought another career, and wrote her first story, "Amos Barton," which was quickly followed by two others, and forms with them the "Scenes of Clerical Life," published originally in 1857 in "Blackwood's Magazine." The success of this ex-

---

[1] [As a faithful translator I keep my author's form. It is needless to say that George Eliot was not Mrs. Lewes; and M. Scherer, as a later essay (*vide infra*) shows, was aware of the fact. — *Trans.*]

periment determined the author's vocation, and she successively enriched the literature of her country with those incomparable masterpieces, "Adam Bede," "The Mill on the Floss," and "Middlemarch." I purposely leave on one side "Romola," an Italian story of the fifteenth century, because general opinion has not ratified the admiration of some and the evident partiality of the author herself for this work, and especially because I have never been able to overcome the aversion, bordering on disgust, with which the chief character inspires me. We have here, if I mistake not, a first trace of the moralizing or didactic tendencies to which George Eliot leans, and which go near to dim the purity of her æsthetic sense. It would seem, too, that this great writer is completely at home, and has the full use of all her resources, in pictures of English life only. "Felix Holt the Radical" was another mistake, though in a different style, and was the only one of George Eliot's novels which public opinion let pass with something like indifference. "Silas Marner," on the other hand, a short story which appeared in 1861, and which I then reviewed, remains one of the most delicate and perfect works of this great novelist.

What marks George Eliot off from her fellows is her possession, in a higher degree, of all the qualities that make the novelist. Her inventive power is shown by stories where the unexpectedness of the situation is not obtained at any sacrifice of probability, and where the development of events always proceeds from that of the characters. Besides, George Eliot does not merely imagine situations; she works them out, and the reader's greatest surprise is to see the writer constantly rising to the height of the catastrophe which she has brought about. She throws her characters into tragic or delicate adventures, she makes explanations imperative, she provokes a supreme crisis, and she gets herself out of the difficulty with so much ease, so much power, and so much nature, that the reader is divided between the emotion produced by the story and the admiration challenged by the writer's success. But this is not her only superiority. In George Eliot description is never there for its own sake, as happens in the produce of inferior art. It is subordinate to the action, which it frames and surrounds, and is none the less full of traits which show an eye as well trained to the observation of nature as to that of the human heart. The dialogue, which in some very great novelists is the weak place, which in their hands so often misses truth and precision of shade, which they make rather an occasion of putting forth ideas and showing wit than a means of dramatic development, is in George Eliot's novels always in its right place. It is fitted to the characters; it varies with them; it is now witty, now pathetic, it expresses the most opposite sentiments, and renders the most diverse individualities. And it does all this without effort, without ever striking a false note, and as if this lady, who has actually lived a life of retirement and work, had felt and understood and gone through everything. It is not too much to say that there is something Shakespearian in this. And yet we have not come to the end of the qualities which make our author the first of contemporary novelists; for it is in creating her characters that she especially shows her genius. There is not one of her works which has not bestowed upon the literature of her country some of those figures which, once seen, abide in the memory of men, more real, more living, than the actual heroes of history. Her sketches of women, as one might expect, are especially wonderful; and yet do the characters of Tito and of Grandcourt come much short of Maggie and of Rosamond? Is there not the same psychological profundity in them? Do we not perceive throughout the glance which divines all motives, which lays bare all feelings, and which would be more pitiless than remorse itself if the author's penetration were not equalled by her tenderness for human weakness and human suffering? George Eliot has created a kind in which she will have no successor, because we shall never again see the qualities of the thinker so combined with those of the artist. Hers is the novel of moral analysis. There is her speciality, there her triumph. Story, description, reflection, dialogue — all in her writings is ancillary to the

painting of the secret movements of the mind, to
the study of the human conscience; while the
minuteness of her observation never hurts either
the vigorous realism of her writing, the personality
of her creations, or the passionate interest of her
drama.

I have as yet said nothing of George Eliot's
fashion of writing. Indeed, it is possible to question whether this author has what we call a style.
Her narrative manner is so simple, and her dialogue
so natural, that we hardly notice in her the writer
properly so called. Even the wit and humor which
she scatters broadcast, the acuteness of her reflections, the felicity of her comparisons, the unexpectedness of her remarks, the tenderness or the
strength of her sentiment, never in any case sink,
with George Eliot, into passages written for effect.
In other words, you must not look, in her writings,
for the eloquent pages, the passages finished and,
so to speak, "hit off," that are met in, for instance,
George Sand. Her talent is more restrained, her
art more severe. On the other hand, we here approach a fault which is obvious in George Eliot's
later writings. Possessing great qualities of diction, and with uncommon and happy phrases at
will, this writer has for some time past taken to
the habit of condensing her thought and her expression to the point of obscurity. This happens
especially at the end of her chapters, when she
speaks in her own person and sums up her own

reflections. Her pen then falls into a mixture of abstract ideas and minutely detailed images in which it is hard to seize the thought. This fault of taste, unaccountable in so great a writer, had appeared already as a blot on "Middlemarch"; it seems to me a little less prominent in "Daniel Deronda." But I cannot understand how there is no adviser of sufficient authority at the writer's elbow to point out to her boldly that she is in danger of entering on a mistaken course. One would gladly cry out to her, "Pray, what on earth are you thinking of? Why so many efforts when what is wanted is just the contrary — straightforward language? Why close your ranks at mere cost of labor when you ought rather to deploy? Break the phrases you are linking so painfully! Divide the periods you are so scientifically building up! Let yourself float, O accomplished artist! on the limpid and copious style which only asks permission to flow from your pen."

However, the fault of which I have just spoken is but a blot which is easy to avoid or to efface; one feels that a mere warning would be enough to make the author correct herself of it. It is not quite the same, I fear, with a peculiarity of George Eliot's intellectual and moral nature, which, after having been one of the elements of her strength and one of the causes of her success, threatens at the present moment to damage her art and her work. It is a curious thing, a paradox which we reject even when it forces itself on us with resistless proof, but the writer's own superiority here turns against her, and she is hurt by the strength of her individuality. In saying this I am thinking more particularly of George Eliot's new novel; so I must begin by giving the reader some notion of it.

In "Middlemarch" there were three stories, somewhat laboriously, but on the whole ingeniously, welded together. In "Daniel Deronda" there are two — two narratives which are simply placed side by side; two works differing in the kind of interest which they are intended to arouse; two novels, in short, one of which is a failure, while the other takes rank among George Eliot's finest creations. The second of these novels, the one we should like to separate from the other, is the history of Gwendolen and Grandcourt. Some inconsistencies have been detected in the outlining of these characters; but, on the whole, the author has certainly added two original figures to the list of her masterpieces. If she has elsewhere drawn others more complete, stronger, more striking from their moral unity, she has created none of such science and of such depth. Here are two names henceforward familiar to all those who read; two beings whose life is inextricably mingled with ours; two types to which we shall involuntarily refer this personage and that with whom we rub shoulders on the world's stage.

I can see Grandcourt before me as I write. I recognize his pale face, his placid and disdainful demeanor. Between his fingers is the eternal cigar, on his lips the oath of ill-temper or the yawn of ennui. A stranger to all moral life, he knows nothing of men but their foibles and their follies; and if he is at any time in danger of being deceived, it will be merely for want of understanding disinterested feelings. A thorough *blasé*, he has no pleasure left but oppressing others; the last enjoyment left to this connoisseur is in ill-treating his dogs, giving pain to his inferiors, tyrannizing over his wife, provoking rebellion in order to crush it. There is meanness under the elegant manners that are never "out," cruelty beneath this well-bred coldness, a monster inside the correct and polished gentleman. Hatred never was so self-restrained, ill-nature so well-mannered. His impassibility as a tormentor, the indifference of his persecution, the phlegm with which he crushes a victim, give an impression of power for evil such as literature did not before contain. It is scarcely possible to lose our temper with a man who never loses his own; we feel that it would give him an advantage; his calm drives one frantic, he is above the very horror which he inspires. A terrible and an astonishing creation!

The portrait of Gwendolen is still more carefully studied, and if it does not strike the reader so much, it is because this character, as George Eliot conceived it, involves a transformation so thorough as to seem like an inconsistency. Gwendolen possesses the formidable power of beauty: she knows it: and she has early acquired the egotism which often accompanies the consciousness of recognized superiority. Accustomed from her infancy to see her mother and sisters the slaves of her caprices, she will carry with her into society the assurance of victory, which is one of its guarantees, the haughty grace which is made more piquant by her spoilt-child's fancies, her impatience, her very imprudence itself. She is wilful, but purposelessly so; ambitious, but with no passionate desires : she asks nothing of life but excitement, brilliant success, the intoxication of flattery, the exercise of despotic power. And yet Gwendolen's nature is not corrupt. Ignorant, frivolous, worldly as she is, living and breathing as she does for nothing but pleasure, she still possesses a kind of innocence. There is in her the germ of a higher life which only waits for the contact of some influence to shoot. It is this germination of the ideal in the heart of a woman given up to society that George Eliot has tried to paint. With a thoroughly feminine intuition, she has represented her heroine as needing some attachment to quit commonplace life, and needing a man to serve her as a conscience. She only begins to be dissatisfied with herself when she recognizes the arbiter of her existence in a strong and pure being. Alas ! this moral revelation is not enough for our poor Gwendolen; she needs, in addition, the hard school of suffering. She marries Grandcourt to escape the mediocrity of her fortune, and becomes the victim of a hateful tyrant. The picture of this hidden agony is terrible. How powerfully does the author show us the beauty, lately envied and worshipped, as she is tamed, little by little, by the cold-blooded ferocity of her husband! She swallows her humiliations, she hates the wealth for which she has bartered her soul; she soon gives up a resistance which she knows to be vain. Overcome by the resentment which springs from forced hypocrisy and by the hatred which springs from habitual fear, aghast at this very hatred against whose promptings she feels herself powerless, urged to despair, and taking temporary refuge in the hope of accidents that my free her, and so open a door of escape from the promptings of revenge, she thus in thought draws near to crime. Then, at last, when Grandcourt one day falls overboard, she hesitates to give him her hand or the rope that might have saved him — hesitates for a second only, but long enough for it to be too late, and then flings herself after him in an agony of despair, remorse, and horror. Even in the work of George Eliot there are few things so powerful as this moral tragedy. A little further, we shall find the author trying (very much in vain to my thinking) to show us a Gwendolen consoled, raised from the dust, ready to seek the expiation of her faults and the business of her life in good works. The Gwendolen who is a sister of charity and the Lady Bountiful of the neighboring schools is not the Gwendolen we have known.   Her conversion almost necessarily strikes a false note in the story, inasmuch as it violates the logical consistency of human character.   Conversion means the introduction of the supernatural and the ascetic: elements which have their place in moral therapeutics, but which are rebellious towards art.

I repeat that the story of Gwendolen and Grandcourt takes its place beside the author's best work: and that, if the character-drawing is not stronger, it is at any rate subtler and more scientific.   Gwendolen's conversation with Klesmer on her vocation as an actress, her interview with Mirah when she wishes to ascertain the truth of the rumors she has heard about Deronda, the tragedy on board the boat in the Gulf of Genoa, the good-byes and the confessions at the moment of final separation, are among the scenes, hard to manage, or even unmanageable, where the genius of George Eliot, compact at once of tact and power, breaks out in all its supremacy.   There is, I am sorry to say, a lack (save in some secondary characters, such as little Jacob, Hans Meyrick, and Sir Hugo Mallinger) of humor.   We are in this respect far from the inimitable creations of the early novels — Mrs. Poyser, poor Mr. Tulliver, the Dodson sisters.   We do not feel in " Daniel Deronda " what the author herself has so happily called " the pure enjoyment of comicality," the amusement which is produced by the sight of innocent foibles, of candid vanity, of things absurd but not evil. The morbid anatomy of conscience, in which the author seems to take more and more pleasure, has in this instance saddened her pencil. But once more, after allowing for all this, and after reducing it to the persons and the things which I have just mentioned, George Eliot's new novel remains a very great and very strong thing. Unluckily, it is mixed up with a secondary story, which is, indeed, clearly distinguished and easily separable from it, but which is its inferior in every way, and the dead weight of which has dragged both itself and its fellow to shipwreck. For a shipwreck I fear there has been. The admiring partiality of the English for their great novelist indeed refuses to recognize any lessening of talent in "Daniel Deronda"; but it cannot help confessing that the author has not succeeded in interesting the public in "her Jews," that all the Israelitish part of the book is wearisome — in short, that there is in it an inexplicable error of taste and of judgment.

The Jewish romance which George Eliot has cobbled on to the history of Gwendolen is composed of certain historical and philosophical theories personified in some half-dozen Hebrews; but the theories are vague, and the personages have no individuality. I cannot recall in the preceding works of George Eliot anything like the feature-lessness of the characters she has drawn here. It is evident that the author has taken every care, has used every exertion, to interest us in Daniel

Deronda, in Mirah, and in Mordecai, and it is painful to see that her pains have been so entirely
wasted.   Mordecai is a mere visionary, who fails
to win us over to his schemes, because he never
explains them, and because the little we can divine
is childish.   Mirah may be charming ; but we have
to take the author's word for it, inasmuch as,
though she tells us so, she never gives proof of the
fact, and has not been able to make anything of
the character but a kind of wax doll which will say
"papa" and "mamma" if bidden.   As for Deronda,
who gives his name to the book, and clearly ought
to be its hero, he is an intolerable kind of Grandison,
with a moral always on his lips, a humanitarian
crotchet always in his head, one of those beings
who are doubtless required for the accomplishment
of all sorts of useful tasks, but whom we should be
very sorry to meet in the world — beings as tedious
as they are estimable, as teasing as they are blameless.   Besides, how describe the mental state of a
man who cannot hide his delight when he learns
that, instead of being an Englishman, as he has
hitherto believed, he is of Jewish birth !   As lief a
Jew as anything else, if you like.   The wise man
attaches but relative importance to matters which
do not depend on ourselves.   But why this particular rapture at finding oneself a member of a
scattered nation, a descendant of a race doomed to
be merged in others, as many nobler nations have
been doomed also ?   One thing ought to have

warned the author that her ideas on Judaism were false — to wit, that she herself has not managed or has not dared to give clear expression to them anywhere. She has left them in the hopeless vagueness of Mordecai's rhapsodies. The only clue to be found on this point is in a passage where it is said that every Jewish family ought to regard itself as fated to give birth to the *Liberator;* and in another, according to which the people of God are to be reassembled and reconstituted in the ancient Promised Land. But what ground has an author for risking views or nourishing hopes like these ? Can it be the Old Testament prophecies ? Does George Eliot share the belief of those fanatical and narrowminded millenarians to be met with now and then among Protestants, who, on the strength of certain texts, imagine that Jerusalem will become the queen of all nations and the centre of the world ? Nothing of the kind, for George Eliot is one of the freest thinkers of our time, one of those most disembarrassed of all theological hypothesis. So that we have here before us the interesting contradiction of a writer who rejects the supernatural element in the belief of the Jews, and yet pleads for the re-establishment of a people whose nationality consists precisely in this belief. We cannot help asking one another what she means — whether Judaism Restored will re-establish the temple of Jehovah and renew the sacrifice of bulls and sheep, or whether it is to be a rationalized Judaism, the

Chosen People without its sacred books, without its institution, without its faith — in short, without everything which has given it existence and character. These reflections supply at the same time an answer to an argument by which George Eliot's mind has evidently been haunted. Struck by certain great facts of recent history, astonished at the force which the sentiment of nationality has suddenly exerted as an historical influence, brooding over the instances of Germany and of Italy, she asked herself why the principle in question should not avail the scattered children of Israel, and failed to perceive that the case of the Jews is altogether peculiar. Of the four elements of nationality — community of race, community of religion, community of language, and community of territory — they lack the two last wholly, and the second itself is at this moment much more a memory than an effectual and living belief.

It is well said by Sir Hugh Mallinger, one of the characters of the novel, when he cries out as Deronda begins to set forth his views on Judaism, "For heaven's sake, don't be eccentric! I can put up with differences of opinion: all I ask is that people will inform me of them without giving themselves lunatic airs." But this is the exact charge I bring against Deronda. This young fellow, who is set before us as at once a model of self-devotion and of good sense, is the slave of a chimera, and of the most uninteresting chimera that imagination ever created. I must dwell on this absence of interest; for, in fact, it is the root of the matter. If these visons on the destinies of the Jewish people are to interest us, they must present either lively strokes of manners, or else some genial conception. The writer would have been entitled to give them a place in her story if the beliefs in question were deeply and distinctively characteristic of Jewish life in the nineteenth century; but we all know that they are nothing of the kind. That being so, she should have confined herself to giving her views on the subject in the piquant shape of a personal paradox. In its actual form, the Jewish episode of "Daniel Deronda" remains one of the most inexplicable mistakes into which a great writer has ever fallen.

In consequence, no admirer of George Eliot has failed, as he read her new novel, to ask himself the question, "Must we note here a beginning of decadence? Can it be that the vein, hitherto so abundant and well-sustained, is beginning to dry up? Can the talent of this incomparable lady be in its decline?" For my part, I do not formulate the problem quite thus: for there might be a failure here, and yet it need not be a proof of lessened strength. Besides, as I have said, there are to be found in "Daniel Deronda" characters, scenes, strokes, which yield in no respect to those which made the reputation of the earlier work. But one thing seems to me undeniable: that certain distinctive elements in George Eliot's genius have at last got the upper hand, and have disturbed the balance of her faculties. She has, as constantly happens, qualities which have become defects. The charm of her work springs in great part from a certain depth of thought; a resigned and patient sense of the conditions of human life; a morality which is at once lofty and kindly, at once implacable in analysis and pardoning much because it comprehends all. George Eliot is an idealist enamoured of good, a philosopher interested in ideas, and a consummate artist all in one—an artist unequalled in creative genius and in plastic force. This co-existence, in the same writer, of the artist and the *savant* is not so rare as may be thought. The work and life of Goethe exhibit the two forces engaged in a singularly interesting conflict, and our own literature gives us at this very moment more than one similar example. The misfortune is that one of the two tendencies almost always ends by dominating and stifling the other. The writer leans more and more to the side to which his inclination tends. Here is an historian and a philologer, devoted, as it seemed, to bare learning, who, nevertheless, breaks, when no one expects it, the bonds of his business and his appointed task, and lets us hear the marvellous accents of fantasy which were thought to be dead within him. There is another who, on the other hand, had early gained the public ear by the boldness of his paradoxes and the vigor of his style, but in whom a taste for formulas has little by little destroyed all attraction of form.[1] Such is also, I fear, the explanation of "Daniel Deronda." The author's taste for ideas carries her into theorizing; her attention to morality turns into purposed didacticism; she introduces political and social views into her novels without restraint, and, finally, the desire of exactitude in her mind produces in her style an intensity of expression which passes into obscurity. And all this turns to the great injury of her art. For art lives not by ideas, but by sentiments, I had almost said by sensations: it is instinctive, it is naïf, and it is by direct and unconsidered expression that it communicates with reality. Among all the contradictions of which life is made up, there is none more constant than this — that there is no great art without philosophy, and that yet there is no more dangerous enemy of art than reflection.

January 1877.

[1] [I think, but am not certain, that M. Scherer is here referring to MM. Renan and Taine. — *Trans.*]

V

TAINE'S HISTORY OF ENGLISH LITERATURE[1]

THIS is a book the like of which is not often seen nowadays : a book boldly conceived, slowly ripened, patiently worked out — a mighty work in which there are to be at once recognized the thought which dominates facts, the inspiration which animates style, the will which accomplishes great undertakings. I could not feel that I had set myself right with M. Taine if, before all discussion, I did not pay homage at once to the value of his work and to the power of his talent. No doubt M. Taine is of those writers who provoke one to contradict them ; but no contradiction will hinder the "History of English Literature" from being, when all is said, one of the most considerable books which have appeared for the last ten years.

Moreover, there are in this book two things very distinct from each other. There is not only a history, but also, and first of all, a certain fashion of looking at history : the author has brought to the study of his subject a mind positively made up on matters of system. It is lucky that he has also brought to it conscientious erudition and a feeling

[1] Paris : Hachette. 3 vols. 8vo. 1863.

for literary beauty. The result is that, if his system and his story have not fully succeeded in permeating each other, the reader will at worst still find in M. Taine a series of critical studies in a very great style.

As for his views on the nature of the historian's task, M. Taine, after setting them forth often before, has reproduced them now in his introduction with a precision which makes it easy to master them thoroughly, and to make a definite estimate of their value. Behind the actions of a man there is the man; and behind the visible man who acts, there is the inner man who thinks and wills. By going back, then, from facts to causes, we arrive promptly at the human soul. For what is man in reality? A living being in whose mind there is produced a representation of things. This representation works itself out and becomes an idea, or determines the will and becomes a resolve. Let us add that this transforming of sensation is carried out in manners more or less clear, vivid, and simple, from which difference arise all the other differences between men. But on what does this first difference itself depend? On a general disposition, on an initial moral state which may be referred to the action of three causes : the race — that is to say, the hereditary temperament, which varies in different peoples; the circumstances — for instance, climate, social conditions, political surroundings; and, lastly, the point which the development, the progress of which is under study, has reached. These ultimate causes, these forces being once recognized, there is nothing left before us but a question of mechanics. No doubt the directions which are taken and the values which are reached cannot be stated as rigidly as in the exact sciences, and consequently the system of notation will not be the same. But we have still in our hands, none the less, the explanation of the characteristics which separate one civilization from another. And when we use the word civilization, we mean religion, philosophy, institutions, arts: everything that goes to make up social life. The whole of it is the result of a moral state which it is our business to discover and formally to describe. Now that is the task of history. History seeks out the laws which govern the life of societies, and all the manifestations of that life. "History at bottom is a psychological problem." It will be understood from this what literary history will be like. A literature is one of the documents which put before our eyes the sentiments of preceding generations. It is the outward sign of a mental stage, the manifestation of the inner and hidden world, which is the proper subject of the historian. To write history is to work from facts up to their psychological causes; but, as the study of a literature is the best means of discovering these causes, literary history will become the principal instrument of history proper; or, still better, it will be history *par excellence,* the real history.

This argument appears to me faulty in two points: it adulterates the notion of history, and it does not completely answer to literary history as M. Taine himself has written it. For history in the sense which the word at once suggests to the mind, and such as it has been at all times conceived to be, is first of all a narrative. Its purpose is to make the actions of men known to inquirers into the causes of these actions, because that is a means of producing a better understanding of them. But its researches are limited to those causes which are matter of documentary evidence. There History stops. We cannot see in virtue of what principle she can be asked to go back to the ultimate causes of events, to consider facts in the light of a problem proposed for solution, to refer them to psychological or mechanical considerations. Besides, what is to become of the story in the midst of these researches, and what have science and literature to gain by such a confusion of kinds? The studies which M. Taine sketches out for us belong not to history but to philosophy. They even constitute a social department of this latter called the philosophy of history — a useful, I will say an important, science, and one which men like Montesquieu, like Herder, like Guizot, like Buckle, have made illustrious; but which cannot be confounded with the art of the great historical narrators without doing violence alike to the interests of philosophy and of letters.

What I have said of history in general is equally true of literary history in particular. Former students of this subject had subordinated general considerations to the special study of authors; and if at any time they thought fit to draw from the state of letters in a country conclusions relating to the political or social condition of that country, it was, so to speak, but a work of supererogation. With M. Taine it is quite the contrary; what was secondary has become principal with him. His book is in essence a history of the English race and of civilization in England. The writer habitually starts from the moral fact, from primary aptitudes, from instinctive dispositions. He shows us conquerors and conquered, blending and forming a new nationality, richer and more complex than the old. Then he puts us in presence of the great events, such as the Renaissance and the Reformation, which affected England as they affected Europe. This is the thread of the story, the substance of the book. The works of his authors, whether they be famous or obscure, whether they be forgotten fabliaux or immortal masterpieces, are merely evidence used to support theories of the writer. Their literary worth is far less in question than the light that they can throw on the manners of an epoch. They are treated, not as products of the art of writing, but as historical documents. There is in this something very novel and very instructive: but, it must also be clear, there is a way of looking at literary

history which is utterly unlike what has hitherto
been understood by it.

A "question of title" it may be said — "perhaps
the mere demand of a publisher!" Besides, has
not M. Taine clearly declared his purpose ? Has
he not said that he undertakes an inquiry into the
pyschology of a people by means of the history of
its literature ? Has he not succeeded in this ? and
if he has succeeded, why quibble with him about
the precise use of a word, or the possibility of a
misunderstanding ?

I should be the first to yield to these arguments
if it were a mere question of title. But there is
something more at stake here : there is the confusion of two methods.

For M. Taine, in fact, has not been so faithful to
his first idea as not frequently to have slipped into
literary history in the common sense of the term.
In vain is his head full of peoples and races. He
is alive also to the greatness of individuals. His
strong and lively imagination is not less struck by
the physiognomy of a writer than by that of an
epoch, and he loves to render the one as well as
the other. He excels at sketching a character, at
defining a talent. He delights in laying hold of a
mighty or strange personality — a Shakespeare, a
Milton, a Byron — in magnifying it as though to
ascertain its nature better, in observing it in the
isolation which comes of genius, in discovering its
strength and its weakness, in seeking for the secret

tie which unites its different parts.   At such times
he hits upon phrases, vividly picturesque or sculpt-
ural, to express the peculiar nature of each mind
and of each work.   Now all this biographical and
critical part of the work is at bottom but a *hors
d'œuvre;* it does not enter into the primary plan,
it cannot be referred to the *idée mère.*   The individual, considered in his proper genius — that is to
say, strictly as an individual — has no place in a
book which aims at being a philosophy of history.
One of two things must be true.   Either the race
explains all, even individual character (and in that
case the product of general causes in these characters ought to have been pointed out), or else a man's
genius is a fact which we are powerless to explain,
which we must accept without attempting to determine its laws (and in that case it is proper to neg-
lect it in a treatise which underneath works of
literature proposes solely "to seek the physiology
of a people ").   Besides, it must not be thought that
when M. Taine betakes himself to the study of the
individual he gives up his fixed ideas of system.
He makes a change in them, that is all.   He has at
one moment been busy in identifying the instincts
of a race in the general characters of a literature.
He will at the next try to discover, in the genius of
a man, the dominant feature whence he thinks he
can deduce the others.

It is well known with what resourceful paradox
M. Taine once upheld a similar thesis on the sub-

ject of Livy. Now, the leaders of English literature are subjected to the same process. Is the subject Shakespeare? "Let us seek the man," says our author, "and let us seek him in his style. The style explains the work, and by showing the chief features of the genius, it announces the others. When you have once seized the master faculty, you can see the whole artist developing himself like a flower." A little further on it is Milton's turn. "His emotions and his reasonings, all the forces and all the actions of his soul, draw together and array themselves under one single sentiment, that of the sublime; and the mighty flood of lyric poesy runs from him, impetuous, unbroken, in splendor like a sheet of gold." Obviously this process has nothing to do with that of which I was speaking above. The one consists in working back from the poetical creations of a people to the natural dispositions characterizing that people; the other consists, on the contrary, in a logical deduction of the qualities of a writer from his predominant aptitude. To speak frankly, these are two methods opposed to each other, connected only by the author's fancy for abstract reasoning, and possessing the special fault of being heaped on one another here without interdependence and without mutual subordination.

Let me be understood. I do not reproach M. Taine with the scientific airs which his thought gives herself. He was entitled to give us a phil-

osophic treatise, even if we might perhaps have preferred a book with its edification better disguised,
with its solidity more adapted to the task of pleasing. Nevertheless, and even if we place ourselves at
his own point of view, we may think that he might
have done more to win his readers' confidence. He
betrays his fixed ideas of system too naïvely and too
uniformly. Instead of consulting the writings of
a period so as to gather from them the strokes
with which he is to draw the picture of the epoch,
he begins by explanations, narratives, descriptions,
so that when literary history at last comes up, it
is only to supply examples in support of the
theory. The effect is that facts seem to bend to
what is asked of them; that the author is (even
against one's will) suspected now of having in-
vented the general rule to explain the particular
phenomenon, now of having twisted historic fact
to suit the exigencies of general views. Let us
not mistake. The human mind and fact are two
matters which have a necessary tendency to draw
together, but which never entirely coincide. Reality
always exceeds our conceptions, and we cannot shut
it up in our private formulas except by mutilating it.
Hence comes a kind of dissembled war, which history
and philosophy have in all times waged against
each other — the war between the man who tries
to adjust facts to laws, and the man who, on the
other hand, busies himself with following men and
things across the eternal surprises of chance.   M.

Taine has set himself to be at once philosopher and historian; he has shown in his work qualities which are very rarely found in union. But he has not succeeded in disguising that feature of his undertaking which was necessarily doubtful, some would say radically impossible. Nay, his methods do not only excite doubt, they sometimes proceed to open violence. Here are two sufficiently amusing examples.

England in the ethnological theories of our author is essentially "the moist country." There earth and air are saturated with water, which explains everything; yes, everything, even to "the enormous whiskers" of the men; everything, even to their "huge feet like those of wading birds, solidly booted, admirable for walking in mud." It will be admitted that this picture of an Englishman obliged to cross marshes, and acquiring the feet of web in the process, pushes the doctrine of the influence of *milieux* a little far.

A few pages later the author brings out in energetic outline the combined habits of independence and order which distinguish the English people. Unluckily, when he is once "off," M. Taine lets himself go, and ends by throwing more than one doubtful touch into the picture. Thus he attributes to paternal authority in England "a degree of authority and of dignity which is unknown to us." He should have said exactly the contrary; paternal authority is with us much severer and much more jealous; but even this is not all. Among the evidence which M. Taine brings in support of his assertions, there is one item which cannot be read without a smile. "The father," he says, is called "the governor." Now this so-called title of authority is, on the contrary, a piece of familiar slang, a nickname which, without being exactly disrespectful, is not easy to reconcile with our notions of filial respect.[1]

I am not certain whether I have made the objections which the idea and the method of M. Taine raise in my mind entirely clear. They may be all summed up thus. The author wished to set before us the formation and the transformations of the English national spirit. He sought out the expressions of this spirit, the documents of this history, in the literature of the people to whom he wished to introduce us. On the other hand, such a literature cannot be reduced altogether to the rather secondary part of witness in support of a thesis, of testimony in favor of an ethnological law. A literature has a life proper to itself: it moves independently, it obeys special influences. It furnishes, I admit, important data to history: but that cannot prevent it from being a literature first of all: that is to say, art, the expression of the sense of beauty. That is its essence: all the rest is, so to speak, but acci-

---

[1] M. Taine, in his *Notes sur l'Angleterre* (p. 120), insists on trying to find a social meaning in this familiar expression, and deducing serious conclusions from it.

dental and indirect.   Now M. Taine has felt this.
He has been unable to remain so faithful to his first
ideas as to study English literature solely as the
monument of a civilization.   He has undergone the
charm of those mighty geniuses in whom he would
at first have seen nothing but mere samples of a
race; he has allowed himself to consider them as
writers and as poets, to question them on the secret
of their conceptions, to describe their methods, to
characterize their style.   In short, he has frequently slipped in his own despite into literary
history, such as it is commonly understood and written.   And this creates two works within his work,
two plans which mutually cross and entangle, two
methods which by no means combine, but on the
contrary oppose each other.   Obviously this is no
mere question of title.   M. Taine, despite the
vigor with which he has realized the master-
thought of his work, has not arrived at an entire
unity of execution.   There is something too much
in him and something too little.   Had he been
nothing if not philosophical, we should not have
thought of demanding from him a complete view of
the history of letters in England: while, on the
other hand, when he permits himself so many excursions into the field of pure art, we feel obliged
to reproach him with omissions.

Shakespeare is a product of the Renaissance;
Milton a representation of Puritanism; the comic
authors of Charles II.'s time the expression of a

licentious reaction against absurd austerities. All this is solidly deduced and set in strong relief. Yet it was inevitable that M. Taine, in thus treating his subject, should mix with it a crowd of views and appreciations which run outside his first intention; and so in these pages one often loses sight of that which was our starting point. We catch ourselves forgetting that what we had to discover was a country and an epoch under the features of individual genius. Then, our taste once whetted for literary discussion, we begin to ask M. Taine for notice of many things which he has not told us, of which his plan did not oblige him to tell us, but which we should have liked to find in these volumes, if only as a kind of half concession and kindly inconsistency. We are surprised, unreasonably I grant, but still we are surprised, not to be put in the way of tracing certain great schools and profound influences. We do not learn what has been the action of the chief English writers on that English literature which, however, forms after all the substance and canvas of the book. And what is the result when M. Taine finds himself in presence of an author who has no very marked enthnological signification — of Johnson, for instance ? Johnson is an original figure : he published numerous works : he founded a school : his style — half-forcible, half-pedantic — long set the fashion. It is true that Johnson represents nothing, is the formula of nothing : and so M. Taine gives not two pages to his writings, and

not a word to the traces he has left. He is less
generous still to Young and to Macpherson, to
Hume, to Gibbon, to Robertson. Poetic influence,
philosophical action itself, innovations in thought or
style, all the capital facts of literary history, our
author neglects them when he does not find in
them the expression of a moral state of society.

We might indeed excuse mere gaps; but the system itself, as M. Taine applies it, sometimes runs
the risk of falsifying historic fact. I need no further proof of this than his picture of modern poetry
in England. At the end of the last century appears
the English Romantic school, "wholly similar to
ours by its doctrines, its origins, and its relation;
by the truths it discovered, the exaggerations it
committed, the scandal it aroused." From this
school issue two kinds of poetry: historical poetry,
illustrated by Lamb, Campbell, Coleridge, Thomas
Moore, Southey, and Walter Scott; and philosophical poetry, to which belong the works of Wordsworth, of Shelley, and of Byron. Here assuredly
we have great names. Walter Scott, not to mention
others, occupied a considerable place in the literature of his country and his time; but Walter Scott
is a man of letters pure and simple, and will not
long occupy M. Taine. Indeed fifty pages will suffice for all this great period of modern poetry in
England. The author is in a hurry: he has found
his "man-formula," he strews all the other reputa-
tions before his feet. One writer only counts in

his eyes, and that is Byron. Why Byron? Because Byron personifies something. "If Goethe was the poet of the universe, Byron was the poet of personality : and if the German spirit has found its interpreter in the one, the English spirit has found its interpreter in the other."

One thing is certain : the English spirit has not been at all ready to acknowledge its interpreter. But, setting this observation aside, how thoroughly does such a manner of writing history disguise the meaning and the march of facts ! I do not think it is at all exact to speak of a "Romantic" school in England. The English have had neither the word nor the thing, neither the discussions which the term recalls nor the innovations which hold so great a place in the French and German literature of this century. Besides, what connection can be established in this respect between the two countries separated by the Channel ? English literature started by independence, and it is in independence that we have ended. Innovation in France has inclined most of all to the theatrical side, while modern English has made its principal effort in narrative poems. And, to come to particular names, who are to be the Lamartines, the Hugos, the Mussets of our neighbors ? Who are to be our Scotts and our Byrons, our Shelleys and our Wordsworths ? I have said that M. Taine divides the recent poets of England into two classes — philosophers and historians. The division is more con-

venient than accurate.   A little arbitrary in itself,
it becomes still more so when all writers are forced
to enter one or other category.   Is it "Gertrude"
to which Campbell owes the privilege of figuring
among historians ?   Is it giving a very exact or a
very full idea of Thomas Moore, of that light and
elegant muse, of that inspiration at once sensual,
sentimental, and satirical, to make of him a traveller
or an antiquary masquerading as a poet ?   And
Coleridge ?   I have found it impossible even to
guess what procured him the honor of being labelled
historian.   However all this is nothing beside the
verdict passed a little later on Carlyle.   Carlyle
classed among the Puritans, "the real Puritans,"
by the side of Pascal and Cowper !   Shade of
Teufelsdroeckh !   I think I see a very curious smile
flitting over your cynical lips.

But, after all, these are only details.   I attach
far more importance to the idea which the author
has formed of the development of modern poetry
in England, to the manner in which he describes
this mighty evolution of the national genius.   M.
Taine, I have said, passes rapidly over other names
to get to Byron.   Byron in his eyes is the last word
of English literature : his contemporaries are but
at most the *di minores* who follow in his train.
Now, has he not, in setting things forth after this
fashion, put his own literary predilections in the
place of facts ?   Has he not rather interpreted
history than told it ?

For the moment the merits of Byron are not
in question. We shall return to them presently.
What we are looking for is the succession of ideas
and the linking together of influences. Now, it is
an established fact that the action of Byron on his
contemporaries was lively, but not durable — indeed, it hardly outlasted his own life. "Don Juan"
— his last work — never has had on the other side
of the Channel the kind of symbolical importance
which it pleases us to attribute to it. Besides, men
were quick to be disgusted with the misanthropic
dandyism, the airs of a *blasé* aristocrat, which the
author of "Childe Harold" was never tired of
ostentatiously affecting. The English genius is
much more active, and as a consequence much more
supple, than we suppose it to be. It passes rapidly
from one hobby to another, and unceasingly seeks
to find its way through contrasts. And so Byron,
hailed in his day as the personification of the noblest
melancholy, ended by seeming artificial and shal-
low. Tired of grand — and false — sentiments, men
turned with delight to a writer whose simplicity
was not free from study, but whose very study had
often enabled him to reach profound thoughts and
a delicate interpretation of nature. Wordsworth
was in his turn proclaimed the greatest poet of the
time. And then, in his turn, he again was found
wanting. Coleridge — a logical enthusiast who
united speculative views to mystical intuitions, a
poet and a theologian — had given his fellow-coun-

trymen many new lights from the German side.
The wind of philosophical systems had made its
breath felt. Emotion was found insufficient; ideas
were called for. And so Shelley, poor Shelley! so
disdained and cried down in his lifetime, succeeded
Wordsworth in vogue. The *amende honorable* was
made to him: he was proclaimed one of the glories
of England. Men became passionately enamoured
of his ethereal, subtle, intangible poetry, and the
hollowness of his humanitarian dreams was for-
given him in virtue of the sublimity and beauty of
his imagination. After which he shared the fate
of his predecessors. As time went on his defects
became more apparent. There was not · enough
human heart-beat, not enough life, not enough of
the dramatic within him. There came a new poet
who, to the science of rhythm, the resources of
expression, the gift of epic narration, the deep feeling for nature, to all the caprices of a delightful
fancy, to all the favorite ideas, noble or morbid, of
modern thought, knew how to join the language
of manly passion. Thus, as it were summing up in
himself all his forerunners, he touched all hearts;
he linked together all admirations; he has remained
the true representative, the last expression and
final, of the poetic period to which ·he belongs.
Tennyson reigns to-day almost alone in increasing
and uncontested glory.[1] Such, at least, is the move-

[1] The evolution of taste and of thought has continued since
these lines were written, and the supremacy of Tennyson has
received (1875) more than one attack.

ment of modern poetry in England as I understand
it.   As for M. Taine, he finds nothing in Wordsworth but limitless boredom, and nothing in Tennyson but an amiable dilettantism.   It will be seen
that an understanding between us is not immediately likely.

But, if M. Taine's systematic views sometimes
lead him to misjudge the interconnection of literary
facts, they also lead him at times to exaggeration
and caricature.   He must needs, to make his historical deductions effective, hit upon individual
characters which represent an age.   And then he
permits himself to endow his figures in a very curious fashion with heroic attitudes, with gigantic
stature, with mystical undermeaning.   So he did
long ago with Dickens, with Thackeray, with Carlyle;
but I know no more notable example of this kind
of hallucination than the chapter in this book
which treats of Lord Byron.

Byron is one of our French superstitions.   Thanks
to distance and to the obstacles which translation
sets in the way of familiar knowledge, we are still,
on this head, in the fashion of 1820.   We insist
upon taking the noble poet seriously.   His name
excites in us an idea of luxury on the great scale,
of brilliant debauchery, of chivalrous character, the
whole mingled with immortal poesy.   Byron is to
us a Don Juan of genius, a splendid and mysterious
Lara, or, as M. de Lamartine sang of old, something
between an archangel and a demon.

M. Taine could not but find his account in accepting the popular legend; for such a figure must put a magnificent crown to the edifice which he had just been constructing.   Here was the English genius, after five centuries of history, on the point of finding its last expression, its incomparable emblem.   Accordingly, see with what expense of metaphors, of contrasts, of hyperboles our author tries to invest his hero with superhuman significance.

" The passion of the moment, be it great or small, swooped down on his soul like a tempest, aroused it, excited it to the pitch of folly or to the pitch of genius.   His journal, his familiar letters, all his unpremeditated prose writings, quiver as it were with wit, anger, enthusiasm.   The cry of feeling vibrates in the very least words.   Since Saint-Simon nothing has been so vividly confidential.   All styles seem dull and all souls seem sluggish beside his." Further on we have a picture "of that splendid impetuosity of faculties, unbridled and let loose, rushing where chance may lead them, and seeming to hurry him without choice on his part to the four corners of the horizon."   Again: Byron ruined himself by despising public opinion; but, singularly enough, this contempt of opinion, which clearly could have done him no harm save in a public which was slave to opinion, this very disdain of the conventional, is one of the characteristics of the English.   "This instinct of revolt is in the

race. It is nourished by a whole bundle of savage
passions born of the climate — a gloomy humor, a
violent imagination, an indomitable pride, the taste
for danger, the desire of battle, the thirst for excitement which is only glutted by destruction, and the
sombre madness which used to urge the Scandi-
navian Berserkers when, in an open boat, under a
sky riven by lightning, they abandoned themselves
to the tempest whose fury they had breathed."

And so the features of the child are still visible
in the maturity of the adult. The Englishman
may measure cotton as he pleases, but he is still
the descendant of the ancient sea-kings, and the
finished ideal of an Englishman will be neither
more nor less than Byron. "Strange and thoroughly northern poetry," cries M. Taine, "with
its root in the Edda and its flower in Shakespeare,
born long ago under an inclement sky, beside a
stormy sea, wrought by a race only too self-willed,
too strong, and too sombre — a poetry which, after
lavishing images of desolation and of heroism,
ends by spreading over the whole life of nature,
like a sable veil, the vision of universal destruction."

According to M. Taine, the poet in Byron is not
less great than the man. He is the only one of
his contemporaries who has "reached the summit."
Manfred is a twin brother of Faust. As for his
style, none has ever better expressed the soul,
"its labor, its expansion, are things visible. Ideas

have boiled in it long and stormily, like the lumps
of metal piled up in the furnace.   They have melted
under the stress of fervent heat, they have blended
their lava with quiverings and explosions, and now
at last the door opens, a heavy stream of fire falls
into the furrow prepared beforehand, setting the
shivering air on fire, while its blazing hues scorch
the eyes that too obstinately gaze at it."

Such is M. Taine's Byron.   No phrase seems too
strong to express his greatness, no image too vivid
to indicate the splendor of his genius.   But it
remains to inquire whether the portrait is as exactly
like as it is brilliantly painted.   For my part, I
own that I can hardly recognize the real Byron in
it at all, and that M. Taine seems to me at once
to have magnified the man and overrated the poet.

Byron, doubtless, is no ordinary bard.   He
possesses fecundity, eloquence, wit.   Yet these
very qualities are confined within pretty narrow
limits.   The wit of "Beppo" and of "Don Juan"
is of the kind that consists in dissonance; that is
to say, in the serio-comic, in an apparent gravity
which is contradicted every moment by drollery of
phrase.   In the same way Byron's fecundity is
more apparent than real.   He wrote a great deal —
poems serious and poems comic, epics and dramas,
visions and satires; but, speaking strictly, he never
had more than a single subject — himself.   No man
has ever pushed egotism farther than he.   Childe
Harold, Lara, Don Juan, Manfred, the Deformed

Transformed, all the poet's heroes, are but so many copies of the same original. Nor is it only his own character that he reproduces continually. It is his domestic misfortunes, his mother and the education she gave him, his wife and the faults which he thinks himself entitled to reproach her with. Now there is in this obstinate determination to acquaint the public with his private life, not only a want of taste and dignity, but also a singular inability to rise to great art, to art which is impersonal and disinterested.

Yet on this point, on the poetical genius of Byron, M. Taine has glimpses of the truth. He begins by extolling him as a giant, but he ends by reducing him to the proportions of an ordinary mortal. At one moment he is a volcano vomiting lava; a little further we shall find him a merely logical and spirited orator. We shall even find acknowledgments that there are some glass beads among the Orient jewelry, some opera choruses among his sombre poetry. There is a confession that it was time for "Don Juan" to come to an end, inasmuch as it was beginning to be a bore. The truth is that Byron's talent is less poetical than oratorical; he has less of imagination than of rhetoric. He always reminds me of the judgment which Schiller passed on Mme. de Staël when he wrote to Goethe: — "The sense of poetry as we understand it is utterly absent in her; she can only assimilate in works of this kind the side which is passionate, oratorical, and general." Exactly so. It is, indeed, a mistake to confound eloquence with poetry. Eloquence is that kind of discourse which serves as an expression for personal emotion; poetry, an infinitely more varied and less interested thing, is the making manifest by means of language of that element of beauty which is in all things and which it is its business to feel and to disengage. We in France are wont to distinguish insufficiently between the two arts. We find it hard to forget ourselves, and give ourselves up to the proper power of the object. We remain the slaves of lyrical declamation. It is the same with Byron, who is of the school of Pope, who himself is of our school. The author of the "Corsair" was not ignorant of the fact; he makes no mystery of his tastes; his admiration for Pope is the fundamental article of his poetical creed, and he is never tired of extolling, as the final effort of genius, the smooth and balanced verses of that artificial writer.

The man in Byron is of a nature even less sincere than that of the poet. Underneath this Beltenebros there is hidden a coxcomb. He posed all through his life. He had every affectation — the writer's, the roué's, the dandy's, the conspirator's. He was constantly writing, and he pretends to despise his writings. To believe himself, he was proud of nothing but his skill in bodily exercises. An Englishman, he affects Bonapartism; a peer of the realm, he speaks of the Universal Republic with

the enthusiasm of a schoolboy of fifteen. He plays
at misanthropy, at disillusion : he parades his vices;
he even tries to make us believe that he has committed a crime or two. Read his letters — his let-
ers written nominally to friends, but handed about
from hand to hand in London. Read his journal —
a journal kept ostensibly for himself, but handed
over afterwards by him to Moore with authority
to publish it. The littleness which these things
show is amazing. You find things purely silly,
like this definition : — "Poetry is the sense of a
world past and a world to come." Women, he
holds, should only read prayer-books or cookery-
books. He will tell you how he met a friend, but
would not ask him to dinner because he wanted
to eat a whole turbot by himself. He makes entries
of his feeding his cats and his raven. He observes
that he has torn a button off his coat. He will
bewail the death of a barber or a dentist, and put
them high above the Duke of Wellington. All this
might be excused if it were sincere — I mean sincere trifling, or sincere folly. But no: it was all an
affectation of trifling, a variety of pose and of mys-
tification. Now this is what M. Taine has not seen
sufficiently or reckoned with enough. A score of
times as I read his eloquent pages on Byron's
stormy soul, I have felt tempted to whisper in his
ear Chamfort's saying, " The great art is the art of
not being taken in."

I have scarcely space to say a few words concerning M. Taine's style, and yet I should have liked to study his fashion of writing — so full of vigor, I had almost said of violence.   I think that by considering its processes closely, one might again trace the effect of the author's ideas of system.   M. Taine is an artist beyond doubt, and a very powerful one : but he is an artist bound apprentice to a *savant*.   He is a man of thought first of all ; he demonstrates, he describes because description is another way of demonstrating, but he does not tell a story.   The picture which he constructs by means of innumerable strokes, ingeniously combined, is only the visible image of his thesis itself. His multiplied descriptions, his accumulated details, his masses of words are but so many arguments which he urges upon you.   His very imagery smells of logic.   I can never read him without thinking of those gigantic steam-hammers which strike redoubled and resounding blows, which send out myriads of sparks, and under the ceaseless blows of which the solid steel is fashioned and wrought. Everything gives an idea of power, a sensation of force ; but it must be added that so much noise is deafening, and that after all, if the style is as solid and as flashing as metal, it is also sometimes as heavy and as hard.

VI

SHAKESPEARE AND CRITICISM

I HAVE just received three new volumes of M.
Emile Montégut's translation of Shakespeare's
works, containing the English history-plays. The
earlier volumes gave us the Comedies, and, with
three or four volumes more for the great dramas,
the pieces with ancient subjects, and the Poems,
the book will be finished. I have subjected M.
Montégut's work to a rigorous examination. I
have not been satisfied with turning it over, but
have re-read some of the original plays, comparing
the translation in all difficult places. And I have
been struck with the care and the success of the
rendering of these passages. It is no small task to
reproduce the good and bad jokes, the inexhaustible plays on words, which the dramatist allows
himself even in the most pathetic situations. But
M. Montégut has, in the great majority of cases,
come out successful. I should add that in the
translation each piece is preceded by an introduction, and followed by notes, in both of which I have
found the best-established results of criticism. I
need hardly say that I do not invariably agree with
M. Montégut; for instance, I could not give him

my adhesion on the meaning of "The Tempest"; for I cannot recognize in it the poet's last will and testament, his farewell to the public, the summing up of his dramatic work. But these are disagreements of detail. As a rule, M. Montégut's judgments are as solid as they are ingeniously supported. It is to be hoped that the translator will not finish his work without adding to it a general essay on the English poet's genius: and I take pleasure in the anticipation of seeing so subtle and so attractive a mind employed in the analysis of one of the most complex geniuses which have ever existed.[1]

I am glad that Shakespeare supplies me with an occasion for speaking of M. Courdaveaux, Professor in the Faculty of Letters at Douai, and author of a volume[2] of literary studies. Most of these studies are devoted to Latin poets, and among them to the Latin poets of love. But Shakespeare also has two articles as his share. In all these pieces the author gives evidence of an elegant scholarship, shows knowledge of his texts, and frames his presentation of them with observations which show good taste and ingenuity. Unfortunately M. Courdaveaux has a thesis. According to him there is a close connection between a man's

---

[1] *Œuvres Complètes de Shakespeare.* Translated by Emile Montégut. The translation is now completed in ten volumes; but the author has not included the Introduction for which I wished.

[2] *Caractères et Talents : Etudes sur la Littérature Ancienne et Moderne.* Par V. Courdaveaux.

talent and his moral character. If Theocritus was not a poet of the first class, it is because he was deficient, not in intellectual, but in moral, qualities. If Chénier is superior to Propertius, it is because Chénier was a much better man. If Virgil and Horace excelled the other flatterers of Augustus, it is because they knew how, even in flattering, to preserve a certain dignity. If, to conclude, Shakespeare deserves to be set above all his contemporaries, it is first of all because he excelled them in nobility of sentiment, in rectitude and elevation of ideas. Even the enigmatical character of Hamlet is explained in the most natural manner in the world by the virtues of the poet. Shakespeare would have been incapable of commiting a murder in cold blood, however much circumstances might have seemed to him to make vengeance a duty. He would have hesitated and drawn back. Well, then, Shakespeare has lent his own feelings to Hamlet, and thence comes the irresolution of which that personage has become the never-to-be-forgotten type. Goethe, Schlegel, and all the rest have given themselves much useless trouble because they forgot that a great poet is a worthy man, and that a worthy man necessarily portrays himself in his works.

I cannot stop to discuss a question which would take me too far, and which does not seem to be well formulated by M. Courdaveaux. There is on this head a confusion of things which ought to be kept distinct. I incline to think that a poet in the

most exalted sense of the word could not be a
knave or a fribble.   The very cultivation of the art,
the direction of mind which it implies, the ideal
cast of thought imply a sort of moral life.   The
conception of the beautiful is a pure thing, and all
impurity is damage done to the æsthetic perfection
of the work.   Great poets are healthy by nature.
But this is a very different thing from saying that
the poet is a good man endowed with talent, or that
genius consists in worthily expressing noble sentiments.   It is still less equivalent to saying that
the end of art is to disseminate good principles or
furnish fine examples.   It must be clear how many
distinctions have to be made to settle completely
the old problem of the relations of the beautiful
and the good, of art and of morality.   But I cannot
dwell on this, and I must pass to a book on Shakespeare which seems to me to mark a new epoch in
criticism.

There is no country where Shakespeare-worship
has been more fervently professed than in Germany.
All schools of philosophy and literature pay equal
homage to the mighty dramatist; all have selected
his personality as the representative of the highest
poetry : and they differ only in the point of view
at which they place themselves for the purpose of
better exalting the genius of the poet.   Thus the
different forms of admiration for Shakespeare beyond the Rhine give us a kind of abstract of the
vicissitudes of criticism in what is the classic land
of theory.

The Romantic School was the first to write the name of Shakespeare on its banners. Lessing had already set the example of the English drama in opposition to the artificial rules of the French tragedy. But the Romantics went further. They put Shakespeare forward as the representative of the middle ages, to which they had taken a fancy. They sought and found in him all the elements of art as they understood it. They acquitted him of all the defects with which he was reproached — slips in history and geography as well as mere faults of taste. Their sun must have no spots; their Bible must remain infallible. Shakespeare had been regarded as an unconscious poet. They claimed for him the full and clear conviction of his own genius and his own work. In short, the author of " Hamlet " was proclaimed the universal poet, the giant of the ages, the supreme exponent of his age, of humanity, of the world.

Philosophical speculation succeeded Romantic mysticism : yet without affecting the new cult, to which it was satisfied with giving a different meaning.   Hegel in his " Æsthetic " followed the development of the idea through the different phases of art — the symbolic art of Asia, the classical art of the Greeks, and finally the romantic art of the Moderns. This latter, in obedience to the ternary arrangement of the system, passed from painting to music, then from music to poetry, and went through the three successive phases of epic, lyric, and drama. Thus drama represented the highest and completest form of art, and Shakespeare, it will be understood, came in at this final term of the demonstration as a personification of the dramatic class. The English poet thus had still to play pretty much the same part, and continued to hide himself from vulgar eyes in uncontested and inaccessible supremacy.

Time brought with it a fresh reaction : the apparent rigor of the Hegelian dialectic had succeeded the fantasies of Romanticism ; but a day came when this dialectic seemed hollow. The Germans were suddenly seized with a great disgust for formulas. They turned eagerly towards active life: they stimulated themselves to become men of action. Public and private virtues recovered in their eyes the place too long usurped by contemplation. Thenceforward nothing was fine unless it was moral. Lucky Shakespeare to find the means of preserving his royalty even in this third evolution ! An eminent critic, Herr Gervinus, hastened to prove (in four volumes) that Shakespeare was the greatest of moralists, the most eloquent defender of the ways of Providence, the surest guide of mankind in the paths of virtue. Not a play of his but, under the commentator's pen, ended by showing some intention of high teaching.

Never had more ability been put at the service of an unluckier thesis. It so happens that Shakespeare is of all the great poets the furthest removed, not merely from any thought of didactics, but from all fixed ideas of the moral kind. A poet pure and simple, he treats good and evil as impartially as Nature herself. But Germany had a fit of utility and didactics upon her; and it was necessary to confirm her in this way of wisdom without disturbing her faith in Shakespeare. This was the origin of Herr Gervinus's book; he gave a new opening to the need for *engouement* which characterizes our ingenious neighbors.

Up to this point, and through all these revolutions of taste and thought, enthusiasm had remained unaffected; the unconscious poet and the learned poet, the unrestrained fantasist and the exalted sage, had been admired by turns; but the genius had been unceasingly declared unique and incomparable. Each vied with other in extravagance of praise; there were no reserves. It would have seemed indecent to pick out faults or even to set degrees between beauties. Men were ready to say with Victor Hugo, "The oak has an eccentric fashion of growing — knotty boughs, sombre foliage, rough and coarse bark — but he is the oak. *And it is because of all this that he is the oak.*" It would have been thought a want of filial piety to treat the master's works like those of any other mortal. But alas! no faith is so deeply rooted in the human soul that it is not shaken at last. There is no movement so unanimous that it does not sooner or later provoke a reaction, and the more blind and excessive the tide has been the more certain is the reflux. In no other way than this can the balance to which all human affairs tend be established; though, more properly speaking, it is never established at all, but consists in this very fluctuation of the mind between opinions which are always partly true and partly false.

Shakespeare-worship is an example of this. Undoubtedly the religion had become a superstition, and the very fanaticism of the believers was sure to end in arousing the objections of sceptics. At the very least independent spirits were sure to claim the right of free examination : and this is what has actually happened. Some two years ago there appeared in Germany a little book which dares to discuss Shakespeare, to distinguish the strong from the weak points in him, to bring him back under the common law of criticism. It is clear that a new error announces itself in the history of the poet's destiny.[1]

The ground-idea of Herr Rümelin's book is the necessity, if we wish to understand Shakespeare, of transporting ourselves into the circumstances in the midst of which he lived and wrote. We make, he thinks, a false estimate of the rank which Shakespeare enjoyed in the esteem of his contemporaries — of the reputation in which his works were held by court and public ; and we thus surround his image with a halo by which we proceed

[1] *Shakespearestudien.* Von Gustav Rümelin. Stuttgart. 1866.

to let ourselves be dazzled. He would have the
truth to be that the theatre was in very evil odor
during those Puritanic times ; that it was attended
only by the populace on the one hand, and by a few
young men of fashion on the other ; that the vocation of an actor was universally despised ; that
Shakespeare does not seem to have enjoyed any
extraordinary vogue during his own life ; that, in
short, the unequalled glory with which his name
is now for ever surrounded dates no further back
than some hundred years ago.

We shall see in a moment the consequences which
Herr Rümelin thinks he can deduce from these
facts. But I must begin by requesting the reader
not to accept the facts themselves too hastily.
The verses in which Ben Jonson equals Shakespeare to the greatest tragedians of antiquity suffice
to show what the contemporaries of the poet thought
of him. The epitaph in which Milton not merely
expresses his admiration for the dead poet, but calls
him

Dear son of memory, great heir of fame,

proves that the succeeding generation were no more
insensible than we are to the beauties of Shakespeare. But Herr Rümelin has been unlucky
throughout this part of his book. He has sum-
moned to support his thesis certain sixteenth-
century documents, and it so happens that these
documents are part of a pretty considerable collection of forged autographs. The English are not

less active than we are in this kind of fabrication ;
it may be added that they are not more skilful, and
that the most cursory reading ought to have been
enough to put M. Rümelin on his guard.

Our author's starting point is indeed in itself
incontestable. It is certain that we appreciate the
work of a writer much better when we strip him
of the halo with which fate has surrounded him
and restore him to the company of the circumstances in which he lived. And it is good, in order
to understand Shakespeare, to remember that he
was an actor and the manager of a theatre. His
plays were not merely pieces of literature, but also,
and first of all, things forced upon him by his business. He did not write for posterity, but for a
special public which he had to please. This is all
true ; but it is not less true at the same time that
it is possible to abuse such considerations, and Herr
Rümelin gives an example of it when he hints that
Shakespeare portrayed his friend the Earl of
Southampton under the features of young Harry
the Fifth. When he guesses that the plays taken
from Roman history were meant to serve as a warning to the same Southampton — "Coriolanus" exhib-
iting to him the dangers of aristocratic insolence,
"Antony and Cleopatra" those of amorous intrigue,
"Julius Cæsar" those of ambition — when, in
short, criticism plunges thus headlong into conjecture, we can only remember that things like these
are pure hypotheses, as incapable of proof as of

disproof. It is the same with this whole class of historical considerations. We may grant that Shakespeare, working according to the needs of the theatre, did not always subject his work to very severe discipline. He wrote scene after scene, developing first one situation, then another, and ending by losing sight of the unity of the whole work. It is certain that there are two distinct dramas in " King Lear," and that most of the pieces drawn from English history are mere chronicles thrown into dialogue. But Herr Rümelin goes much farther. We know in what a questionable shape the part of Hamlet presents itself, in how many ways commentators have sought to explain this mysterious mixture of irresolution and enterprise, of hidden designs and capricious sallies. For Herr Rümelin there is no mystery at all. The character of Hamlet is simply incoherent; and it is incoherent because the poet worked in bits and scraps; because he did not know how to bind the scenes together, to run the shades into one. In a word, we are to see no problem here, but the actual imperfection of the work. Perhaps so; but it will be granted that this is to cut the knot rather than to untie it.

Herr Rümelin explains the great features of Shakespeare's genius in the same way as the defects of his dramas, by the circumstances of his life. We must, he holds, always come back to the one point: the poet was a manager. Everything follows from this. Shakespeare's profession has its inconveniences as well as its advantages. If it assists the knowledge of mankind, it is not favorable to experience of the world. Hence, Shakespeare is distinguished for the creation of a multitude of characters, all living and individual; his theatre is a gallery of portraits which, once seen, can never be forgotten. No writer has ever shown such a faculty of creation. On the other hand (still according to Herr Rümelin), the action in the English dramatist's works is weak. You see that he is ignorant of society and of the secret springs of events; in particular he errs by making situations too much the result of personal character. Experience tells us that things do not happen thus in real life. We must remember, too, that a manager's career is full of agitations. It allows of no rest. And so, assuming that the manager be an actor as well, it makes the most feverish existence that can be imagined. Herr Rümelin has no hesitation in thus explaining the touch of excess and morbidity which he finds in most of Shakespeare's creations.

On the whole, and in spite of many just and striking observations in detail, it is impossible to say that Herr Rümelin has succeeded in his attempt. He has done a service to criticism in protesting against an enthusiasm which refused to argue under pretext of admiring better without argument, but he has not produced any considerable result from the new method which he professed to apply to the works of Shakespeare. The reason is that history never explains a man; that circumstances modify but do not create a living personality. They can at most help us to understand the turn which his genius took, the obstacles which he had to surmount, the limits which were imposed upon him. And so Herr Rümelin's criticism, doubtless altogether unintentionally, has become almost entirely negative; he has principally told us what Shakespeare was not.

And then, since humanity can never do without superstitions, he hurries, in the very process of upsetting one idol, to set up another in its place. What hurts Herr Rümelin most in German Shakespeare-worship is, it seems, its preference of Shakespeare to German poets, Goethe in particular. The last chapter of the book draws a parallel between the two writers in which the German is naturally allowed to have the best of it. I do not care to follow M. Rümelin in this kind of comparison, neither the use nor the interest of which have I ever understood : not to mention that here the terms of juxtaposition are almost wholly points of contrast. What can there be in common between two authors of whom one lived fifty, the other eighty-four years ; of whom the first gave himself up almost wholly to drama, while the second attempted every style, busied himself with all science, exercised himself in every path; of whom, finally, the latter carried into art every resource of erudition, while the former still belongs to art which is simply creative ?

Strange to say, Herr Rümelin has no sooner arrived at Goethe, than he loses all the faculties of measure and discretion which he had shown in speaking of the English poet. This is the way of the Germans ; they will end by spoiling Goethe for us by mere dint of exaggeration. I, for my part, know few writers for whom I feel a greater admiration, to whom I owe deeper and more lasting delight ; but I am bound to say that neither do I know one in whose case I am more convinced of the necessity of allowances and reserves. The day of reasoned criticism must surely come for Goethe, as it seems to have come for Shakespeare at last; and then men will wonder at the complaisance with which we now shut our eyes to his faults. We are too prone to forget how much littleness is compatible with greatness, and how many parts of weakness and dulness the highest genius may contain. Goethe is one of the most striking examples of this truth. He is the author of some of the most perfect work that any literature has produced, and of some of the most tiresome books that have been written in any language. Side by side with profound and admirably expressed thoughts, there are to be found in his books a multitude of pompously enunciated commonplaces. He is wanting both in critical precision and in creative power. Exquisite, accomplished, and extensive as was his culture, he lacked

more than one of the principal elements of thought.
History was a stranger to his meditations. He was
acquainted neither with the society of great cities,
nor with the policy of great states. His genius at
first showed an admirable combination of sentiment
and reflection.; but in the long run reflection got
the better and cast a chill over the whole. His
finest works belong to that period of his life when
the consummate science of the artist was balanced
by passionate ardor. But afterwards the intention
of teaching and the calculation of effect got the
upper hand so much that he revelled more and
more in symbols, in ideas, in dissertation. Let us
say it boldly, the second part of "Faust" is insup-
portable, the second part of "Wilhelm Meister" is
painful, and the last half of the "Memoirs" simply
presents us with the portfolio of an old man who
wishes to make the very utmost of his former studies.   Goethe, who is assuredly not so mighty a
genius as Shakespeare, is a genius of greater extent
and universality : but Shakespeare at least did not
outlive himself.

VII

MILTON AND "PARADISE LOST"

I

Who knows not the visit which Candide and Martin paid to Signor Pococurante, a noble Venetian?[1] When they had talked of painting and music they went into the library, and Candide, perceiving a Milton, could not prevent himself from asking his host whether he did not look upon this writer as a great man. "What?" said Pococurante, "the barbarian who constructed a long commentary on the first chapter of Genesis in ten books of harsh verse? The clumsy imitator of the Greeks who caricatures creation and who, while Moses represents the Eternal Being as creating the world by his word, makes the Messiah take a big compass out of a cupboard in heaven to trace out the work? What? *I* admire the man who has spoilt Tasso's hell and Tasso's devil; who makes Lucifer masquerade, now as a toad, now as a pigmy; who puts the same speech in his mouth a hundred times over; who represents him as arguing on divinity; who, in attempting a serious imitation of Ariosto's comic invention of fire-arms, makes the devils fire

---

[1] [*Candide,* Chap. xxv. — *Trans.*]

cannon in heaven? Neither I, nor anybody in Italy, has ever been able to take pleasure in all these dismal extravagances. His marriage of Sin and Death, and the snakes of which Sin is delivered, make any man of tolerably delicate taste sick, and his long description of a hospital is only good for a grave-digger. This obscure, eccentric, and disgusting poem was despised at its birth: and I treat it to-day as it was treated in its own country by its own contemporaries. Anyhow, I say what I think, and I really care very little, whether others agree with me or not."

A mere fling, you will say, and not of any consequence. Wait: here is another bright spirit of the eighteenth century, who takes the fling quite seriously and eagerly indorses it. "I hate devils mortally," writes Mme. du Deffand to Voltaire, "I cannot tell you the pleasure I have had in finding in 'Candide' all the evil you have spoken of Milton. It seemed to me that the whole was my own thought: for I always detested him." Thus we see that once upon a time French taste found itself face to face with "Paradise Lost" and straightforwardly expressed its repugnance for a poem which is, it must be frankly confessed, very foreign to the habits and traditions of our literature. It is the way of taste to deliver judgments like these — judgments which are all the more positive from the very fact that they merely render an impression. Admiration, when things are regarded in this way,

is not more reasonable than aversion; or, if either
reasons, it starts equally from a personal sentiment.

But let us go from France to England, from the
detractors of Milton to his panegyrists.   Addison
does not deign to ask whether "Paradise Lost"
merits the name of a heroic poem.   " Let us call it
a divine one," he says, " and say no more about it."
It lacks none of the beauties of the highest poetry,
and if there are also spots in it we must remember
that there are spots in the sun.   But perhaps it
will be said that Addison is obsolete.   With all my
heart.   Let us, then, open our Macaulay, a modern
surely, and one who has read and compared everything.   One of his essays — indeed, the first that
he wrote for the " Edinburgh Review " — has Milton for its subject.   Good heavens, what enthusiasm !   The whole English language is ransacked to
supply the Whig critic with admiring epithets.
Even " Paradise Regained " receives his homage.
The superiority of " Paradise Lost " over " Paradise
Regained " is not more certain than the superiority
of " Paradise Regained " over any poem that has
appeared since.   Well done ! that is something like
having an opinion.   One recognizes in this dogmatic
judgment the writer of whom Lord Lansdowne [1]
said once, " I wish I was as cocksure of anything
as Tom Macaulay is of everything."   Still the
writer's assurance is here reasonable enough : he is

[1] [It was Lord Melbourne, was it not?   It is certainly more
in his way. — *Trans.*]

expressing his tastes, translating his impressions, and, so long as we keep to this region of personal literary sentiment, Macaulay has as much right to admire as Pococurante to depreciate.

Of this, criticism has now convinced itself. It has perceived the barrenness of these positive tastes, of these contradictory judgments. It has felt that there is a method at once more decisive and fairer : the method which sets to work to comprehend rather than to class, to explain rather than to judge. Such criticism seeks to give account of the work by means of the genius of the workman and of the form which this genius has taken under pressure of the circumstances among which it has been developed. Yet, therewithal, it denies not the eternal poetic substance, the creative power in face of which we find ourselves, when all is said, in the case of any masterpiece. But, by the side of this element, which is, so to speak, irreducible, it makes allowance for date, for country, for education, for dominant ideas, for the general course of events. From these two things — the analysis of the writer's character and the study of his age — there arises spontaneously an understanding of his work, instead of a personal and arbitrary estimate made by the first comer. We see that work, after a fashion, pronouncing judgment on itself, and taking the rank which belongs to it among the productions of the human mind. This rank it occupies — I repeat the fact and shall take good care not to forget it —

thanks to poetical beauties appreciated by the reader's emotion. But that very emotion, it must equally be remembered, depends on the point of view at which we place ourselves, on the allowances which we make for the author and his epoch, on the secret transposition by which we adjust his music to our own voices. All this is the business of the historic intelligence. The "Iliad" has gained more than it has lost by being regarded as a national saga, and the representation of a still barbarous society. The exquisite poetry of the "Æneid" is enjoyed better when we have given up demanding originality of epic conception in it; and Racine exercises his power over our emotions more certainly when we have once allowed for the artificial *ars poetica*, the conventional language of the period, in "Andromaque" and in "Phèdre."

II

Milton was born in 1608, ten years after the death of Spenser and eight years before that of Shakespeare. He died in 1674, fourteen years after the Restoration. He thus went back nearly to the reign of Elizabeth, and he saw the beginning, the triumph, and the fall of the Commonwealth. Thus, also, he belongs at once to the Renaissance and to Puritanism. The whole character of his genius and of his work is explained by this double filiation. He is a poet, not of the great creative age,

but of that age's morrow, a morrow still possessed
of spontaneity and conviction. Yet he is a didactic
and theological poet, that is to say, the only kind
of poet which it was possible for an English republican of the seventeenth century to be.

The Renaissance and Puritanism were two powerful movements, at once in alliance and in opposition
— two epochs diversely memorable. I can hardly
understand why the history of the Renaissance has
not yet employed some eminent writer. There is
no greater theme, no more varied subject. There
comes a day when humanity re-discovers its patents
of nobility. It finds antiquity in the dust of libraries as Pompeii has since been found under the
ashes. A whole new world issues from these tat-
tered parchments, a new ideal arises in the soul of
man. Forms of marvellous beauty rise like an
apparition. There had been no idea earlier of such
clear wisdom, of such fascinating speculations, of
such a consummate art of poetry. Men came little
short of adoring as divine immortal writers like the
great Plato, like the sweet Virgil. But the worship of beauty is contagious. These masterpieces
naturally became models; or, rather, in this commerce with the ancients there was kindled an inspiration which in turn produced its own poets,
and gave new examples for the succeeding centuries. Nor was this all. To the enchantments
of taste were promptly added the satisfactions of
reason and the conquests of science. Scholarship

was born from the use of ancient tongues and the familiarity with texts. Men taught themselves to compare opinions, to distinguish epochs, to subject traditions to doubt. The historic sense of things was aroused. A breach was made in authority. Finally, and as though the rediscovery of this old world were not enough, a new world disclosed itself. Sailors transformed the prevalent idea of the terrestrial globe, and astronomers the prevalent idea of the universe. Add to all this the great industrial inventions, with, at their head, that of printing, which stands to writing as writing does to speech, which gives the means of fixing the acquisitions of the human mind, which thus constitutes the instrument of instruments for what is called progress. And now put on the crown and, as it were, the aureole of this marvellous time, in the shape of the produce of its own special art, of the masterpieces of its architects, its sculptors, its painters most of all. Picture in this way all the restorations, all the conquests, all the glories of the time, and say if there was ever in the history of humanity a stranger spectacle or a more exciting surprise. Mankind made a backward leap of fifteen centuries to recover its true traditions. It freed itself at last from the Semitic spirit. It said good by to scholasticism and asceticism, it cast off the monkish gown in which its limbs had been prisoned. It left the cloister — long and damp and sombre — to bask once more in God's sunlight. Weary of striving and struggling, of tragical repentance, of funereal meditation, men opened their breasts to the breath of the spring. After long being in leading-strings to priests, they tried to walk alone, and bathed deliciously in truth, in beauty, in nature and its simplicity. Oh, period truly incomparable! Lasting enchantment! Excusable intoxication! Second and unspeakable youth of the world!

But also what a transition was that from the Renaissance to Puritanism! And yet the one sprang from the other, for Puritanism is but Protestantism in an acute form, and Protestantism itself is but the Renaissance carried into the sphere of religion and theology.

Yet again, what a difference! The Puritans are men to whom the curtains of the heavens are opened, and to whose eyes the realities of the invisible world have been revealed. They have seen Jehovah on His throne, the Son on His right hand, and the angels prostrate before them. Thenceforward, they live as if in the presence of this terrible God and in the expectation of judgment. They have but one care, the salvation of their immortal souls. Life for them is but the service of the Lord, who has predestinated them to destroy idols, to establish the true faith, to bring a rebellious world into conformity with the Divine Will. Such is the mission of the faithful here below. He is equally ready to suffer pillory or prison, and to gird on the sword like Gideon to slay the impious. Like all

men who are the slaves of a single idea he is
at once heroic and ridiculous. Observe these long
faces, these mourning garments, these shaven heads.
Listen to this Biblical jargon, these hymns droned
through the nose, these endless prayers, wiredrawn
discussions, curses of the world and its amuse-
ments. You will turn away your head with a smile
of pity or of disgust. Agreed: but these same men
are stout soldiers and zealous citizens. There are
generals and statesmen among the fanatics who
kneel there smiting their breasts and seeking the
Lord. It is impossible not to admire their sagacity
in counsel, their constancy in undertakings, their
valor and their discipline in the field. It would
seem that, certain of the reward which awaits them,
they carry into mundane affairs all the freer spirit
and all the more entire devotion.

The Puritans are the Jacobins of Protestantism.
In both there is the same abstract conception of
things, the same tyranny of the idea, the same
craving to realize half-seen visions. In both you
find the twin tendencies, radicalism and idealism.
In both there is an equal faith in the Absolute,
the source of all fanaticism. Both invoke the
name of Liberty, but both also invoke her rather
as a means than as an end, and truth is set by both
above her. Nay, the very Hebrew names with
which the Puritans deck themselves recall our
Brutuses and our Aristides. The two Utopias,
classical democracy and the theocracy of the Bible,

are face to face. For the Bible is the Koran of Puritanism. The Bible is to the Puritan a religion, a prophecy, and a code. It is the rule absolute for the individual and for the State. It foresees all, provides for all, has a text for every use and every circumstance. It is no more lawful to supplement it where it is silent, than to act against its spoken commands. Imagine, if it be possible, this venerable collection of prophets and apostles, this sublime Hebrew Book with its histories, its poems, and its precepts, raised as a whole to the importance of a revelation from the Almighty, imposed as a law upon society, applied to the life of a modern people, and supplying the type of its institutions, the rule of its morals, the guidance of its State. The object is to establish a Christian republic, and, with that end, to pass the level of the Bible over all existing things. The Church and the Monarchy alike must go down before it, and then, on the ground that has been cleared, there shall be built the city of the saints, the town where the Eternal, though unseen, shall dwell!

And now, can the reader imagine a contrast more complete than that between the Renaissance and Puritanism? On one side every curiosity of intelligence, every research of language, every refinement of taste; poetry, with its mythology, its sports, its license; the cultus of pagan antiquity; a false wisdom and false gods; madrigals, novels,

the theatre. On the other ardent fanatics, sombre
anchorites, fanatic levellers, full of hatred for
Satan and his pomps, caring for nothing but long
sermons and excited prayers, broken in to the
dogmas of Predestination, of the Fall and of Justification, burning to make of Englishmen a new
people of Israel. Such are the powers which are
to fight for Milton; or, rather, such are the different
inspirations to which he abandons himself simultaneously and without a struggle. He is an elegant
poet and a passionate controversialist, an accomplished humanist and a narrow sectary, an admirer
of Petrarch and Shakespeare and a cunning exe-
gete of Biblical texts, a lover of pagan antiquity
and devoted to the Hebrew spirit. He is all this
at once, naturally, and without an effort — a problem
in history, an enigma in literature!

III

Milton passed ten years of his life in study, in
travel, in brilliant literary experiments. He spent
ten more in the fiercest struggles and the most
technical controversies of Puritanism. Yet he was
never exactly a Prynne or exactly a Petrarch; if
there was something of the theologian in the poet
there was also something of the poet in the theologian, and the two inspirations blended in him after
the closest and most natural fashion in the world.
And when old age draws near, when the drama of

the Republic is played out, when the Restoration has put an end to Utopias, Milton will at once satisfy art and faith, the two passions of his life, in one grand epic.

That life is well known. We are not in his case, as we are in Shakespeare's, reduced to a few insignificant facts and a few doubtful traditions. We might say that he has written his own biography. His poetry is full of personal memories, and his polemical works become at times memoirs of his life, passionate and naïf memoirs, where the writer reveals himself without any disguise.

Milton, I have said, was born in 1608. His father was a notary, or something like it, and affluent. Himself a man of letters, he put his son through an excellent course of study. There is extant a Latin letter in which the young man thanks his father for not having forced him to read law or to enter a lucrative profession, but for letting him learn not merely Greek and Latin, but French, Italian, Hebrew and even the sciences. Nor is this the only passage where Milton has taken pleasure in recalling his early and vigorous education.[1]

In one of his tracts against episcopacy he dwells with even more complacency on these fair years of

[1] [M. Scherer here and afterwards quotes and translates long passages from the *Defensio Secunda*, the *Areopagitica*, the *Apology for Smectymnuus*, and other works of Milton. As these are well known to English readers, it has not seemed necessary to encumber the text with them. — *Trans.*]

study. He went, he says, from historians to poets, from poets to philosophers, and in this long commerce with ancient and modern writers, he was able to preserve the native purity of his soul; nay, more, to form a sublime ideal blent of purity, poetry, and fame. It is a memorable passage[1] where we seem to see the bard of the "Paradise" preparing himself by mystic washings for the work to which the Most High has charged him.

Yet let us hasten to say that the innocence of Milton's morals was not the result of excessive occupation in study nor of an extravagant severity. His youthful poems show traces of more than one affair of the heart. In a Latin elegy addressed to his friend Diodati he describes the young girls whom he has seen passing. Their eyes are torches, their necks of ivory, their fair hair is a net spread by love: Jove himself would feel young at the sight of so many charms. "To the virgins of Britain," cries the poet, "belongs the palm of beauty," and he was caught by this beauty. Another elegy tells us how. He despised Love and his arrows; but Love avenged himself. One spring as he was walking, he did not watch his own glances enough, and the sight of a girl set his heart on fire,

> "Protinus insoliti subierunt corda furores
> Uror amans intus, flammaque totus eram." [2]

[1] [The famous one from the *Apology for Smectymnuus.* — *Trans.*]

[2] [" My heart forthwith unwonted passions tame,
Love burns my soul within, and all was flame." — *Trans.*]

Unluckily the beauty vanished, and he could not discover her. What would he not give to see her again and speak to her! Perhaps she might not be deaf to his prayers. But there, his vexation is already forgotten. He is at the University, under the groves of Academe, and thenceforward his heart wears a corselet of ice.

Milton left Cambridge in 1632 after having spent seven years there. He withdrew to his father's, accompanied, he says, by the regret of most of the fellows of his college, who showed him much friendship and esteem. He often returns to this subject, stung to the quick by the taunts of his enemies, who accused him of having been expelled from the University. So far from this, he says, they wished to keep him there, and he long continued in affectionate correspondence with his Cambridge friends. But let us follow our poet, who is now three-and-twenty years old.[1]

*   *   *   *   *

Let us halt here for a moment and endeavor to put the separate traits together, and construct an idea of the poet. Milton, at his return from Italy, was exactly thirty years old. He was short, his height being below the middle stature, and also

---

[1] [A cento from the above-named sources, part actual quotation, part paraphrase, part summary, follows in the original. As it is very difficult to find a satisfactory rendering for this blending of Milton and Scherer, and as the facts about Milton's Horton period and his travels are well known to the English reader, it seemed simpler to omit it. — *Trans.*]

very thin; but strong, dexterous and courageous.
He was a practised fencer, and sword in hand
feared nobody. Such, at least, is the portrait he
drew later of himself. Tradition adds that he was
remarkably handsome. He has also described his
manner of life, for the fury of his enemies, by
attacking his person and his private life, obliged
him to enter into the most minute details of refu-
tation. He rose, so he tells us, early — in summer
with the lark, in winter with the bells that called
men to work or prayer. He read or listened to
reading till attention and memory failed. Then
he betook himself to exercises suited to maintain
the health of the body, and by that means the
strength and independence of the mind. We must,
as I have said, take care not to look on Milton as
a gloomy fanatic or an ascetic. At Cambridge he
had written tender Latin elegies; he had, when in
Italy, no scruple in rhyming madrigals after
Petrarch, and celebrating in them real or ficti-
tious loves. At Rome, in the very city where he
prided himself on holding high the banner of his
faith, he had listened with transport to the singer
Leonora Baroni. His epitaph on Shakespeare, "My
Shakespeare" as he calls him, is well known, with
its passionate expression of the emotions he owed
to the reading of this "dear son of memory." Nor
was this all; Milton on occasion shows himself
quite ready to put on one side deep study and
serious occupations in order, with his friends, to

give himself up to "mirth that, after, no repenting draws"—a light repast, good wine, some Italian music, that is the programme. "Mild heaven," says he, "disapproves the care, That with superfluous burden loads the day, And when God sends a cheerful hour refrains." So there is nothing in him repulsive or morose. He is pure without too much severity, grave without fanaticism: full of original sanity, of gracious strength. He is a son of the north who has felt the Italian influence: an after-growth of the Renaissance, but a growth full of strange and novel flavor.[1]

IV

Milton returned to his country at the very moment when the Monarchy was about to begin a death-struggle with the Parliament, and in the midst of the ecclesiastical controversies by which that struggle was embittered. He could have no hesitation as to the side which he was to join: but he had to ask himself with some embarrassment what he was going to do now that the day of pre-

---

[1] Milton allows his taste and admiration for Shakespeare to appear in *L'Allegro*, published in 1645, but doubtless written some years earlier (See v. 135). The same poem exhibits him in his least austere light. Our author makes Joy, daughter of Bacchus and Venus, mother of the Graces. He bids her bring with her "Sport that wrinkled Care derides" and even "Laughter holding both his sides." It is true that the pleasures he expects from Joy and Freedom are "*unreproved* pleasures." Cf. *Paradise Lost*, iv. 293, 294.

paratory studies and of travel was passed, and that it was time to fix an object for his life.

At any other time his choice would have appeared easy. He seemed destined for one or other of the learned professions, more especially for the service of the Church. But at that day this career was closed to him. "None could take orders without devoting himself to slavery." But he had cherished dreams dearer still. The most curious passage of the memoirs of which I am here piecing the fragments together, that in which he recalls the poetic aspirations of his youth, lets us see what it cost him in effort to renounce them, and betrays the hope of still some day paying the debt of genius to his country and his God.[1]

We may believe Milton when he expresses the regret with which he renounced immortal songs for the polemics of the moment. But he thought he heard the call of the Church and of his country. He postponed to another season the accomplishment of his poetic mission, and plunged headlong into the struggle of the Parliament against King Charles and Archbishop Laud. Others had drawn the sword : his weapon was the pen. His learning and his practice in writing marked him out for the part of controversialist : and he poured forth a

---

[1] [M. Scherer here translated the long passage in the *Reasons of Church Government*, about the vulgar amorists and parasites, comparing with it the exordium of Canto ix, *Paradise Lost.* — *Trans.*]

crowd of pamphlets on every subject which events made actual. He began by Church questions, attacking ceremonies, the episcopate, tradition, and striving to bring the Church back to its primitive simplicity. A few years later he married, and, as is well known, was soon deserted by his wife. The cause of this separation is not known, but is it rash to seek it in the very character of the poet? Serious, living on the heights, given up to long work and sublime meditations, he was likely to make a rather poor husband. Moreover, he had drawn from Holy Writ quite Oriental and very decided notions on the inferiority of woman and her subjection to man. At any rate, the young bride did actually desert her husband's house, and did not return till two or three years later. Then something happened to Milton which has often been seen in similar cases: his personal grievances were raised in his own eyes to the height of a question of public interest, and he set himself to write on marriage and divorce as he had written before on episcopacy and formal worship. It seemed to him, as he explained later, that men must begin by being free at home before being so in the market-place, and that the vilest of slaveries is that of a man bound without remedy to an inferior being.[1]

---

[1] " Frustra enim libertatem in comitiis et foro crepat qui domi servitutem vero indignissimam inferiori etiam servit," *Defensio Secunda.* As for Milton's ideas on marriage, see *Samson,* l. 1055, and *Paradise Lost,* i. 635 sq., vii. 539 sq., 565 sq. ; but note

The last debate which Milton maintained in his fifteen years of polemic, was that in which he engaged with Salmasius on the subject of the death of Charles I. To the scandal of the whole of mo-narchical Europe he was seen defending, with cold-blooded erudition, the right of peoples to punish tyrants. For the rest, the style of all these writings of his is the same. The author unfolds the treasures of his learning, heaping up the testimony of Scripture, passages from the fathers, and quotations from the poets, laying sacred and profane antiquity alike under contribution, and subtly discussing the sense of this and that Greek or Hebrew term. But it is not only in the crudity of his erudition and in his religious prejudices that Milton is of his age. He belongs to it also by the personal tone of his polemic. Morus and Salmasius had attacked his morals, gibed at his short stature, made odious references to his loss of sight: Milton retorts on them the money they have pocketed and the servant girls they have debauched, seasoning the mess with coarse epigrams, with vulgar terms of abuse. Luther and Calvin themselves, experts as they were in insult, had never done better.

And yet with all this Milton, I must repeat, is by no means a fanatic pure and simple, like most of the Puritans. He is not, as they were, impelled by

at the same time vii. 546 sq. for his deep sense of feminine seductions. Adam becomes so eloquent on this subject that Raphael "contracts his brow," and thinks it necessary to remonstrate with him.

a base and blind desire of levelling. He is an iconoclast, but one with his wits about him : a Radical, but fully conscious of the principle from which he starts, and of the end for which he is making. The very worship of the letter which shocks us in his books, his Biblical narrowness, his childish attempt to reform Church and State by dint of a few texts laboriously marshalled — all these weaknesses are in him but, as it were, the form, the accidental clothing, of a 'most lofty conception of things. At bottom Milton is an absolute spiritualist, and this is the essence of his thought. He idealizes and abstracts everything. A stranger to the world, he does not trouble himself about the distance which separates his visions from reality. He allows nothing for human weakness or for political necessity. He never understands that societies can only subsist by a perpetual declension from the principles of right and truth. He sees all things, so to speak, in God, and the earthly State confounds itself in his mind with Jerusalem which is on high.

But we should give an incomplete idea of Milton's prose writings if, after having spoken of the temperament of his mind and his polemical excesses, we did not say a word of the magnificence of his style. For magnificence is not too strong a word. There are moments when, shaking the dust of argument from off him, the poet suddenly bursts forth and carries us off on the torrent of an incomparable eloquence. It is not rhetorical phrase-making, it is poetic enthusiasm, a flood of images shed over the dull and arid theme, a wing-stroke which sweeps us high above peddling controversy. The polemical writings of Milton are full of such beauties. The prayer which ends the "Treatise of Reformation in England," the encomium on zeal in the "Apology for Smectymnuus," the portrait of Cromwell in the "Second Defence of the English People," and, lastly, the whole treatise on the liberty of the press, are counted among the most memorable pages of English literature and among the most characteristic examples of the genius of Milton.[1] The dryest of Milton's writings are thus constantly illuminated with flashes of poetry.

And so we come back to our conclusion, that Milton was born a poet, and one of the greatest of poets. He had long before written some short pieces which would have been enough to make him immortal, "L'Allegro" for instance, and "Il Penseroso." He was now approaching a green old age; but he preserved his inner fire and a kind of heroic and magnifical spirit, which breaks out in the midst of the wretchedest wranglings. Yet none the less he is a polemic and a theologian in his heart. Some years ago there was discovered a stout treatise on "Christian Doctrine," on which he worked throughout his life; and it is not certain that this was not his

[1] [M. Scherer here gives the immortal "mewing her mighty youth" passage from the *Areopagitica.* — *Trans.*]

favorite work. For he was before all things a Protestant scholastic. He rejoices in the pet dogmas of Puritanism, in Original Sin, Predestination, Free Will. Not that he does not carry even into this region a kind of natural independence. Thus, he dared to follow St. Paul and Arius in making Christ a sort of secondary or intermediary God, and he was not afraid to push his views on divorce to the point of apologizing for polygamy. But his theology is none the less that of the time — bound to the letter of the sacred writings, without grandeur, without horizons, without philosophy. He never quits the written word; and he will cut the knot of the most exalted problems by the authority of a single obscure or isolated passage. In short, Milton is a great poet, doubled with a Saumaise, or a Grotius; a genius, nourished on the marrow of lions, on Homer, Isaiah, Virgil, Dante, but also, like the serpent in Eden, chewing the dust of dull polemic. He is a doctor, a preacher, a pedagogue, and when the day comes for him to be able at last to realize the dreams of his youth, and endow his country with an epic, he will construct it of two matters, of gold and of clay, of sublimity and of scholasticism, and will leave us a poem which is at once the most extraordinary and at the same time the most intolerable in existence.

V

I shall not follow the life of Milton any further. It grew more and more sombre with age and circumstance, and everything seemed to combine to overwhelm that mighty heart. He lost his sight in 1651 as a consequence of the obstinate labor which his "Defence of the English People" cost him. The doctors had warned him of the consequences in vain. "Their warnings," he says, "caused me neither fear nor hesitation. Urged by the heavenly Counsellor Who dwells in conscience, I would have shut my ears to Æsculapius himself speaking in his Epidaurian temple." A year afterwards, Milton's wife died. He married twice again : but he had by his first marriage three daughters, who did not get on well with their stepmothers, and disturbed the household by their domestic dissensions. And we may suppose that the *coup d'état* by which Cromwell substituted the Protectorate for the government of Parliament could not but sadden the soul of Milton. It was the first blow dealt to the republican ideal which he had cherished. Alas! his generous dreams were to be still more rudely dissipated. A *coup d'état* can only establish a government by setting this government at variance with its own first principle: it can only form a regular civil order by condemning the violence which gave its own success. What is certain is that Cromwell's son ruled but a moment after his father. At the date of the Restoration Milton was fifty-two, and it is reasonably enough supposed that about that time he began the composition of the poem which he had projected twenty years earlier. His friends had disappeared, his dreams had vanished, his sight was quenched, old age made itself felt. But he had kept the faith; and, turning his eyes towards the heavenly light, he dictated songs which he knew were fated to be immortal.[1]

Such was Milton; himself a poem, to use his own expression. Grave, serene, wholly given up to the contemplation of heavenly things, slowly maturing the work of his life, isolated in his generation by the very force of his genius. His soul, as Wordsworth has said in a fine sonnet, was "like a star, and dwelt apart."

VI

"Paradise Lost" is a work of the Renaissance, full of imitation of the ancients. The plan is modelled upon the consecrated patterns, especially on that of the "Æneid." There is an exposition, there is an invocation; after which the author plunges *in medias res.* Satan and his accomplices are discovered stranded on the floor of hell, like Æneas on the coast of Carthage. At this point the action begins. It is and will be very

---

[1] Read the Introductions to Bks. iii. and iv. of *Paradise Lost.*

simple throughout. As Æneas triumphs over
Turnus, so Satan will ruin humanity in the person
of our first parents. This unity of action is
demanded by the rules; but it is necessary, on the
other hand, that the poet should tell us what has
gone before, and what will come after, otherwise
there would not be material enough. So resource
is had to narratives. Æneas tells Dido of the
Fall of Troy: Raphael narrates to Adam the
revolt of the angels and the creation of the world.
Thus we are posted up as to the past: but the
future remains. The poet cannot leave us with
the death of Turnus or the Fall of the first human
beings, because the true interest of the two poems
lies in the relations of Æneas with the destinies of
the Roman people and in the relations of Adam's
sin with the lot of all mankind. Patience! a new
device will get us out of the difficulty. Æneas
descends to Hades, and there finds Anchises, who
shows him the procession of his posterity. The
archangel Michael leads Adam to a hill and
delivers a complete course of lectures to him on
sacred history, from the death of Abel to the
coming of Christ, and even to the Last Judgment.

Such is the plan of "Paradise Lost": there is
nothing more regular or more classical. We recognize the superstitions of the Renaissance in this
faithfulness to models. But the result is that
Milton's poem presents a sort of tertiary formation,
the copy of a copy. It is to the Latin epics what

these are to Homer. We shall see presently what
Milton has succeeded in throwing into the traditional mould ; but as for the form of his poem he
did not create it for himself, he received it. It is
a legacy of antiquity.

VII

If the form of "Paradise Lost" was supplied by
the Renaissance the substance was furnished by
Puritanism. "Paradise Lost" is an epic, but it is
a theological epic, and the theology of the poem is
made up of the favorite dogmas of the Puritans —
the Fall, Justification, the sovereign laws of God.
Moreover, Milton makes no secret of the fact that
he is defending a thesis : his end, he says in the
first lines, is to "assert eternal providence And
justify the ways of God to man."

There are, therefore, in "Paradise Lost" two
things which must be kept distinct : an epic poem
and a theodicy. Unluckily, these two elements —
answering to the two men of which Milton was himself made up, and to the two tendencies which his
age obeyed — these two elements, I say, were incapable of thorough fusion. Nay, they are at complete variance, and from their juxtaposition there
results an undertone of contradiction which runs
through the whole work, affects its solidity, and
endangers its value. It would be vain to plead the
example of the classical epic. The Gods no doubt

hold a great place both in the "Iliad" and the "Æneid"; but Christianity is in this respect very differently situated from Paganism. Christianity is a religion which has been formally "redacted" and settled; and it is impossible, without doing it violence, to add anything to it or subtract anything from it. Moreover, Christianity is a religion serious in itself and insisting upon being taken seriously, devoted to ideas the gravest, not to say the saddest, that imagination can form : those of sin, redemption, self-denial, good works — all of them things which, as Boileau says, are not fitted for being smartened up by ornament.

> L'évangile à l'esprit n'offre de tous côtés
> Que pénitence à faire et tourments mérités,
> Et de vos fictions le mélange coupable
> Même à ses vérités donne l'air de la fable.[1]

But this is not all. Christianity is a religion of dogma: in place of the fantastic and intangible myths of which the Aryan religions were made up, it has abstruse distinctions, paradoxical mysteries, subtle teachings. In short, it amounts to a metaphysic, or, to return to the expression I used at first, a theology. And theology has never had the reputation of being favorable to poetry. Lastly, and as a climax, this theology is still alive. It is for

[1] [In Gospel truth nought's by the mind discerned
But penance due and punishments well-earned;
And when your art a blameful blend supplies
You give its very truths the air of lies. — *Trans.*]

thousands an object of faith and hope : it is not "to let," if I may so speak, there is no vacancy in it; and the poet who carries into it the creations of his fantasy has all the appearance of committing sacrilege.

This, as it is, looks ill for Milton's poem; but we have not yet said all. "Paradise Lost" is not only a theological poem — two words which cry out at finding themselves united — but it is at the same time a commentary on texts of Scripture. The author has chosen for his subject the first chapters of Genesis, that is to say a story, which the stoutest or the simplest faith hesitates to take quite literally, a story in which serpents are heard speaking, and the ruin of the human race is seen to be bound up with a fault merely childish in appearance. In fixing on such a subject, Milton was obliged to treat the whole story as a literal and authentic history; and, worse still, to take a side on the questions which it starts. Now, these questions are the very thorniest in theology : and so it comes about that Milton, who intended to instruct us, merely launches us on a sea of difficulties. What are we to understand by the Son of the Most High, who, one fine day, is begotten and raised to the rank of viceroy of creation ? How are we to comprehend an angel who enters on a conflict with God, that is to say, with a being whom he knows to be omnipotent ? What kind of innocence is it which does not prevent a man from eating forbidden

fruit ?   How, again, can this fault extend its effects
to ourselves ?   By what effort of imagination or of
faith can we regard the history of Adam as part of
our own history, and acknowledge solidarity with
his crime in ourselves ?   And if Milton does not
succeed in arousing this feeling in us, what becomes
of his poem ?   What is its value, what its interest ?
It becomes equally impossible to take it seriously
as a profession of faith (since this faith escapes us)
and even to regard it as the poetical expression of
a theodicy which is out of date, because that theodicy could only become poetic on the terms of being
intelligible.

"Paradise Lost" has shared the fate of its hero,
that is to say, of the devil.   The idea of Satan is
a contradictory idea: for it is contradictory to know
God and yet attempt rivalry with Him.   Accordingly, the flourishing time of belief in the devil was
a time of logical impotence.   The devil at this time
of day has been riddled through and through, he has
become a comic character, he supplies us with our
little jokes.[1]   As for "Paradise Lost" it lives still,
but it is none the less true that its fundamental
conceptions have become strange to us, and that if
the work survives, it is in spite of the subject which
it celebrates.

[1] [There is, however, a proverb in M. Scherer's language,
Rira bien qui rira le dernier ; and one may also think of Sandy
Mackaye's very pregnant and luminous protest against the pre-
mature interment of this personage.— *Trans.*]

VIII

Nor is this the only trick which Milton's theology has played upon his poetry. The marvellous is an essential part of classical poetry, and this is intelligible enough. In a certain sense Paganism is more religious than Christianity, and associates the Deity with every act of human life more naturally and more of necessity. From the very fact that it has Gods for everything — for the domestic hearth, for love, for marriage, for fighting — there is not a circumstance in which these Gods have not a *locus standi*. Much more is this so when the subject is a hero whose valor is inconceivable without divine protection, or a great historical event, whereof the decrees of Zeus supply the sovereign explanation. It is by no means the same with the moderns, in whom the much more exalted, but much vaguer idea of divine Providence has replaced the crowd of special deities. If there is in this a metaphysical progress, there is at the same time a poetical impoverishment. It is not that Christianity also has not produced its own mythology : we have a whole Catholic Olympus, pretty well populated. But the attributes are uncertain, the parts ill distributed : and, in spite of everything, there clings to these creations a sort of inborn spiritualism, which is proof against the materialism of popular beliefs. Christianity, I have said, is a religion wanting in ductility. Since it damns those who do not believe it, it perceives the necessity of offering them clearly defined doctrines. Everything in it is more or less settled and agreed upon. Imagination, therefore, can only assign very narrow limits, or, so to say, a circle drawn beforehand, to the utterances of God or the actions of angels. Hence the awkwardness of poets who have tried to draw from the Christian theology the marvels of which they had need. They satisfy the demands neither of piety nor of poetry. They are hampered by the fear of going too far; and, however timid they show themselves, they still have an air of temerity. The "Gerusalemme Liberata," the "Henriade," the "Messiade," "Les Martyrs," show the faults of the kind palpably. Dante alone escapes, because with admirable tact or, if anyone pleases, art, he has brought into play only the sinners and the saved.

Yet Milton has been more fortunate than most of the epic poets of the Christian period. Indeed, there was no necessity for him to make a shift to supply his epic with the element of the marvellous, since the whole was already placed straight off in the region of the supernatural. God and his Son, the devils and the angels, were not kept in the background and reserved for the denouement. They themselves filled the principal parts. Even our first parents, placed as they were in the garden of Eden and in a state of innocence, shared in a kind of superior existence. Thus there was from the first no need to introduce the divinity arbitrarily.

The author of "Paradise Lost" had but to remain within the conditions of his subject and to extend a little the outlines of the sacred history.

But if Milton avoided factitious marvels it was at the cost of inconvenience elsewhere, of baldness in story, of poverty in ethical quality. Not only is the reader lifted into the sphere of religious abstractions, where the eye of man cannot see or his breast draw breath; but the whole action and actors alike are too destitute of complexity. In strictness there is but one personage in possession of the stage — God the Father; since God cannot show Himself without eclipsing all the rest, nor speak without His will being done. The Son is but a double of the Father. The angels and archangels are but his messengers; nay, they are even less — personifications of his decrees, supers in a drama which would have gone on equally well without them.

Milton did not yield without a struggle to the conditions of his chosen subject. He tried to evade them, and only made the defect more sensible. The long discourses with which he fills the gaps between the action are only sermons, and do but make evident the absence of dramatic matter. Then, since after all some sort of action, some sort of contest was necessary, the poet had recourse to the revolt of the angels. But, unluckily, the fundamental defects of the subject were such that this expedient turned in a fashion against him. What the drama gains in movement, it loses in verisimili-

tude. We see a battle, but we cannot take either
the fight or the fighters seriously. A God who can
be resisted is not a God. A struggle with Omnipotence is not only rash, but silly. Belial saw that
very well when, in the Infernal Council, he rejected
the idea of a contest, either open or concealed, with
Him who is all-seeing and all-powerful. Nor can
one, indeed, comprehend how his colleagues did
not at once give way to so self-evident a considera-
tion. But, I repeat, the poem only became possible
at the cost of this impossibility; and so Milton
bravely made up his mind to it. He urged to the
last, he accepted, even in its uttermost consequences, the most inadmissible of fictions. He presents to us Jehovah anxious for His omnipotence,
afraid of seeing His position turned, His palace
surprised, His throne usurped.[1] He sketches for
us angels throwing mountains, and firing cannon,
at each other's heads. He shows us victory evenly
balanced till the Son arrives armed with thunder
and mounted on a car with four cherubs harnessed
to it.

We have still to inquire whether Milton had an
epic imagination, or whether his subject did not do
him good service by dispensing him from drawing

---

[1] *Paradise Lost*, v. 719, *et seq.* In fact and in fine Satan *has*
won something, and *has* succeeded. His own lot is made no
worse, and, on the other hand, a great many men will be damned,
x. 375. It is useless, therefore, to represent Evil as merely passing, or even as a means to good, x. 629.

more largely on his own resources. As a matter of fact, he scarcely ever strays from this subject without falling into burlesque. His prince of the rebel angels, who changes himself into a toad and a cormorant; his demons, who become dwarfs in order to be less crowded in their Parliament house; the punishment inflicted on them, which consists of being changed once a year into serpents; the Paradise of Fools; the famous, but extravagant allegory of Sin and Death — all these fictions give us but a feeble notion of Milton's inventive genius, and make it permissible to think that he would not have succeeded in a subject where he had to create his heroes and imagine his situations.

IX

Let me not be misunderstood. I do not reproach Milton, because, with his sixteenth century Calvinism, he is found out of harmony with nineteenth century thought. I care very little about his believing in witches and in astrology. Where would Homer be, where Dante, if, refusing to place ourselves at their point of view, we judged them from the level of our modern criticism? Not a single work of art could support such a trial. But the position of Milton is not exactly this. Milton wants to prove something, he is sustaining a thesis, he means to do the work of a theologian as well as of a poet. In a word, whether intentionally or

merely as a fact, "Paradise Lost" is a didactic
work, and, as a consequence, its form cannot be
separated from its matter. Now, it so happens
that the idea of the poem does not bear examination; that its explanation of the problem of evil
verges on the burlesque; that the characters of its
heroes, Jehovah and Satan, are incoherent; that the
fate of Adam touches us little; and finally, that
the action passes in regions where the interests and
the passions of our common humanity have nothing to do. I have already pointed out this contradiction in Milton's epic. The story on which it
rests has neither meaning nor value unless it
retains its dogmatic import, and at the same time
it cannot retain this import without falling into
theology, that is to say, into a domain foreign to
art. The subject of the poem is nothing unless it
is real, unless it touches us as the secret of our
destinies ; and the more the poet tries to grasp this
reality the more it escapes him.

So intangible in character are these conceptions,
that Milton knew not even where to pitch the
scene of his drama. He is obliged to forge a system of the world on purpose, a system in which
he himself only half believes. He is hampered by
the science of his time. Men are no longer in the
fourteenth century, when Dante could image hell
as a great hole burrowing beneath the surface of
our globe. Copernicus and Galileo have inter-
vened. So the cosmology of the Scriptures must

be modified and accommodated to the enlightenment of the day. There is nothing more curious than to read "Paradise Lost" from this point of view, and to note the modifications imposed by science on tradition. Milton regards space as infinite, but divided into two regions, that of light or creation, and that of darkness or of chaos. On earth, in the country of Eden, is the Earthly Paradise, communicating by a staircase with the abode of the Most High. Chaos surrounds the whole of this created world, but on the edge of chaos, in the twilight, is the Limbo of vanity, and beyond chaos, in the depths of uncreated space, is found Hell, with a gate and a bridge constructed by Sin and Death, over which is the road from earth to the abyss.[1]

A vague conception, half literal, half symbolic, whereof the author had need as a scene for his personages, but in which he himself has no entire confidence — a striking example of the kind of antinomy with which I charge the whole poem, of the combined necessity, and impossibility of taking things at the foot of the letter.

X

Let us sum up. "Paradise Lost" is an unreal poem, a grotesque poem, a tiresome poem. There

---

[1] Milton introduced not merely his cosmology but also his politics into his poem. See on republicanism and tyranny, xii. 64-101.

is not one reader in a hundred who can read Books
Nine and Ten without a smile, or Books Eleven and
Twelve without a yawn. The thing does not hold
together: it is a pyramid balanced on its apex, the
most terrible of problems solved by the most childish of means. And yet "Paradise Lost" is immortal. It lives by virtue of some episodes which will
be for ever famous. In contrast with Dante, who
must be read as a whole if we wish really to grasp
his beauties, Milton ought not to be read except in
fragments; but these fragments form a part of the
poetic patrimony of the human race. The invocation to Light, the character of Eve, the description
of the earthly Paradise, of the morning of the
world, of its first love, are all masterpieces. The
discourses of the Prince of Hell are incomparably
eloquent. Lord Brougham used to cite them as
worthy to be set side by side with the greatest
models of antiquity, and another orator of our
time, Mr. Bright, is said to be a constant reader
of Milton. "Paradise Lost" is, moreover, strewn
with incomparable lines. The poetry of Milton is
the very essence of poetry. The author seems to
think but in images, and these images are grand and
proud as his own soul—a marvellous mingling of
the sublime and the picturesque. Every word of
his vocabulary of expression is a discovery and
unique. "Darkness visible" is well known. If he
would paint night he shows us the fairies dancing
by the woodside:

> while overhead the moon
> Sits arbitress, and nearer to the earth
> Wheels her pale course.

The sun shines on the expanse of the deluge waters
and begins to evaporate them :

> And the clear sun on his wide watery glass
> Gaz'd hot, and of the fresh wave largely drew,
> As after thirst.

Peace follows fighting :

> The brazen throat of war had ceased to roar.

The chaste happiness of the wedded pair is drawn
in a word :

> Imparadised in one another's arms.

Verses of this kind, always as exact as they are
beautiful, are innumerable in Milton, and one is
almost ashamed to cite them, so capricious does
choice seem in the midst of such riches.

Besides, all is not said when some verses of
Milton have been quoted. He has not only imagery
and vocabulary, but the period, the great musical
phrase, a little long, a little loaded with ornament
and convolved with inversions, but swaying all with
it in its superb undulation. After all, and above
all, he has an indefinable serenity and victorious-
ness, a sustained equality, an indomitable power;
one might almost say that he wraps us in the skirt

of his robe and wafts us with him to the eternal regions where he himself dwells.[1]

November 1868.

[1] Milton himself has given the rule of poetry. According to him, it must be "simple, sensuous, and impassioned," which comes to the three conditions of simplicity, fulness of imagery, and movement.

VIII

LAURENCE STERNE,[1] OR THE HUMORIST

I

THE name of Sterne suggests not merely the memory of a talent, but also the idea of a class : Sterne is the representative of something definite. Now, it is this representative value which in literature constitutes fame. The merits of Sterne may be discussed as much as anyone likes, but he has a substantive existence : he is there, with his own character, and with a certain rank and prestige as a founder.

Everything about him is odd — his life, his personality, his work. He was born in Ireland, of an Irish mother, and, as far as concerns blood, the Englishman in him is crossed with another race, a careless race, and a light one. His father was merely an ensign, had gone through the war in Flanders, and when peace was made carried his wife and his children from garrison to garrison. He died from the results of a duel. Having picked a quarrel with a certain Captain Philips, the fight came off at once in the room where they were, and a story

[1] *Laurence Sterne: his Person and his Writings.* By Paul Stapfer. 1870.

is told on the subject. The adversaries had engaged so furiously that Philips's sword, piercing Roger Sterne's body, actually stuck in the wall. Thus pinned to it, the luckless wounded man lost neither his presence of mind nor even a certain humorous pleasantry; for he begged his conqueror to be so kind as to wipe the point of his sword and take the plaster off before drawing it out of his body.

Young Sterne had been put to school in Yorkshire at eleven years old, and after his father's death he was taken charge of by a relation, who sent him to finish his studies at the University of Cambridge. As soon as he had graduated, he was provided with a benefice; for his uncle, the archdeacon, an uncle well to pass in the world, and able to serve his nephew if his nephew would let him, had destined him for the church. Once provided for, Sterne lost no time in marrying, falling in love, like a sentimental person as he was, with a girl in the neighborhood, and so finding himself tied for life to an insignificant and unattractive woman. Let us run over these facts, for we have already got the whole Sterne before us: middle-class extraction; garrison memories; means, those of a fairly well-off man of letters; a rather narrow domestic circle; the career of a country parson. We ought to add the neighborship of Hall Stevenson, a college friend, at whose house Sterne met very lively, not to say very unreverend,

companions, with, a little later, some travels in
France and Italy; and we shall have almost all the
elements of "Tristram Shandy" and the "Sentimental Journey" before us. M. Montégut has
very neatly analyzed these influences in his study
on Sterne: — "The best passages of his story,
its most ingenious episodes, its most sympathetic
personages, are due to these reminiscences and
emotions of childhood. It was in the life of the
regiment, by the side of his father and his father's
comrades, that he succeeded in securing those singular and touching growths of honor and humanity
which the military career more than any other
fosters in souls well born."

And again: — "At least a good half of 'Tristram
Shandy' is incomprehensible, unless it is considered as the direct chronicle of an old English
family of the upper middle class, concerned for
some generations with the political disputes of the
country, and with sufficient experience of life to
have more than once known the vicissitudes of
fortune. Old family stories handed down from
father to son, relics pathetic or comical, old receipts
for the cure of disease, treasured scraps of paper
yellowed by time, quaint and original opinions
founded on some immemorial adventure or some
distant experience — all these oddities fill 'Tristram
Shandy,' and constitute one of the principal charms
of the book."

Sterne long remained the obscure parson of an

obscure Yorkshire parish. It must be confessed
that a stranger minister of religion never climbed
a pulpit. With a flighty temperament, an ill-
regulated imagination, an invincible inclination to
drollery, few principles, and less dignity of be-
havior, it is hard to imagine such a preacher at his
task. As a matter of fact, Sterne's sermons are
not out of harmony with their author's eccentricity.
He published them: so that we know what we are
about. He is still the buffoon of genius, restrained,
no doubt, a little by the gown he wears, but in-
demnifying himself by the very strangeness of the
contrast between the tone of a religious harangue
and the liberties he takes. He has digressions on
polygamy, digressions on travel. The preacher
amuses himself by full descriptions of the disorders
and disappointments of the Prodigal Son. One day
he takes for his text this passage of Ecclesiastes:
"It is better to go to the house of mourning than
to the house of mirth," and starts his subject by
crying, "That I deny!" At the same time he has
real merits, if they are not exactly the merits of a
sacred orator. "He knew," says M. Stapfer, "how
to be interesting without making people laugh: he
could even be serious and profound. He never, it is
true, has any Christian unction; but he has a delicacy of moral analysis, and a talent for putting
things before his audience, which show no common
knowledge of the human heart, together with dramatic aptitude still less common." For the rest —

still according to M. Stapfer — Sterne as a preacher
was only "an amateur in sacred literature, studying in the Bible stories the motives of the wicked
and the just with the disinterested curiosity of a
philosopher, and drawing little pictures of their
good and bad actions with the passionate imagination of an artist."

But with all this we must not fancy that Sterne
was a freethinker who preached only from the lips
outwards, and as a matter of business. On the contrary, M. Stapfer insists on the sincerity of his
preaching. He believed what he taught. "I do
not say," continues our critic, "that he practised
what he preached — that is quite another matter:
but he believed it. Hypocrisy never entered into
his nature, and however odd such a minister of
religion may seem, nothing would be falser than to
represent him as a Tartufe, nor would it be much
more exact to imagine him simply as a joker.
Sterne in his pulpit, clad in the black gown of the
Protestant preacher, was still an artist and a philosopher, a wit and a sentimentalist, an enemy of
quacks and pedants, of superannuated methods and
commonplace ideas. He was also an enemy of
gravity, because it is nine times out of ten affected,
interested, and false : and a friend of pleasantry in
season and out of season. Yet, again, he was an
irregular personality, liable to sudden changes of
humor, gay one moment and the next serious or
even sad ; an optimist now, and anon a misan-

thrope; the most whimsical of writers and of men
in his ways of thinking, feeling, and writing."

I may interrupt myself here to remark that while
we make acquaintance with Sterne we also make
acquaintance with M. Paul Stapfer, his critic and
biographer, and that this young author's book has
already commended itself to me by more than one
trait of exact and delicate observation.[1]

Rousseau became an author at thirty-seven:
Sterne was forty-seven when he published the two
first volumes of "Tristram Shandy." It is difficult
to understand inspiration so late in the day, but
it was written that everything about our author
should be unique. Anyhow, his success was immediate and very great. Though the volumes appeared
modestly enough at York, two hundred copies were
sold in two days, and when, a short time afterwards,
Sterne went to London, he found himself famous.
Everybody wanted to see him: he was invited
everywhere, and to secure him it was necessary to
take steps two months beforehand. The name of
"Tristram Shandy" was given to a new salad, to a
new game of cards, to several racehorses. The
book lay on all tables: it was pirated and imitated,
attacked and defended. A peer, Lord Falconberg,

---

[1] [I hope it is not impertinent to add another interruption.
M. Stapfer, who, at the time M. Scherer wrote these words, was
a friend and colleague of my own, and whose doctoral thesis is
the subject of this essay, has since held Professorships in Letters
at Grenoble and Bordeaux, and has produced capital work on
Shakespeare, Rabelais, and other subjects. — *Trans.*]

thought he could not show his admiration for the author better than by bestowing on him a benefice worth a hundred guineas a year; a bookseller for his part offered him 650*l.* for two new volumes.

From this time Sterne passed a considerable part of his time in London — in the drawing rooms that pulled caps for him, with the wits of the time, in the gardens of Ranelagh, and behind the scenes of Drury Lane. Nor was he less well received in Paris, whither Englishmen were then fond of coming to have their renown ratified. I do not know how it happened that our eighteenth-century letters and memoirs preserve hardly any trace of his passages there. Garat, however, has drawn him in a few lines, and shows him to us as we already know him, "always and everywhere the same: never influenced by plans, and always carried away by impressions; at the theatre, in the drawing room, on the bridge, always somewhat at the mercy of things and persons; always ready to be amorous or pious, burlesque or sublime." He was at Paris when he burst a bloodvessel in his chest, and his health, already delicate, was henceforth wholly precarious. In vain he sought a cure in the south of France and in Italy; consumption, without vanquishing his levity or his gaiety, held him between life and death. The "Sentimental Journey" appeared in February, 1768, and three weeks afterwards its author died at London in furnished lodgings. It has been asserted that his corpse was stolen by resurrection men, that he was dissected, and that one of his friends coming in during the demonstration recognized the body, and swooned with a shriek of horror.

No one can have a complete or even a sufficient idea of Sterne who does not know what a pitch, both of passion and fickleness, he had reached. Never was there a more inflammable heart. "I must," he wrote, "positively have some Dulcinia in my head. It is a condition of moral harmony for me. I am firmly persuaded that, if ever I do a base thing, it can only be in the interval between one passion and another." As a matter of fact he went from one Dulcinia to another, without taking any trouble to engineer the transitions. It is said that he included the whole sex in his passion. "After all the weaknesses I have seen in women, and all the satires I have read against them," wrote Sterne towards the end of his life, "I love them still, persuaded that the man who has not a kind of affection for the entire sex is incapable of loving a single woman as he ought." His very marriage was nothing but a love passage, and he dealt with it no otherwise. We possess the letters which he wrote to "his Lumley," as he called his betrothed, full of sentimental assurances and of tears; but we possess also a letter in dog Latin which he wrote twenty years later to his friend Stevenson "Sum fatigatus et aegrotus de mea uxore plus quam unquam." His second passion was for Catherine

Béranger de Fourmentelle, a girl of French extraction, who lived at York with her mother. For her Sterne does not in the least beat about the bush; he ardently desires that God may soon relieve him of his wife, so that "his Kitty" may at last be wholly his. "There is only one hindrance to our happiness," he writes to Kitty, "and what that is you know as well as I. God will open a gate which will allow us to be one day much nearer each other." This attachment, which was to be eternal, lasted but a year. The success of "Tristram Shandy" put everything out of Sterne's head, and when the poor woman left York to join him in London, he could not find time even to see her.

I fancy that M. Stapfer does not pretend to be exhaustive on this subject. It is impossible to enumerate all the conflagrations which successively devoured this celebrated humorist. " 'Tis like the stars in the sky," said Sainte-Beuve to me once, speaking of Chateaubriand's attachments; "the more you look at them, the more you discover." So it is with poor Yorick. In 1764, Sterne was at Paris on his return from a two years' stay in the south of France, and it is easy to guess what kept him there for eight weeks; he writes to Stevenson, "I have been under the yoke of the tenderest passion whose empire heart ever underwent." But the most famous of his affairs of the heart was that which made Eliza Draper immortal. Eliza had been born in India. As she was consumptive, her husband had sent her to England for medical care, and though she had not been cured, she was on the point of returning to Bombay when Sterne made her acquaintance. She was a young woman who seems to have possessed in the highest degree the grace and indefinable charm of languor. Raynal celebrated her in one of those pompous apostrophes which we cannot read nowadays without a fit of laughter. " O territory of Ajinga! thou art naught, but thou hast given birth to Eliza! A day will come when the marts of commerce founded by Europeans on the Asian coasts will exist no longer. Grass will hide them, or the Indian, at last avenged, will build upon their ruins. But if my writings have any life, the name of Ajinga will abide in the memory of man," and so forth. Sterne's own letters to Eliza are less burlesque, but not less enthusiastic. Alas! they had at last to separate; Eliza went to join Mr. Draper, and Sterne remained at London. It is impossible, is it not, to refrain from pitying them ? We imagine the immense and lasting desolation :

Que le deuil de mon âme était lugubre et sombre !
Que de nuits sans pavots ! Que de jours sans soleil !

Why, to think so would be to know nothing at all of Yorick's nature ! Eliza had not been three weeks gone when Sterne wrote another declaration to another beauty : — " Beloved fair ! What a dish-clout hast thou made of my soul ! Less than an

hour ago I fell on my knees. I swore never to
come near thee again, and after saying the Lord's
Prayer for the sake of the end, ' Lead us not into
temptation,' I rose up like a Christian soldier,
ready to fight the world, the flesh, and the devil,
and assured of trampling all these foes beneath my
feet. But now that I am so near you, a mere stone's
throw from your house, I feel myself seized with a
giddiness which turns my brain upside down."
Diamond cut diamond! It is but too clear that
Sterne, as Warburton said, was an incorrigible
blackguard. But Eliza Draper, for her part, was
nothing but a coquette, for she had kept Sterne's
letters, and it was she who published them.

II

It is time to come to the works of an author who
has been depicted to us as so bizarre and capricious.
We have already seen that he did not take pen in
hand till very late, when he was forty-seven years
old. He died nine years afterwards, and within
this short space of time he published the nine volumes of "Tristram Shandy," the "Sentimental
Journey," and the "Sermons." Both the novel
and the "Journey" were left unfinished; but had
their completion ever been intended? For taking
your hero, as the author does, so many months before his birth, for halting so long on the steps of a
staircase, for discussing so learnedly noses, knots,

and moustaches, would even the forty volumes that
the biographer promised have sufficed ?   Is not the
sudden dropping of the story and the reader the
necessary climax of all the practical jokes which
the writer has arranged for us ?   We have no right
to complain of anything when we go on board with
such a shipmate unless he happens to bore us, for
the buffoon is condemned to be always amusing.
It must be confessed that Sterne has not paid quite
attention enough to this law of the style.   He is
tedious, lengthy, wearisome, obscure, repellent, to
such an extent that his books, "Tristram Shandy"
especially, are little read nowadays.   And yet
"Tristram" is a masterpiece: the characters of
my Uncle Toby and of Corporal Trim are real
creations.   There is nothing more original, nothing
more thoroughly worked out, in any literature; but
nothing less than these admirable portraits and
some charming passages could have succeeded in
saving Sterne's books.   The mere style which he
created, and to which his name remains in some
sort attached, the style of humorous fantasy, would
not have sufficed to do it.

There are three things to distinguish in Sterne —
his sentiment, his humor, and his method; for there
is deliberate method in this writer.   Sentiment and
pleasantry flow freely and at first hand from him;
but mannerism mixes with them at the last, and
hurts the first inspiration.

Sterne is a sentimentalist: in the same way as

the whole eighteenth century was, as Diderot is in
his passionate apostrophes, as the whole of France
became in the following of Rousseau. Men talked
of virtue and sentiment just as they wore powder
and matches. Virtue, for her part, held her ground
till far into the Revolution, and supplied the material of endless harangues, those of Robespierre in
particular. Sensibility was not so long lived;[1] she
gave place to the heroism of Brutus and his kind.
Yet Madame Roland was still a " sensible" woman,
and Olympe de Gouges, when she wrote to the Convention asking for permission to defend Louis XVI.,
spoke of examples which had "excited her heroism
and aroused her sensibility." Sterne is at once
tender-hearted and sentimental; that is to say,
naturally susceptible of sympathetic emotions, and
inclined at the same time to invite them for the
pleasure that he feels in them, and the credit they
gain him. He was very early familiar with the
tone of tenderness. See how he describes the solitude in which "his Lumley" has left him. "A
solitary plate," he writes to her, " only one knife,
one fork, one glass! I bestowed a thousand pensive
and penetrating glances on the chair that you have
so often adorned with your graceful person in our
tranquil and sentimental repasts." He insists that

---

1 [I think M. Scherer brings the abhorred shears to Sensibility too early : but as I could only refer to an essay of my own on
the subject, it is, perhaps, better to confine myself to this simple
remark. — *Trans.*]

when his time comes, he will die alone, far from
home, in some inn.[1] If you will believe him, the
suffering of friends at such a moment, nay, the last
offices of affection, would torment his soul and suffice
to kill him. "Thank God!" he cries, "for my sensibility; though it has often caused me suffering, I
would not give it for all the pleasures of coarse sen-
sualists." We can now understand what Sterne
means by a "Sentimental Journey."[2] The traveller
à la Sterne is a man who troubles himself but little
about the goal for which he is making, or the regions
which he traverses. He hardly visits remarkable
monuments, he says nothing of the beauty of places;
his objects of search are sweet and affectionate
emotions. Everything becomes to him matter for
sympathy : a caged bird, a donkey sinking under
ill treatment, a poor child, an old monk. A sort
of universal benevolence makes him take his share
of all small sorrows, not exactly for the purpose of
consolation, but to enter into them, to taste their
savor, and, if I may say so, to extract the picturesque from them. Sentimentalism is perfectly compatible with a certain strain of egotism, and the
sentimental traveller is at bottom much more his
own master than is thought. It is for this reason

---

[1] [It is fair to observe that he *did*. Few persons of sensibility
thus kept their word. — *Trans.*]

[2] [Here M. Scherer quotes, in a note, the well-known passages from the *Journey* as to "the man who goes from Dan to
Beersheba" and the "quiet journey of the heart." — *Trans.*]

that he paints so excellently, for this also that he so often exaggerates and strikes into falsetto. The history of Father Lorenzo is an example of these exaggerations. Lorenzo had given Sterne his snuff-box, and some months afterwards our traveller, revisiting Calais, learns that the poor monk is dead. He " burst into tears "[1] at the tomb. Well and good, but there are too many of these tears in Sterne. I like him better when his tenderness keeps better measure, or when he contents himself with a simple humane impulse. In this style of touching simplicity, he has told stories which are, and deserve to be, famous, being pure masterpieces, such as the story of Le Fevre, the death of Yorick, the two donkeys, the dead donkey of Naimpont, and him of the pastry-cook. Did Sterne ever write anything more exquisite than Uncle Toby's fly ? Is not the hero of the siege of Namur all in this trait ?[1]

To sum up, Sterne is a tale-teller of the first order and excellent in sentimental scenes. But he has the faults of his style: he abuses the trick of interesting the heart in trifles: he enlarges little things too much: he scarcely ever declaims, but he sometimes whimpers.

Let us go on to the form of his pleasantry. Sterne is a *humorist*. Humor is so distinctly the characteristic of his writings that they have been useful in

[1] [These celebrated passages are translated in the original. — *Trans.*]

fixing the sense of the word. But if Sterne remains the type of humor, he is, notwithstanding, by no means the sole representative of it : antiquity, it has been observed, knew it not : the Latin peoples appear less capable of the feelings which it implies than the Germanic nations. Yet Spain has Cervantes and France Rabelais. Germany possesses Jean Paul; in England Shakespeare is full of this kind of wit, and Carlyle has taken great trouble to inoculate himself with it.

What, then, is humor ? In other words, what have the writers whom we have just mentioned in common ? M. Stapfer has devoted the whole of an excellent chapter to the subject. He fixes for his own part on a definition according to which the humorist is the tragi-comic painter of humanity and of human absurdity. That is pretty exact, save that it is subject to the drawback of not telling us very much. I think it is possible to go somewhat deeper ; for humor seems to be an idea in æsthetics which admits, as well as another, of analysis and definition. Let us start from laughter, since laughter is a thing familiar to us. It is excited by a sense of the ridiculous, and the ridiculous arises from the contradiction between the use of a thing and its intention. A man falls on his back : we cannot help laughing unless it so happens that his fall is dangerous, and so one sentiment is driven out by another. The terrors of Sancho, the brags of Falstaff, the rascalities of Scapin, amuse us because of their disproportion with the circumstances, or their disagreement with facts. Such is the law as well of the finest wit as of the coarsest punning : at bottom of the pleasure we experience whenever we laugh there is the surprise produced by a disparity. As for the physical effect determined by this surprise, it is sufficiently well known for there to be no need of describing it : in our amazement and amusement we experience a slight spasm of the muscles of the face and the vocal organs. That is the analysis of laughter; it is complete ; we have the whole phenomenon before us.

Let us now take matters on a larger scale, and extend our terms. The disparity lies no longer in the double sense of a word, between an attitude and our usual decorum, between the madness of a moment and the rational conduct which forms the main substance of life. It is between the man himself and his destiny, between the whole of reality and the ideal which, rightly or wrongly, imposes itself on our minds as the law of things. The contrast is glaring on all sides. We hold ourselves formed for happiness and virtue, destined for everything that is true, noble, and sublime; and if we have the least touch of sincerity, we are obliged to recognize that we are weak, vacillating, limited, prosaic, fickle. No one is a hero to his *valet de chambre*, because the *valet de chambre* knows what is beneath and behind the hero. Whence comes a great and all-pervading comedy, the human comedy, " Vanity Fair."

Now, let us suppose that an artist has grasped
this irony of fate in all its lively qualities. Yet
the result must not be irritation or indignation.
He has learnt to be tolerant. He has no special
grudge at nature for corresponding so little to an
ideal which is perhaps, after all, arbitrary. He is
even able to bestow compassion on the strange shortcomings of our poor species. He puts up, pitifully
and even sympathetically after a fashion, with all
these examples of the mean, the base, the small, the
poor. At bottom he discovers that everything is
not so bad, that humanity is not altogether so much
to be complained of, that there are other persons
here below besides rascals and ruffians. Nay, more,
he takes pleasure in discovering everywhere vestiges
of an original and indefeasible nobility. Still he
knows at the same time that all of it has a seamy
side, and he delights in turning that side out: in
showing the tribe of narrownesses and absurdities
that accompany virtue, the grotesque that pushes
its way among things venerable and venerated. The
views of our artist are tempered by a kind of melancholy : he laughs at humanity, but with no bitterness. The perception of the contrasts of human
destiny by a man who does not sever himself from
humanity, but who takes his own shortcomings and
those of his dear fellow-creatures cheerfully — that
is the essence of humor.

It is easy to understand the kind of pleasantry
which results from it — a kind of gall-less satire, a

mixture of things touching and things merry, a
mutual permeation of the comic and the sentimental. But this is not all. The humorist, if he be
analyzed to the end, is a sceptic. The tolerance of
the wretchednesses of humanity by which he is characterized can only come from a certain weakening
of idealism in him. He sees perfectly well that
our absurdities are often excusable or even the
cloaks of virtue; but he sees also that our virtues
have their absurd sides, and this is hardly compatible with a vigorous moral conviction. For him
the fact eclipses the ideal to which the fact corre-
sponds so imperfectly and so awkwardly. Whence
it comes that our humorist is very apt to play with
his subject: he does not take very seriously a
spectacle which to him is only a spectacle, hollow
enough, and petty enough after all. His heart is
but half in his business as a moralizer: his sincerity is not unmixed : his first object is to amuse
himself and other people. And this is why he is
so very likely to exaggerate the kind of pleasantry
to which he gives himself up. He will pile on the
contrasts and the dissonances, seek oddity for
oddity's sake —find it necessary to be droll at any
price, invent what is burlesque, fall into what is
equivocal and even merely buffoonish. Yet this
does not prevent the temperament of the humorist
from being, on the whole, the happiest that a man
can bring with him into this world, and the humorist's point of view the justest from which it can be

judged. The satirist grows wroth: the cynic ban-
ters : the humorist, for his part, by turns laughs
and sympathizes.

He has neither the fault of the pessimist, who
refers everything to a purely personal conception,
and is angry with reality for not being such as he
conceives it; nor that of the optimist, who shuts
his eyes to everything missing in the real world,
that he may comply with the demands of his heart
and his reason. The humorist feels the imperfections of reality and resigns himself to them with
the good humor which knows that our own satisfaction is not the rule of things ; that the formula of the
universe is necessarily larger than the preferences
of a single one of the accidental beings of whom
the universe is composed. The humorist is beyond
all doubt the true philosopher — always providing
that he is a philosopher.

Without going about to do so, we have just
drawn the portrait of Sterne. He had neither ill
nature nor egotism; but (which is much more
human) he had weakness and levity. His, says M.
Stapfer, was a kind of optimism which believed in
the good of human nature and the moral government
of the world, without denying the evil and the disorders in both — I should add, especially without
taking either tragically or troubling himself much
about them. He writes, " 'Tis a good little world,
the world in which we live. I take Heaven to witness, after all my jesting, my heart is innocent, and

the sports of my pen just like those of my infancy
when I rode cock-horse on a stick." And elsewhere:
"*Vive la bagatelle!* O my humor, never hast thou
painted in black the objects I met in my way. In
danger thou hast gilt my horizon with hope, and
when death itself knocked at my door, thou didst
tell him to call again with so gay an air of careless
indifference that he doubted his mission."

There we have him — a light and easy humor, a
man who looks at once with amusement and sympathy at human affairs, who loves the world without
forming too high an idea of it. And we have, as
the result, a kindly satire, where bitterness is replaced by good humor, contempt by affection, the
spirit of detraction by sensibility, a satire which
inspires us with interest and even affection for the
very persons of whom it makes fun.

Besides this fundamental characteristic, which
is the property of humor, and which constitutes
Sterne's originality, he has a notable talent as a
moralist and a tale-teller. "He possessed" (I am
still quoting M. Stapfer) "a delicate psychological
faculty; the power of creating character and arrang-
ing situation; the talent of drawing personages and
of making them speak; a knack of sentiment,
noble, touching, or absurd; pathos, color, truth,
nature, style." Indeed, M. Stapfer is never tired
of returning to Sterne's creative genius, and especially its finest instance, the two brothers Shandy.[1]

---

[1] [Here M. Scherer inserted a long passage, or rather cento,
from M. Stapfer. — *Trans.*]

For Sterne does not merely outline characters; he sets them at work, as I have already said, in delightful scenes; or rather his manner of showing them is by making them speak or act. I have mentioned my Uncle Toby and the fly; but how many little pictures of the same kind there are! How charming a thing, for instance, is the history of the adventure by the roadside between Nîmes and Lunel! The traveller hears music, alights from his mule, finds peasants dancing to the music of the tambourine; mixes with them, skips with Nanette. "Why," cries he, "could I not live and end my days thus? Just Disposer of our joys and sorrows, why could not a man sit down in the lap of content here, and dance, and sing, and say his prayers, and go to heaven with this nut-brown maid." Elsewhere there are dialogues inimitable in their droll spirit. Thus, the hero of the book has been called Tristram instead of Trismegistus; it is the result of a mistake, and Tristram's father, who attaches a superstitious importance to proper names, takes the thing tragically. My Uncle Toby, for his part, cannot share this feeling, and relieves himself on the subject to his honest servant, who is of his master's opinion.[1]

To all these qualities we must add those of style. Sterne is no ordinary writer; in his best passages he has a fashion of writing — straightforward and natural, and at the same time exact and picturesque

---

[1] [The passage is well known. — *Trans.*]

— which implies either very true instinct or very great art. There is within his smallest detail "a certain grace of originality, which makes things unexpected and delightful blossom in the midst of exact pictures of reality."[1] Unluckily Sterne is never natural for long; if he possesses a style of his own, a substratum of real originality, he possesses also affectations, a method, and a great deal of both. He is a mannerist. He tries to be odd, which is the worst way of attaining oddity. He lays himself out to astonish us, which is the worst way of succeeding in doing so. He begins his story by the first end he can catch hold of, and then goes on anyhow, dropping the clue every moment, piling up interruptions, digressions, discussions; affecting not to know what he is going to write next sentence; building his theatre before us, and insisting that we shall see its tricks and dodges; appearing in person on the scene with

[1] As I am speaking of Sterne's style, I will say a word of the unpublished fragment which M. Stapfer has given us, and which seems to him to be due to the author of the *Sentimental Journey*. The handwriting of the original is said to be like that of Sterne, but the piece is unsigned, and there is no sufficient information as to its origin and its history. The manner and the style are yet to be dealt with. I must say that I have difficulty in recognizing therein the humorous writer we all know. It *might*, at a pinch, be Sterne's; nothing makes the supposition impossible: but I must add that nothing obliges us to accept it, for nothing recalls the thought or the manner of the supposed author.

[This note referred to a fragment which had been supplied to M. Stapfer by a Yorkshire friend in whose family the MS. had long been. — *Trans.*]

fool's cap on head, and warning us that he is going
to do so; jingling his bells, pirouetting, shouting
words of double meaning at us, playing tricks on
the audience.   These devices are by no means
invariably amusing — very far from it.   How is
one to be amused by chapters in reverse order,
blank pages, blacked pages, haphazard diagrams ?
Can Sterne possibly have thought all this quaint
and witty ?   Can the exquisite author of the story
of Le Fevre have mistaken, as so often happens,
the strength and the weakness of his genius, holding as its true originality what was only slag and
dross ?   What is certain is that Sterne keeps afloat
to-day on the current of literature with some difficulty, and that it is the fault of the very eccentricities on which he plumed himself.   For he does
plume himself on them, and this is what sets us
against him; his drolleries are sought for, his
caprices deliberate.   There is affectation in his
letting himself go; he is the most learned of buf-
foons, the most sophisticated of simpletons, so
much so that you are sure of nothing in him,
neither of his tears nor of his laughter.   But why
seek to grasp a personality so mobile, to define so
subtle a talent ?   M. Stapfer has collected in
more than one fine passage the result of his study
on Sterne, and has really left nothing to be done
after him.   It would be impossible to put in a
judgment a nobler conception of humanity, more
reason, or more grace.

May 1870.

IX

WORDSWORTH AND MODERN POETRY IN ENGLAND

I

I HAVE need of all the interest with which the subject of this article inspires me to enable me to surmount the difficulties which I foresee in it. It is always hard to speak of a foreign poet, even though he be a Shakespeare, a Goethe, or a Byron; for one cannot suppose all readers familiar with the work which is to be the subject of discussion, and yet it is impossible to discuss this work without supposing it known already. How much greater does the difficulty become when the writer to whom it is desired to call attention has no European reputation, when he has not been translated, and when as a consequence his name carries no meaning with it to the reader! We must quote him to give any idea of his genius, and to quote him we must translate him, unless we wish merely to address the small number of persons who understand his language. Now, how are we to translate a poet? In verse? My opinion on this point is known;[1]

[1] [One of M. Scherer's very best critical essays ("De la Traduction en Vers," *Etudes,* v. 319-341) is a vigorous defence of the opinion here expressed. — *Trans.*]

it is only a Marc Monnier[1] who can allow himself
experiments of this kind, and even then this prince
of translators inspires us rather with admiration
for his skill as a virtuoso than with a feeling that
we really grasp the authors he has rendered.   Shall
we have recourse to a prose version as more within
our reach, and at the same time able to keep closer
to the original ?   Yes ; but if we then keep the
sense, we voluntarily give up the form ; and is not
the form in poetry the very essence of the thing ?
We sacrifice the color to keep the outline ; but what
becomes of a painting when the color has vanished ?
In such straits does the critic find himself when he
tries to serve as interpreter between two languages ;
and yet we must give him license to attempt it
sometimes.   It is really not admissible that names
which are illustrious but a few leagues beyond our
frontiers should never be uttered in France, or
should be uttered without carrying with them even
a tolerably precise connotation.   Now the name of
Wordsworth is incontestably one of the great
names of English literature.

II

I confess that my pleasure in speaking of Wordsworth is increased by the pleasure of mentioning

[1] [A Genevese *littérateur* of great ability, erudition, and
elegance (*b.* 1829), who has died since M. Scherer's own death.
His translated *Faust* had pointed some remarks in the essay
noted above. — *Trans.*]

the eminent writer to whom we owe the recent publication of the poet's selected works. Mr. Matthew Arnold himself occupies a high place in the contemporary literature of his country. He presents a singular example of that modern curiosity which explores all paths, touches all subjects, and tries all ways of expression. He has been by turns a theologian, a poet, and a critic, and (a rarer thing) he has attempted nothing in which he has not excelled. His religious conceptions are distinguished by a combination of freedom of thought, historical intelligence of fact, and lively sentiment of moral beauty. Christianity is for him only a form of what he calls Hebraism; but Hebraism itself is one of humanity's titles of honor. Mr. Arnold's theological essays have often made me think of that most original enterprise of the German Schleiermacher. With very different methods, with less science and dialectical apparatus, but on the other hand with far more lightness of touch, fineness of perception, and sympathy for the needs of the age, they present the same effort to disengage from religious beliefs their divine and permanent substratum, and to raise religious thought to a height where it becomes equally independent of critical investigation and speculative philosophy.

We have accustomed ourselves to paradoxes in modern culture; and the same writer, the same theologian, who has discussed so pertinently God and the Bible, the authenticity of St. John's Gospel and the teaching of St. Paul, is also a poet. Indeed he began as such, and in this guise he has quite recently showed himself again by publishing a complete edition of his poetical works. Here, as everywhere, for the matter of that, his position is at once high and peculiar. Mr. Arnold is neither the disciple of a school nor the slave of his own mannerism; he possesses the originality which sincerity gives when it is helped by natural and divine gifts. I may add that in Mr. Arnold the poet has the same elasticity as the thinker; he takes all manners and leaves them by turns, by turns he tries all instruments. We have from him epic stories and attempts in drama, elegies of no common savor, great philosophical pieces. And in every style he has a certain absolutely personal accent and note of distinction. The language of verse has seldom clothed thought at once so ample and so easy.

Have we done with him? Not yet. From the marriage of such a thinker and such a poet sprang a critic — the liveliest, the most delicate, the most elegant of critics, the critic who has given out most ideas, has conferred upon them the most piquant expression, and has most thoroughly shocked the sluggishness of British thought by wholesome audacities. There is one other point on which everybody is agreed. Mr. Arnold is a delightful writer; full of limpid clearness and unaffected grace. We never catch him in the act of trying set attitudes or ambitious tricks. It is refreshing to open his books when one has just been reading the great mannerists on whom the literature of our neighbors so falsely prides itself — Carlyle, with his conscious deliberate, calculated jargon: Ruskin, with his affectations of profundity, with his laborious quest after expression, with all the studied poses of a quackery saddening to see in conjunction with merit which is often great, and constituting a sin against true sincerity and lofty taste.

There is a kind of ingratitude in the way in which we in France ignore the works of Mr. Arnold. For there is no foreign writer who is better acquainted with the literature of our country, or who has on the whole such a sympathy (I had nearly said such a weakness) for our ways of thinking, our manners, our institutions. He envies us our political equality, and he even extols the services rendered by the French Academy. His reading is not limited to our classics; he enjoys our intermediate[1] writers, and has introduced to his countrymen, Sénancour, Joubert, Maurice de Guérin and his sister. I fear it is true that he is less orthodox on the subject of our poetry; he has somewhere in one of his articles an awkward phrase about Lamartine, and I should not be surprised if Racine did not appeal to him. But far be it from me to owe him a grudge for this. I have long laid my account with such matters, and have seen without disgust the indifference of for-

---

[1] [Intermediate, that is to say, between the Classical school and the Romantic revival. — *Trans.*]

eigners to beauties which, from the very fact that they are not generally perceived, are only dearer and more sacred to their true adorers.

There is one idea — that of culture — which recurs frequently in Mr. Matthew Arnold's works. He has defined what he means by it. The man of culture in his sense is not the man who possesses a mass of erudition, nor the man who is distinguished by more or less intellectual strength. Culture, as he understands it, is that fineness, that delicacy, that sureness of perception which is given by familiarity with the great thinkers of all times, which is produced by the knowledge of the best things which have been said in the world. It is easy to understand how at this level of thought literature connects itself with morality ; how poetry finally blends with religion ; and it is easy also to discern the higher meaning of certain of the writer's assertions, which seemed at the first blush to be mere genial eccentricities. Mr. Arnold, who is far from endowing himself with any kind of mission, who is the simplest and least affected of men, has none the less become in his own country the representative of the higher function of letters. No one has recognized their humanizing influence as he has, and no one was so fit as he to become the apostle of what I may call intellectual civilization. At the present moment Mr. Arnold is the most seductive product that English literature has to offer, by reason of his union of thought and fancy, of solidity and grace, of self-respect and liberty of mind.

III

In the graceful preface which he has set in front
of his selection from Wordsworth's works Mr.
Arnold endeavors to fix the poet's place. This to
his thinking is a very high one. Wordsworth seems
to him to have the marks of poetical *greatness;* and
these marks Mr. Arnold accordingly defines.

The *great* poet, in our critic's sense, is the poet
who expresses the noblest and profoundest ideas
on the nature of man, who has a philosophy of life,
and who impresses it powerfully on the subjects he
treats. The definition is obviously rather vague.
It is true that Mr. Arnold adds that the philosophical
conception of things ought, in the poet's work, to
be produced within the eternal conditions of poetical
beauty and truth. Only, he does not tell us what
these conditions are, and it is exactly this that we
ought to know, in order to determine whether Wordsworth is an artist as well as a thinker.

What is poetry? And what do we mean when
we say that a site, a picture, a book is poetical?
We must, indeed, observe that the word fits things
very different. It is with it as with another æsthetic
category, that of beauty. We apply the term beautiful to the most diverse objects — a tree, a horse,
a thought, a speech, an action, a character. There
must clearly be something in common between the
uses, different as they are, of the same term; but in
what does this element of resemblance lie? Is it

not that we call a thing beautiful when it approaches the typical notion that we form by spontaneous abstraction of individual traits ?

By proceeding in a similar manner we may, I think, reach the conclusion that the poetical element of things is the property they have of setting the imagination in motion, of stimulating it, of suggesting to it much more than is actually perceived or expressed. The poet is he who sees through his imagination, and the special quality of imagination is to increase everything that it sees, everything that it touches, to expand or to abolish limits, and so to idealize. Yet we must not say that it embellishes ; nor must we generally lend ourselves to the confusion of the ideas of poetry and of beauty. A cathedral, for instance, is more poetical than beautiful; and the Parthenon, on the other hand, is more beautiful than poetical. Indeed, imagination can increase horror as well as charm.

To speak shortly, then, and taking it by itself, poetry is the sight of things through the eyes of imagination; and poetical expression is the reproduction of them under the form most capable of arousing the imaginative powers of the reader. And so imagery is the special language of poetry. Let the reader try to recall the finest passages of his favorite poets, and he will see that it is by the choice and the charm of metaphors and comparisons that they delight him. Why is the exclamation of Antiochus, in Racine, a favorite quotation ?

> Dans l'orient désert quel devint mon ennui !

What is it that makes this verse of Lamartine one
of the finest in the language ?

> Dans l'horizon désert Phébé monte sans bruit ?

Whence comes the admirable melancholy of this
passage of Victor Hugo ?

> Qui peut savior combien toute douleur s'émousse
> Et combien dans nos cœurs un jour d'herbe qui pousse
> Efface des tombeaux ?

Join to the imaginative conception of things the
expression proper to arouse this conception in others,
submit this expression to the laws of rhythm, give
it the cadence which by a secret connection puts
nervous sensation in accord with the movement of
thought, and you will have poetry in the complete
and concrete sense of the word.

IV

To enjoy a poet, there is no need to do more than
take his works and read them ; to judge and to
comprehend him (which is the proper task of the
critic) we must also place ourselves at the time
when he wrote, must explore the influences under
which he was formed, and those which in his turn
he exercised. We must, in short, assign him his
place in literary history.

One thing is clear at the first reading of Wordsworth, and this is that he belongs to the reaction
against the Classical school, the school personified
by the great names of Dryden and Pope, represented also honorably by Thomson, Goldsmith, and
Gray — the school which, with Campbell, Rogers,
and Byron himself, threw up suckers even in the
very heyday of the Romantic period. The characteristics of the Classical school in England were
pretty much the same as among ourselves — in
point of matter, more rhetoric and eloquence than
feeling or fancy; in point of form, the sonorous-
ness of skilful periods and the surprises of a perpetual antithesis. But if Wordsworth was the
most industrious and noteworthy of the innova-
tors he was by no means the earliest. That place
should rather be given to Cowper, whose chief
poem, "The Task," dates from 1785, and really
marks an epoch in the destinies of English poetry
by setting the example of simplicity and nature,
by choosing very simple subjects, by adopting a
fluent and familiar versification. A curious thing,
indeed, that this hermit, with his sorrowful soul,
his morbid piety, his reason always struggling
with madness, should have left so unquestionable
a mark on the literature of his country! There
can be no hesitation in connecting, if not with
Cowper's example yet with the same yearning for
innovation and the same general and hidden tendencies, the tales of a poet, George Crabbe, whose

numerous works had immense popularity at the beginning of this century, but who for his part sinned by excess of simplicity. In his hands, the natural style became merely and placidly prosaic, and so we only make mention of the author of the "Parish Register" as a matter of history. On the other hand, we must take Burns as of the first importance in respect of the influences which acted on Wordsworth and help to explain him. Not that this admirable lyric poet takes rank in the pedigree which we are trying to draw up. He had nothing to learn and nothing to unlearn; he shot up as spontaneously as the daisy of his own mountains. Yet it is to the breath which was then blowing on English letters that Burns owed the welcome given to his poems, and being thus naturalized on the south of the Tweed, he himself became one of the authors of the revolution which Wordsworth completed.

We now know Wordsworth's origins, the family of which he sprung. His first poems, the "Lyrical Ballads," date from the end of the eighteenth century; but he was not thirty when they appeared, aud he definitely belongs to the movement of poetic renovation which has left glorious traces on the literature of his country during the first quarter of the nineteenth. It is true that he continued, long after this period, to be prolific without any notable change of style, and without any sensible weakening of his genius. In his life of eighty years,

he saw many a revolution in the conception of art,
and in the admirations of the public. His own
career, let me repeat, offers no appreciable distinction between the works of his youth and those of
his maturity, nor any of the transformations which
are observable in the life of some artists. His
poetic fame, on the other hand, had its phases
and its vicissitudes. Wordsworth first appears to
us as one of the most noted champions in the
struggle wherein his friends, the other Lakers, Coleridge, Southey, John Wilson, fought in a lower
rank than his; but in which he also met noisier
and more brilliant competitors who eclipsed him
for a while. From this time forward he had his
admirers, even his devotees; but he had also his
contemners. One side held him up as the prophet
of a new poetical religion, the other mocked at his
style. But these very controversies proved that
he had already excited and arrested public opinion;
that is to say, that he was already famous. As
for fashion, which is a different thing, that was
for the moment entirely on the side of two writers,
one of whom, in a series of poems full of brilliancy
and music, poured forth an inexhaustible vein of
chivalry; while the other dressed up the gloomy
caprices of a *blasé* in the turban and the caftan.
We in France are now too wont to forget, or, to
speak more exactly, we never quite knew, the
enthusiasm excited by Walter Scott's legendary
epics until their popularity was shadowed by the

stronger and more romantic conceptions of Lord Byron, and by the prodigious success of Scott's own prose stories.

The progress of literature, a subject hitherto insufficiently studied, is dominated by three great laws. The first turns on the modifications which are produced in the moral and intellectual state of the public. The point of view, especially in our modern societies, changes incessantly, and with the point of view in general everything changes likewise — taste as well as ideas, the starting points of art as well as those of thought. Yet it sometimes happens, and here we come to the second of the laws of which I speak, that progress is brought about, not by simple development of ideas, but, on the contrary, by more or less pronounced reaction, the human mind eagerly and willingly running in the opposite direction to that which it had formerly followed. The third and last law — one which applies no less frequently than the others — consists in the satiety produced by custom, and the yearning for innovation which comes of satiety. The human mind wants to be interested, and there is no interest, or at least no forcible stimulant, except in surprise. The intelligence demands novelty as the body demands action: or else the man falls into ennui — the most terrible of evils, the evil which all seek to avoid, and do avoid at all hazards. I must ask pardon for going back so far in order to explain a thing simple enough in itself,

but it is precisely because it is simple that sufficient attention has not been paid to it. But, however this may be, my readers will easily guess the
application I wish to make of these principles to
literature. A great poet cannot escape imitators.
He has opened a way into which everybody is sure
to rush; some to profit by the public taste, others
because their talent naturally and spontaneously
takes the shape which genius has just consecrated.
And so come secondary, even tertiary, forma-
tions. After Homer comes Virgil; after Virgil,
the modern epics from Tasso to the "Henriade."
After Sophocles comes Racine; after Racine, Voltaire and the whole classical tragedy up to 1830.
But the imitators are so busy, that at last readers
are sick of them, cry "Hold!" and insist on something new. It is impossible that something new
should not come — something grandly and really
new if the national genius is strong enough; some
affected and puerile imitation in wording, costume,
local color, if genius refuses to revive an exhausted
literature.

There is no country of our time where the succession of poetical masters, and with them of poetical influences, tastes, schools, and methods, has
been so rapid as it has in England. The reason is
that (contrary to the notions of our Continental
ignorance) the English are the most poetical nation
in Europe, and, what is more, that Englishmen,
reading much more than we do, are much more sub-

ject to the needs of change of which I spoke just
now. In France we have not got beyond Byron.
For us modern poetry is still embodied in the
works — brilliant enough and easily understood —
of a man whose disorderly life, whose ostentation
of misanthropy, whose pretentious dandyism — in
a word, whose littleness and affectation, have never
succeeded in diminishing his ancient vogue with
our countrymen. But the English are long past
Byronism. As Byron succeeded Scott, so in his
turn he was himself succeeded by other inspirations. The author of "The Lady of the Lake"
and "Marmion," after enchanting one generation,
ended by seeming insufficient to a society which
was still excited and moved by the Revolution and
the wars of the Empire. However superficial
Byron's passion may seem to us now, its tone of
intimate appeal answered the prevalent demand
better than the exterior and objective poetry of the
Scotch *chansons de geste.* Men were drawn back,
with a power which could not be denied, to the
inner world, to the hidden drama, to restless aspirations. Only, this too wore itself out, and that
quickly. The factitiousness of this ostentation of
boredom and despair was felt before long; Byronism was too violent, and for that reason not true
enough, to answer the lasting needs of the soul.
The abuse, as always, invited the reaction. After
such a debauch of exaggerated sentiment, men were
seized with a thirst for sincerity and simplicity.

Besides, they had not the inconvenience of waiting for the epiphany of a preacher of the new gospel. He was there at hand; he had been writing for thirty years; he had already a share of influence and renown; a party had actually formed round him. And it was from this moment, about 1825, that the second epoch of Wordsworth's influence dates — the epoch which was at once that of his uncontested popularity and of his acknowledged supremacy in literature.

Then, as always happens in these cases, men thought they had discovered the last word of art in him. Philosophy of the most exalted kind had met its final form in the most perfect poetry; and the result was full of simplicity, sincerity, beneficence. For some fifteen years Wordsworth, in his remote retreat of Rydal Mount, enjoyed glory which, though it has certainly grown less bright since then, was after all deserved, and admirably free from alloy.

Yet he was not the less bound to be in his turn the victim of a new evolution of taste and thought. As Byron had succeeded Scott by working with more energetic stimulants on men's minds; as Wordsworth later had attracted, by his contrast of healthy simplicity, imaginations jaded by Byronism; so Wordsworth himself in the long run began to seem unsatisfying. His defects were more clearly seen. The need of a wider thought, of a more brilliant fancy, was felt. This was the moment for the rehabilitation of two poets who had both died in the flower of their age, unknown or disdained, some twenty years earlier. Shelley and Keats in their turn became prophets and leaders of schools. The first and greater of the two had been drowned in 1822, at the age of thirty, in the Gulf of Spezzia; but his genius had been of a rare precocity, and he left a great number of poems in very different styles. The dominant — unluckily by far the dominant — note in them was that of a social Utopia. Shelley's naïve and generous soul was possessed with the idea of a world governed by justice and by reason. He had conceived an immense pity for all suffering, and in consequence an implacable wrath against the creeds and the institutions which he took to be the causes of such suffering. He was still an undergraduate when he bade defiance to the orthodoxies of his country : the results were a quarrel with his family, an ill-starred marriage, exile, poverty, persecution — altogether a state of affairs in which it was difficult for the public to separate the poetical genius from the revolutionary Utopist. Moreover his earlier works, and even some of his later, were penetrated to the core of their substance with the fault of didactic intention, and hardly permitted their readers to enjoy their exquisite poetical beauty, smothered as it was under the apparatus of visions, personifications, and allegories. At least half of Shelley's work is spoilt by intolerable humanitarian "purpose."

It was only at intervals, when the sentiment of nature overpowered him, or when, here and there, some earthly love mingled with Platonic dreams in his heart, that pure poetry got the upper hand in this writer's mind. Yet, on the whole, after saying all this, after making all these allowances, Shelley is a poet of the first order, and it is no wonder that his star when it once rose in the heaven of English poetry dimmed that of Wordsworth. It was, we must allow, the stronger of the two. It was not more various, for Shelley, like Wordsworth, is not free from monotony. There was not much more vibration of the string of human passion; for, if Shelley is sometimes what Wordsworth never is, in love, his loves are of a very ethereal kind. But Shelley had more freedom, his thought was more daring, he touched higher questions, he expressed deeper anxieties, more actual needs of contemporary humanity. And he did all this in a poetical tongue of wider range, of deeper resonance, of greater imaginativeness, of a melody simply marvellous — a thrilling and subtle melody, now like the slow and solemn murmur of the wind in the pine forest, now like the liquid and pearly notes of the lark soaring in the sunbeams.

A resemblance in fate rather than in talent is the reason of the fact that one involuntarily thinks of Keats and Shelley together. Keats, a little younger than Shelley, died before him, when not yet six and twenty, and leaving but two substantive poems

(one of them unfinished) and a small number of
exquisite lyrics. His faults are numerous and
glaring. The mythology which supplied him with
his *mise en scène* is elementary and almost puerile.
His stories are lacking in human interest. In fact,
he does hardly anything but describe, and he
describes with an exuberance which is unluckily
not incompatible with the most painful monotony.
The enthusiasm for nature which is the soul of his
verse is certainly sincere, and yet Keats writes with
effort. His naïveté is not feigned, but there is
something in it of deliberation, and therefore of
exaggeration. In short, there is affectation in him,
and I cannot regard as wholly unjust the reproach
of cockneyism which critics used to throw at this
poet and his friends. Yet, with all these faults,
Keats is very far from being an ordinary person; his
posthumous popularity is very far from being inexplicable, and the influence which he still exercises is
very far from being a mere matter of coterie and
engouement. He has a special feeling, a feeling of
extraordinary intensity, for nature and for beauty.
It seems as though he saw woods, streams, fields
for the first time, so full of novelty and of the marvellous is the spectacle to him. There is at once
sensuousness and religion in his communion with
the life of all things. There would seem to be a
perfume which gets in his head, an intoxication to
which he gives himself up, a ritual into whose mysteries he is trying to break, a baptism, a whelming

in the eternal *natura naturans*. Wordsworth himself, as we shall see, can lay claim to a deeper
understanding of nature : but it is easy to understand that his idyllic piety, his patriarchal philos-
ophizing, must have at last seemed terribly grovel-
ling to a generation which had drunk the heady
philtres of Keats's descriptive poetry.

Do I mean that modern poetry in England has
stopped at Keats and Shelley ? Not at all; for,
once again, there is no finality in art, and no man
has ever been able to boast of having said the last
word on anything. Great writers, as they enlarge
the fields of the human soul, only create new needs
and excite to new experiments. Keats and Shelley
have certainly not been thrown into the shade by
Tennyson; but it is equally certain that Tennyson
has climbed on their shoulders, and has, in some
respects, reached a higher level. If he is not superior in strength or grandeur to Shelley, the metal
of his poetry is purer, its workmanship is more
ingenious and more exquisite, the work taken as a
whole is of a more surprising variety. Tennyson
possesses a consummate science of rhythm, the
rarest resources of phrase, taste, grace, distinction,
every sort of cleverness, of research, of refinement.
He is the author of lyric pieces unequalled in any
language, some of infinite delicacy, some of engross-
ing pathos, some quivering like the blast of a
knightly horn. He lacks only one thing, one supreme gift, the pinion-stroke which sweeps Gany-

mede into the empyrean, and casts him panting at
Jupiter's feet. He sins by his very elegance; he
is too civilized, too polished. He has tried every
style — grave, gay, and passionate — the idyl, the
ode, and the elegy, mock-heroics, epics, drama.
There is no style in which he has not had brilliant
success, and yet it may be said that he has explored
nothing thoroughly. There are ardors in passion,
troubles in thought, bankruptcies of the ideal in
life, which Tennyson's note is not equal to expressing. His poetry (whether as matter of inspiration
or of determination I do not 'know) keeps too
strictly to the region of decencies and conventions.
And so we must not be surprised if an adoring public came at last to doubt its idol; in some cases,
indeed, to carry its devotions elsewhere. For these
persons, when they were once in the mood to be
faithless, the thickets and obscurities of Browning
were sure to be only an additional attraction. Are
not the most fashionable cults those which can
only be reached after a process of initiation? But
it is not our business to follow the development
of modern poetry in England further. What we
have said is intended solely to mark out Wordsworth's place in this great and splendid movement.
He was one of its chiefs, one of its illustrations;
and, even putting this aside, he abides in the literature of his country as one of its chosen authors,
relished and read for the sake of his own peculiar
beauties.

V

It may seem at first sight that life is necessarily modelled on each man's inborn tendencies; but as a fact it is made up of two things. It is, as I think I have remarked elsewhere, as it were the confluence of two currents, the point of intersection between the trajectories of two forces, those of nature and of destiny. No matter what we are; what we shall be depends on the accidents of education, the chance meetings of life. There are even moments when this thought is a troublesome one, "What will the future bring?" "How shall I come out of the trial I cannot avoid?" For, in fact, destiny is the stronger, and in the case of most men she seldom allows nature to exercise her rights fully. How rare, for instance, is a poetical life, even with the sincerest poets! In this respect Wordsworth is altogether an exception. It is impossible to imagine either a life better suited than his to his genius or a soul better adapted to relish the charm of this life, to gather up its inspirations, to tell its inner joys. He was born and he spent the greater part of his days in the Lake District of the north of England, where nature is graceful and charming, not violent enough to crush the imagination, but bold enough and varied enough to give it gates of escape to the infinite. He had travelled, and seen other skies besides those of England; but without going far enough to bring back with him the regrets which sometimes pursue the traveller who has walked under the palms. He was born in a middle condition, and some friends procured him independence and leisure. To conclude, he was early notorious and later famous, and if his star paled a little before his death, we may believe that he had confidence enough in himself not to perceive it, or, at least, not to trouble himself about it.

His works — very numerous and sufficiently dissimilar — present a certain difficulty to those who try to class them according to the kinds to which they belong. I think, however, that I am neglecting nothing, and at the same time observing a natural order, in making three classes: narrative poems, lyrics, and sonnets. Wordsworth's predilection for the sonnet, and the success wherewith he has cultivated a kind which might seem somewhat artificial for a poet of nature and of the fields, are things to be observed, and important to take account of in the final estimate. He has really excelled in it, and many of his sonnets approach perfection. Although English literature is singularly rich in poetical jewels of this kind, Wordsworth, to my taste, has in this respect rivals, but no superiors. The piece on the sonnet itself, that composed on Westminster Bridge, that addressed to Milton, and half a hundred others (he wrote four hundred), show that combination of ingenious turn and victorious final touch which is the triumph of the kind.

Sainte-Beuve, who loved the sonnet in his character of "reflective" poet, and who loved Wordsworth for that vein of poetry at once familiar and full of feeling, which he would have liked himself to acclimatize in France, translated or imitated several of our author's sonnets. He returned to the practice at all times of his life, inserting one or two in each of his collections. Such a windfall is lucky for me, and I make the most of it by citing one of these free translations : — [1]

> Je ne suis pas de ceux pour qui les causeries,
> Au coin du feu, l'hiver, ont de grandes douceurs ;
> Car j'ai pour tous voisins d'intrépides chasseurs,
> Rêvant de chiens dressés, de meutes aguerries,
>
> Et des fermiers causant jachères et prairies,
> Et le juge de paix avec ses vieilles sœurs,   ˏ
> Deux revêches beautés parlant de ravisseurs,
> Portraits comme on en voit sur les tapisseries.
>
> Oh ! combien je préfère à ce caquet si vain,
> Tout le soir, du silence, un silence sans fin ;
> Etre assis sans penser, sans désir, sans mémoire,
>
> Et, seul, sur mes chenets, m'éclairant aux tisons,
> Ecouter le vent battre, et gémir les cloisons,
> Et le fagot flamber, et chanter la bouilloire.

[1] [To re-translate this translation would, of course, defeat the object of citing it. It represents, it need hardly be said, the famous "Personal Talk," and the translation is "free" in more senses than one. Neither the gratuitous introduction of and aspersion on the "deux revêches beautés," nor the omission of the beautiful image of the "forms with chalk," is the best possible instance of Sainte-Beuve's taste as a translator. — *Trans.*]

We might also take from the "Consolations" the piece beginning

Les passions, la guerre, une âme en frénésie.

But we must allow that the sonnets translated by Sainte-Beuve are chosen in a rather narrow circle of subjects, and that the comparison brings out the difference set between two poets, who in sincerity, and even in depth of thought, approach each other, by the want of that commanding plastic spirit with which Sainte-Beuve, to his bitter regret, knew himself to be insufficiently endowed.

Wordsworth's narrative poems include large compositions such as " Peter Bell," " The Waggoner," " The Prelude," and, chief of all, " The Excursion," a long story in several books, which is itself a fragment of a still vaster whole, a kind of philosophical epic.   To the same class belong a great number of shorter tales, idyls, eclogues, ballads, or mere anecdotes in verse, among which are many of the author's most characteristic and best known poems.

We must also draw a subdistinction among his lyrics, Wordsworth's chief title to admiration.   Our poet wrote some odes of a character more classical and (if I may venture to say so) more ambitious than seems consistent with his usual manner. They are, however, much and justly admired; as, for instance, " Laodamia," the religious symphony on a Platonic theme, and the ode to " Duty." The other lyrics, much more numerous, are in kind

purely subjective, and disengage themselves in all
sorts of forms — elegies, inspirations, invocations,
memories, landscapes. There is not an aspect of
the country, not an object in the fields or in the
woods, which does not evoke enthusiasm in this
melodious soul. Wordsworth is as much ravished
at the sight of a buttercup or daisy beneath his
feet as at the rainbow on the horizon: and all his
work is shot through with a deep note of meditation, the comment of the sage on the teachings of
life.

This work, as I have said, is considerable. There
are seven volumes of his poems, many of which
are mediocre. But there are few poets who have
left so many precious pieces. And he has, besides,
his own incontestable originality. He created the
class of the childish ballad, the rustic pastoral, the
idyl of the poor: and he drew from the contemplation of nature tones of sweet and grave fervor, the
secret of which he kept. No poet puts the reader
so thoroughly in communion with nature, because
none has felt a more religious love for her.

VI

I shall point out at once what is wanting and
what is faulty in Wordsworth, the qualities which
he lacks, and the imperfections which disfigure his
poetry. Let us begin with the qualities lacking.
No one acknowledges more fully than I do the injustice, not to say the absurdity, of asking a man

for something else than he has chosen to give, or, worse still, reproaching him with not being somebody else, and not what nature has made him. Therefore, it is not as a reproach, nor even as a regret, that I examine what is wanting in Wordsworth; it is merely to characterize his genius better, to set his poetical physiognomy in stronger relief.

To great troubles of mind he was a stranger, and his nearest approaches to tender sentiment are the pieces to the memory of that Lucy whom he has himself described. As for political emotions, he had, like many others, hailed in the French Revolution the dawn of a new era for humanity. His sonnets bear witness to his wrath against the conqueror who dispelled his dreams, who put an end to the Venetian Republic and the independence of Switzerland, and who menaced England with invasion. There is nothing in all this which goes beyond respectable Liberalism and patriotism.

Let us then make up our minds not to expect from Wordsworth either that knowledge of the human heart which is given by life in the world, or that inner and dramatic working of passion which no man describes well unless he has been its victim, or those general views on history and society which are formed partly by study, partly by experience in public affairs. Our poet was as much a stranger to the harassings of thought as to those of ambition, to the pangs of love and of hatred as to the resignation at which men arrive when they have seen how small are the great things of this world. He has nothing of the sublime melancholy, the ardent inquiry, the audacious revolt in which the poetry of half a century ago delighted. Still less has he the mocking scepticism, the raillery now gay now bitter, which followed the "songs of despair." He will never rank with those who like Byron, disturb the soul; who like Heine, arm it with irony; or who like Goethe, calm it with the virtues of knowledge. Wordsworth is simply a hermit who has studied nature much, and has constantly analyzed his own feelings. We could hardly call him a philosopher; his mind is too devoid of the element of reasoning and speculation. Even the name of thinker but half suits him: he is the contemplative man.

I have thus made a list of the qualities which Wordsworth has not, with all the less intention of casting them up against him that the qualities which a writer lacks are usually the conditions of those which distinguish him. It is otherwise with the positive defects which disfigure work, and in regard to which it is equally impossible not to suppose that they could have been avoided and not to wish that they had been.

Mr. Arnold cites a remarkable expression of Wordsworth's. He remembers having heard him say that Goethe's poetry does not possess the supreme character of being "inevitable." By this Wordsworth meant that poetry ought to have in it

something spontaneous, that one ought to feel in it
sentiment rather than reflection, the spurt from
the inner fount rather than will and design. The
saying was admirably just in relation to Goethe,
whose "Lieder," perfect as they are, and perhaps
by reason of this very perfection, give us the effect
of something crystallized. It is learned, correct,
brilliant; the things, I grant, are diamonds, but I
see not in them the shapes of life.[1] Besides, the
distinction which Wordsworth's *mot* suggests is of
very wide application. It does not merely divide
poets into two classes; it serves to mark off, even
in the works of the same poet, many things which
must be scored to the account of deliberate purpose,
not to say of business. Our three great contemporary French poets have all, though in different
degrees, the note of inevitableness; yet all is far
from being equally true in them. As for Wordsworth, he has by no means escaped the effect of his
own remark.

In this there is something strange enough. If
ever a writer had a claim to be held sincere, it was
this man of genius, whose heart was at once austere
and simple. Yet, beyond all doubt, not everything
in his writings is genuine. Wordsworth gives himself certain airs; he has manufactured a mannerism; he exaggerates what he feels; he is too liberal
of his own fashions of thought and of speech; he

[1] [And the *König in Thule?* and *Freudvoll und leidvoll?* and
a dozen others? — *Trans.*]

appears in a guise which is certainly his own, but of which he has, nevertheless, made up the outlines and studied the expression. He is naïf; but his naïveté often looks calculated. His enthusiasm for nature, however deep and real it be, becomes now and then declamatory. For instance, take the ode which I have mentioned, and in which the author assumes with Plato that the child brings into the world the memory of an anterior existence. This piece, noble, magnificent as it is, has always seemed to me to ring a little false. We can hardly help seeing in it a thesis adopted with a consciousness of the poetic developments of which it is capable, rather than a serious belief of the author's. I may say as much of his ecstasies over a fawn, of his tenderness *à propos* of a girl he has met in the mountains: —

> Thee neither know I, nor thy peers,
> And yet my eyes are filled with tears.

All Wordsworth's faults have the same source, and are of the same kind. He has an ideal of life, and involuntarily adjusts his moral attitude to it; he has an ideal of art, and exaggerates the style he admires. His habit of seeking and finding lessons in the smallest incidents of his walks passes into didactic mania. He draws morals from everything, delivers sermons on every text he meets. Nor is this preaching vein by any means always a poetical one. We seem sometimes to hear the psalmody of the conventicle: —

> Oh ! there is never sorrow of heart
> That shall lack a timely end,
> If but to God we turn and ask
> Of Him to be our friend.

That is like one of Watts's hymns.[1]

The titles of Wordsworth's poems often bear a trace of his moralizing tendency. There is one called "Anecdote for Fathers, Showing how the Practice of Lying may be taught"; another — an admirable piece, by the way — bears the stupid title, "Influence of Natural Objects in Calling forth and Strengthening the Imagination in Boyhood and early Youth." Wordsworth is not exactly lacking in wit; he has sometimes touches of gaiety and of acuteness, but he has no sense of the ridiculous.

The contradiction which lies at the bottom of his work is, that while he shows in it the truth and spontaneity which befit a poet of nature, he is at the same time conscious of his part. He has a system, and deliberately takes up the position of an apostle; his prefaces are filled with an ostentatious purpose of bringing men's minds back to simplicity in subject and language. He is the professor of a

---

[1] [And not very unlike these verses:

> Sur cette terre ou tu veux que j'habite,
> O mon Sauveur, mon Dieu, je suis à toi;
> Et dans le Ciel où ta grâce m'invite
> Encore à toi, toujours à toi.

The author of which, M. Gréard tells us, was Edmond Scherer. — *Trans.*]

Poetic which consists in discovering beauties in the commonest objects of nature, lessons in the humblest beings, and in clothing these subjects with a new interest, in restoring them to the domain of art by dint of intense observation and forcible expression. And it is certain that Wordsworth, as far as he is concerned, has actually realized this programme. But, unluckily, he has not only reached his end, he has gone beyond it. The simplicity of his subjects and of his manner too often passes into triviality, the simplicity of his style into poverty. He showers puerile anecdotes on us; he tells us stories of dogs, he narrates what a little girl said to her sheep. He affects not merely an enthusiasm for flowers and birds, but a predilection for beggars, idiots, and cripples. The lower a being is in the scale, the more he labors to awake our sympathy in its favor. There is no detail so minute, so insignificant, that he does not delight in taking note of it. If he tells of a summer walk, he must needs speak of the cloud of insects which surround his face and follow him as he advances.

It is easy to understand that, with all his efforts, he does not always succeed in making such themes poetical. Prose breaks in against his will. He has passages where matter and form vie in commonplace, as this on the career of a *mauvais sujet :* —

> His genius and his moral fame
> Were thus impaired, and he became
> The slave of low desires ;

> A man who, without self-control,
> Would seek what the degraded soul
> Unworthily admires.

What a pity to find verses like these (and they are not rare in Wordsworth) in a great poet! The exaggeration and the affectation with which I reproach him have, moreover, done him infinite harm. We are able now to distinguish the lasting beauties of his work from the parts of it where his system of view has hurt the sincerity of his inspiration; but for a great many years he was chiefly famous by the absurder sides of his pastorals, and by the parodies to which they lent themselves. It happened to Wordsworth in England as with us to the poet who had already long since written the "Nuits," while men still obstinately refused to see in him aught but the author of the "Ballade à la Lune."

VII

Let us leave these imperfections and faults alone, and seek nothing in Wordsworth but what, in sum, he is — one of the poets who have best loved, felt, and rendered nature. Now there are many ways of loving her. There is that of youth. The young man loves nature as a field open to the exercise of his energies. To grasp the world, the great world, to succeed to the inheritance of oneself in the consciousness of one's own strength, is the highest delight at this time of life. And so country pleas-

ures stand, then, in the ratio of the play they offer
to activity, of the excitement into which they
throw the animal spirits.   Exercise on foot, gallop-
ing a horse, hunting, swimming, are so many joys
into which sun, greenery, the tints of wood and
field, no doubt enter to some extent, and contribute
to the intoxication of days of delicious fatigue; but
nevertheless they remain as but the background of
the picture.   It is the opportunity of asserting
himself that the young man seeks in nature.
When he comes to the serious part of life, when he
is absorbed in his task, and in the struggle for
existence which is now carried on at such close
quarters, man does not yet necessarily lose his
taste for nature, but what he now asks of her is
repose.   He loves her for the contrast which she
makes with the noisy town, with absorption in
material interests, with the meanness of rivalries,
the disturbance of passion.   If only the soul is not
world-worn in the great game of hazard which each
man plays against society, there is no wandering in
the alleys of a great park, no sitting on the brink
of a quiet pond, or in sight of a vast champaign,
without the sudden feeling of a kind of refresh-
ment.   The calm of things communicates itself to
the spirit; we fall insensibly into unison with the
universe which cares so little for what agitates us
so much.   Universal order brings us back to a
juster sentiment of reality.   Over our obstinate
preoccupations, our harassing regrets, our stubborn

anxieties, our disgusts, our jealousies, our hatreds, over all the workings of a brain on fire, the contemplation of nature drops an appeasement which belongs to nothing else.   As happened of old with the Master's touch, there comes forth from it a virtue which heals.

For the old man himself, or for him in similar plight, the sick man whose days are numbered, nature still has her charm, a sadness of special savor, a sweetness dashed with bitter : —

Aux regards d'un mourant le soleil est si beau !

There is a strange pathos in the contrast between the unchangeableness of things and the feebleness of the thinking being who contemplates them. There is perceived at such times, in the aspects of the country, as it were a bitter pleasure mingled with resignation and disdain.   A melancholy triumph is felt in the inequality of the fight in which we are succumbing, in the paradox of the defeat, in the simultaneous superiority over what is lasting which is given us by the consciousness of our own caducity.   We taste the strange and horrid joy of having gauged the worth of life, and of feeling ourselves and the world of thought and passion we carry in our breasts as vain as the ripple which forms on the surface of the lake, and vanishes with the same puff of air that caused it.

Young men see in nature an empire to be overrun ; men of mature years seek in her a truce to

inner troubles; old men find in her a funereal consolation. But the artist? Is it not for herself
that *he* loves her? Is it not on her alone that he
lives? Is he not solely enamoured of her beauty?
Does he not set his whole ambition in comprehend-
ing and expressing her, in feeling and translating
her, in entering into all her moods, seizing all her
aspects, penetrating all her secrets? Who, if it be
not the artist, can flatter himself with being initi-
ated in the mysteries of the great Goddess?

And yet it is not so. What the artist pursues is
not so much nature as the effects to which she
lends herself, as the picturesque, as art. If he
throws himself at her feet, it is but to hasten elsewhere and boast of the favors he has received. The
artist is a man who has the rare and fatal gift of
doubling himself, of feeling with half his soul and
employing the other half in telling what he feels;
a man who has experienced emotion, but who has
afterwards slain it in his bosom in order the better
to take it as a model, and sketch it at his leisure in
strokes which are a transfiguration.

Is there not something of a similar kind in many
a religious conception of nature? Does not, for
instance, the theist also look at her from the outside, as at an object which is exterior and foreign
to himself? He thinks to exalt her dignity by
making her come from the hands of the Supreme
Artificer, and he does but strip her of her proper
life. The watchmaker is skilful, a wonder-worker,

omnipotent; but the watch is, after all, only a masterpiece of mechanism. Religious anthropomorphism carries within it a contradiction which secretly gnaws it, a soulless Universe and an unsubstantial God, a dead Universe and a God of abstraction.

The sentiment of nature in Wordsworth does not exactly resemble any of the kinds which I have described. "Wordsworth's poetry," says Matthew Arnold, "is great because of the extraordinary power with which Wordsworth feels the joy offered us in nature, the joy offered to us in the simple elementary affections and duties, and because of the extraordinary power with which, in case after case, he shows us this joy and renders it so as to make us share it." This definition suits the Wordsworth of the pastorals; it is not enough to characterize the poet's highest inspirations, those of the verses composed on the banks of the Wye, of the Platonic ode, or of the admirable piece beginning

Wisdom and spirit of the Universe.

I should myself rather say that Wordsworth is the poet who has most profoundly felt and most powerfully expressed the commerce of the soul with nature, the dialogue of the human mind with the spirit of things, the "obstinate questionings" of which he himself speaks, the vague disquietudes of a creature moving in "worlds not realized," the high

instincts which surprise ourselves.   If the view of
the humblest flower at his feet softens his mood, it
is because it suggests to him

> Thoughts that do often lie too deep for tears.

Wordsworth's love for nature, then, is not that
of the man of culture who admires a landscape ;
nor is it that of the man of speculation who lets
himself float on the universal current.   He brings
to it something more intimate than the one, something more personal than the other.   True, nature is
for him the great mystery, but she is a living mystery ; not an abstraction or a concept, but a being,
a soul.

> The being that is in the clouds and air,
> That is in the green leaves among the groves.

He never generalizes her, never allows her to be
attenuated into a mere idea; on the contrary, he
individualizes her in every one of her manifestations, the wood, the rock, the torrent.   And he
recognizes her sovereignty ; he interrogates her as
an oracle; he gathers up her inspirations like the
accents of a higher wisdom.   Science for him consists in endeavoring to decipher her enigmas,
virtue and happiness in placing oneself under her
influence and setting oneself at unison with her.   I
know no one but Rousseau and Lamartine to compare
with him in point of this submissive and passionate adoration.   Only, Rousseau introduces into it
something morbid, and Lamartine fully intends to

get some fine melodious verses out of it. Wordsworth, for his part, has a healthy soul, and never
listens to himself as he sings. It is true that as a
compensation Lamartine has more tragedy of sentiment, and a greater sublimity of expression. He
has an element of interior drama which is wanting
to Wordsworth. Lamartine is the greater when,
with finger raised to heaven, he bids us attend to
the voices from on high : —

> Adore ici le Dieu qu'adorait Pythagore,
> Prête avec lui l'oreille aux célestes concerts.

He is more pathetic when he retraces the vain
revolts of the Childe : —

> Triomphe, disait-il, immortelle nature !

VIII

The whole of Wordsworth's life was spent in the
worship of nature, and his works are nothing else
than the celebration of the mysteries of this religion. He must not, therefore, be confused with
the descriptive poets, even though his works
abound in descriptions, and though these descriptions are fine and often picturesque. He had an
observing eye ; he seizes the aspect of objects, the
distinctive character of things, and he marks them
off with precise and personal strokes. In especial
he has admirable sketches of his own country —
Westmoreland. All the same, we are, with him,
a hundred leagues away from the descriptive

school, whether of the older or the newer variety. Description in Wordsworth is not there for its own sake, intended to show the artist's craftsmanship, but is bound up with the impression which objects make upon him as a man, with the emotions that they arouse, the sentiments they inspire, the influence they exercise. For Wordsworth, once more, does not love nature as a painter occupied with line and color, but as a devotee. He approaches her with a pious intention; his love for her is a charm with which he saturates himself, a power to which he gives himself up, a life which he aspires to live.

Wordsworth is a hermit who listens to the heavenly voices. Instead of seeking an intellectual solution of the great problem of the Universe, he trusts to the intuitions opened by nature, or, better still, to the moral disposition she produces, the serenity she communicates, the harmony she sheds in the heart. The intensity of the sentiments she arouses is an all-sufficing revelation. Intimate emotion, secret ravishment, silent enthusiasm, have need neither of proofs nor of reasoning. We must also note that Wordsworth makes man fall back into nature as one of the elements of which she is composed. The peasant, the mountaineer, the poor and their ways of life, form part of the total effect of the scenes he draws and the feelings he evokes. They are, so to say, the figures of his landscape, and are only there to play their part in the general impression. Such is the mean-

ing of Wordsworth's narrative poetry. His rustic
idyls set before themselves not so much the interesting of the reader in a scene as the acquainting
him with the hidden aspects of universal existence,
with the manifestations of wisdom and goodness,
which make, in the poet's eyes, the true meaning
of the world. The unity of his work lies in the
tender interest which he takes in everything that
lives, from the shrub in the hedges to the blind
and the lame on the highways. As for towns, he
would fain ignore them. He holds them as a
jarring note which it is specially necessary to
merge and disperse in the general harmony of
creation.

Wordsworth adored nature from his youth up,
and he loves to recall the intoxication of his first
impressions, the joy which the rainbow made him
feel, the solemn beauty of the country in the
midst of which he and his companions disported
themselves, the contrast between the noisy games
and shouts of youth re-echoed by the rocks, and
the approaching silence of the night : —

> While the distant hills
> Into the tumult sent an alien sound, etc.

He described these emotions of childhood with still
more fondness in the admirable verses, composed
in 1798, on the banks of the Wye. All the poet is
in this piece, where depth of sentiment has found
perfect expression, and which is almost sufficient

when translated to give a knowledge of Wordsworth and of his genius.[1] Later, his love for
nature took a different, but not a stronger, form;
and he delights in connecting his present joys with
those of his infancy, in linking, as he says, his
days each to each by natural piety. If things had
once a freshness and a splendor which he feels no
more, the glory of a dream which vanished at the
waking, they have in compensation an attraction
which was not known to youth. The experience
of life opens the heart to a kind of affection for all
created things, even to "the meanest flower that
blows."[2] Thus nature acts by secret but beneficent sensations, by a physical calm which is
always ready to translate itself into universal
benevolence. Wordsworth owes to his rural reminiscences

> In hours of weariness sensations sweet
> Felt in the blood, and felt along the heart, etc.

That is fine, but I half think that I prefer the
hymn to the Spring which the poet addresses to
his sister, to bid her join him in a country excursion : —

> It is the first mild day of March, etc.

Such ideas are fundamental ones with Wordsworth. Nature is holy and she sanctifies. She

[1] [The famous passage telling how "the sounding cataract
Haunted me like a passion." — *Trans.*]

[2] [That from "The Old Cumberland Beggar" about the
"spirit and pulse of good." — *Trans.*]

attunes the soul to herself, and thus she heals, she consoles, she elevates. She breathes indulgence and tenderness. We have but to give ourselves up, "in a wise passiveness," to her influence, to approach her with a humble and receptive heart, to regard her "with a superstitious eye of love." There is in the first book of the "Excursion" a fine passage on the property, possessed by the beauties of creation, of humanizing man, by transporting him into a calmer and loftier region, whither comes neither dislike nor disdain, and where the only form of blame is compassion. But I will rather cite another as less didactic : —

> Nature never did betray
> The heart that loved her, etc.

Yet the religion of nature has still profounder secrets. If she is wisdom and goodness, nature is also understanding and revelation. She brings, besides soul-health, knowledge ; a higher knowledge, a gnosis which mere reasoning cannot reach. She helps us to penetrate the laws of the Universe's being. It was not often that Wordsworth permitted himself to hint at these utmost heights of his thought, at

> that blessed mood
> In which the burthen of the mystery, etc.

A little farther, after recalling the emotions of childhood in the verses I have quoted above, he says : —

> I have learned
> To look on nature not as in the hour, etc.[1]

Here we have what is highest in Wordsworth's thought, as well as sublimest in his poetry.

IX

I have still to speak of Wordsworth's poetical expression. Not that, to my thinking, the diction of a poet is separable from his thought; it would be more exact to say, on the other hand, that the one is the soul of the other, and constitutes its personality. Here, more than anywhere else, the boundary between matter and form is a mere abstraction. Let rhyme be the proof of this. English poetry admits blank or unrhymed verse; but the difference between the poetry which is rhymed and the poetry which is not is as far as possible from being a secondary one. I would almost affirm that it is a difference of kind, and I do not want any other example of this than Wordsworth's own.

Rhyme—and the same may be said of the stanza or the strophe—is the natural expression of lyrical inspiration. As often as there is in the poet's soul a livelier movement or a more profound emotion he has involuntary recourse to musical language, to assonance and to cadence. "There is so much analogy," says Madame de Staël, "between physi-

---

[1] [All these latter quotations are from *The Wye.*—*Trans.*]

cal and moral nature, that all the affections of the soul have an inflection of voice which is proper to them — a melody in words which is in accord with the meaning of the words themselves." Take away these melodic elements on the pretext that they are not essential to the thought, and you will see that the thought itself will have lost its characteristic quality. All Wordsworth's readers know his fine verses in honor of Lord Clifford, the shepherd to whom a royal decree in 1485 restored the titles and the rank of his ancestors: —

> His daily teachers had been woods and rills,
> The silence that is in the starry sky,
> The sleep that is among the lonely hills.

Why does the literal translation[1] which I give of these verses in no degree render their striking beauty? No doubt because a translation always alters the physiognomy of the original by making use of words which cannot possibly be the equivalents of those which they replace; but it is also because the translation at the same time tampers with the musical value and relation of the words, because it preserves neither rhythm nor rhyme,

---

[1] [In this case a literal retranslation of M. Scherer's "literal translation" seems suitable and indeed necessary. It runs thus: — "His only masters had been the woods and the streams, the silence which reigns in the starry skies, the sleep which reigns among the lonely hills." Of course, however, even this has not the full inequality to which M. Scherer refers, because some of the "musical values" reappear in the English.]

because the sonorous quality is no longer there. This is so true that Wordsworth himself could not have written the passage which I just cited in blank verse. The effect would have been completely different. A very curious thing is rhyme, and very complex is the pleasure which it procures us. Men do not like to acknowledge how great a part is played in the arts by the mere fact of a conquered difficulty. Yet it is the conquered difficulty which produces the impression of surprise, and it is surprise which produces interest. It is the unexpected which gives the feeling of the writer's power. The expectation of the reader of poetry is perpetually kept on the alert by the risks of the enterprise which he is contemplating. He asks himself (unconsciously, of course) at each verse how the author will manage to give a good account of the phrase within the conditions of the versification, to keep the natural line of the discourse and the beauty of the thought, while at the same time observing certain despotic rules; how he will keep up the supply of rhyme, full of beauty, richness, and sonority, without sacrificing reason in the slightest degree. If the poet wins this kind of wager, if his verse still flows freely, if his turn of words is happy and his imagery striking, if the assonance ends the verse as though of its own accord, without an effort, adding to the idea instead of subtracting aught from it, why then the reader's pleasure continually increases. His expectation,

each moment fulfilled and exceeded, becomes enthusiasm — an enthusiam, we must boldly acknowledge, which is not free from analogy with that
excited by a *tour de force*. The difference is, that
here an intellectual *tour de force* is in question, and
that the joy experienced is, when all is said, an
intellectual emotion. The poet is not merely an
acrobat. Still the paradox is none the less there;
and the sublimest art, the profoundest emotions,
rest on conditions which, when analyzed, seem a
little puerile.

All this leads me to draw a distinction between
the rhymed and the unrhymed poems of Wordsworth, a distinction, moreover, coinciding with that
which I have already set up between his narrative
and his lyrical pieces, and especially between his
long poems, such as the "Excursion" and the
"Prelude," and the little pieces which are in all
men's memory. Unquestionably, the first are not
as popular as the second, and this has to do not
merely with their length. They are a little heavy,
a little monotonous, and, despite their incontestable beauties, it is hard to read them without ennui.
Something of this same ennui has finally clung to
the name of Wordsworth, and has injured his
glory. The fact is that our poet, when he writes
without the help or the restraints of rhyme, is subject to a drawback which is connected with his system, and, one might almost say, with his genius.
Blank verse, which is, when rightly considered,

only cadenced prose — which lacks what I should call the dramatic interest of the poet's struggle with rhyme — needs to be relieved by the greatest intensity of thought and expression. The creative power of the author must reinforce the poverty of the instrument he uses. This is the case, for instance, with Milton, whose imagination triumphs so victoriously both over the ungrateful character of his subject and over the monotony inherent in the versification he has chosen. As for Wordsworth, he cuts himself off from this resource. He possesses, at a pinch, as we have seen, sublimity of sentiment and of language; but it is only as an exception, and by a kind of infraction of his principles. For he has a theory, and, what is more, is the head of a school. He undertook the mission of rehabilitating simplicity, as well in tone as in feeling. He renounced the artificial diction of the classics, their antitheses, their abundance of epithet; attempting to make up for the nakedness of his form by the charm of an absolutely sincere emotion, and by the originality of an absolutely natural language. Unluckily, his success is not invariable. His stories of country incidents and his description of rustic scenes did not always admit the beauties or the ornaments which might have relieved their monotony, and the consequence is that Wordsworth's poetry, with the tendency which it already had to the prosaic, sometimes falls bodily into it, and that chiefly in the unrhymed poems.

Having made this distinction between the work of our author in his prosaic and in his poetical style, we can come to his poetic diction in the narrow sense of the word. It is well known that in this respect there are two schools among contemporary poets. The one class has sincere and genuine feeling, which expresses itself in a fashion appropriate, and consequently original. Poetry, with them, goes from within to without, from thought to expression. With others, on the contrary, the first business is not profundity of sentiment or truth of idea, but rather the picturesque effect possible to extract from the subject. This is so true that the latter class does not even recoil from the vulgar or the ignoble, provided that they find in either material for descriptive novelty. Poetry in their work goes from without to within; it is the expression which has to give value to the thought. I need hardly say that the first of these two manners is Wordsworth's. His feeling is always genuine, and his expression always subordinated to his idea. He never sacrifices anything to the desire of showing his skill. His affectations — for, as we have seen, he has such — are in the other direction; they come from the desire of remaining simple and humble, not from the wish to appear a clever craftsman.

I have just distinguished between legitimate art, which only speaks because it has something to say, and art become ostentatious, which says nothing except to show how well it can speak.   There is a final distinction to draw, this time between desires which are equally legitimate, between ancient or classic art, which attaches itself to the beauty and nobility of things, and so even indulges in abstraction of individual traits, and modern art, which, on the other hand, delights in throwing up the particular physiognomy, the characteristic feature, of the model furnished to it by nature.   There is this remarkable thing about Wordsworth, that he unites the two methods.   His poetry is distinguished, and that to a rare degree, by the interpenetration of the two elements which are mingled in different proportions in the temperament of all true artists, the perception of the personal and real life of things, and the sense of the general signification which idealizes them.

Such contradictions are proper to rich natures. Wordsworth, the prolific and discursive poet who expands himself in slow and boundless strides, is the same poet who condenses his thought in admirable sonnets.   We shall find the dreamer, who seems to have no eye but for natural objects, able to define the genius of a Burns or a Milton in a few words of rare felicity.   The first verse of his magnificent sonnet addressed to the author of "Paradise Lost" —

Thy soul was like a star and dwelt apart —

has always seemed to me admirable at once for

exactness and for majesty. There is something
very special in the delicacy of the characterization
joined to the sublimity of the image.

Wordsworth is inexhaustible in passages which
depict now the scenes of nature, now the emotions
to which those scenes give rise. And the proof of
the fidelity with which he translates his feeling,
the proof that his fashion of speech has something
indefinably definite which forces itself on the reader,
is that many of his verses have passed into current
and, so to speak, proverbial quotation. He is an
attentive observer, his emotion is sincere, and,
finally, he has the faculty of expression, the divine
part of the art of writing. And so there comes
about in him the perfect fusion of the landscape, of
the feeling inspired by this landscape, and of the
trait by which the whole is expressed : —

> At length towards the cottage I returned
> Fondly, and traced with interest more mild
> That secret spirit of humanity
> Which, 'mid the calm oblivious tendencies
> Of nature, 'mid her plants, and weeds, and flowers,
> And silent overgrowings still survived.
>
> *The Excursion.*

Never has there been expressed as a whole, with
such puissant simplicity, and with plasticity so
sovereign, the whole gamut of sentiments which
nature awakes, from the thoughts

> whose very sweetness yieldeth proof
> That they were born for immortality,

to the inner ravishment, the secret enthusiasm, experienced by man

> when wedded to this goodly universe
> In love and holy passion.

I hope I have given some idea of Wordsworth's merits. Taking him where he is pure and without blemish — that is to say, somewhere half-way between his deliberate simplicity, between his propensities of a somewhat didactic kind, and between the lyrism, also too conscious and slightly declamatory, of the great odes — you find something of altogether superior quality. Wordsworth is a very great poet, and at the same time one of those who lend themselves best to everyday intercourse — a puissant and beneficent writer who elevates us and makes us happy. We must not be astonished if his renown has passed through vicissitudes of admiration and disdain, for his work is certainly unequal. But we must also not be astonished if, after these vicissitudes, he is in the way of taking rank among the classics of his country; for his beauties are of those which time consecrates instead of aging them. I should not be surprised if the selection of his poems published by Mr. Matthew Arnold, and the attention thus recalled to him, serve to fix his place definitely in the heaven of British glories. If Shakespeare, as I hold, remains absolutely and forever peerless, Wordsworth seems to me to come after Milton; decidedly, I think, below him, but still first after him. He is of the stuff whereof the immortals are made.

X

THOMAS CARLYLE.

CARLYLE has written a great deal, and in very different styles. There are some among his works which belong to pure literature : and these are the earliest in date, the "Life of Schiller," and the critical articles which the author contributed to reviews and collected later. Then come the great historical compositions on the "French Revolution," on "Cromwell," and on "Frederick the Great." The fixed ideas which are customary with the writer, and which appear in all these works, found political and social application in the volume on "Chartism," in "Past and Present," and in the "Latter-day Pamphlets." As for the directer expression of Carlyle's philosophy, we must go to "Heroes and Hero-worship" for that, adding, if we please, "Sartor Resartus," which is a philosophical sally, as well as a literary fantasy, and the "Life of John Sterling," in which the author has put much of himself.

Thus Carlyle touches on very different subjects, and yet in hardly any writer is there more unity. In every work I have mentioned there is the same special manner of feeling and of expression. I am

very far from denying that this originality is
sought for, is deliberate both in matter and form.
On the contrary, I shall have to insist on the feature of *parti pris*, which we cannot fail to recognize
in Carlyle without deceiving ourselves. But the
fact remains, all the same, that the writer is a
thinker, and that his teaching has founded a school.
As for bringing his ideas under any precise formula,
we must not think of it. The very property of
Carlyle's ideas is to set at defiance definitions, distinctions, all the logical and critical apparatus in
use with common folk, in order to take refuge in
the regions of imagination and sentiment. Carlyle
is a mystic. The world appears to him as clothed
in obscurity and bristling with problems. He can
see nothing but abysses. Nature, history, man,
everything gives him matter for wonder. His customary mental attitude is veneration: and to adore
is necessary to him. This taste for the mysterious
and the sublime lends itself necessarily to exaggeration. Humanity is engaged in a titanic struggle
between good and evil. The littlenesses of real life
become a spectacle at once grotesque and hateful.
Modern society is abandoned in the lump to plati-
tude and lying. The nations seek their welfare in
constitutions, in balancings of power, in parliamentary talk, in the devices of so-called liberalism and
so-called progress, while there is nothing real and
true in the way of government but the supremacy
of the strong man. The hero and the hero's right

— that is the sum of Carlyle's thought of human things.   He must have Mahomets, Cromwells, Fredericks, Napoleons, the men who force their way because they are the genuine and direct products of nature.   It will be seen here what is the link between Carlyle's theory of heroism and his general views of the world.   The man destined by providence, with the superior gifts which mark him out for sovereignty, is a natural reality set against social fictions, and at the same time one of the mysterious forces of the universe into the contemplation of which our author loves to plunge.

If it is natural to refer Carlyle's work to the thought by which it is inspired, it would be unjust to the author to insinuate that the whole merit of his books lies in the mystical preaching which we have just described.   There is in him, speaking of him as a man of letters, an historian, and there is also a satirist.   The historian is remarkable for conscientious research, and for the lively manner in which he seizes and renders the physiognomy of events.   His power is beyond dispute.   Through all his oddities there appears the gift of evoking the past, of making it live, of making out of it a drama which cannot be seen without emotion.   The truth is that Carlyle, in spite of his would-be philosophy, possesses a talent which is essentially dramatic and picturesque.   In the midst of all his moralizing sallies, of his habit of denouncing, adjuring, and objurgating, we see that his object in his histories was but to tell his story, and to tell it so as to please. He is an artist, and has done artist's work. His airs of grandeur and solemnity are but part of his style as a painter. They are but a refinement —I had almost said a set-off or seasoning.

In two or three of his works Carlyle is a historian; he is a satirist in all. His idealist prepossessions, as I showed just now, peep through everywhere, in the shape of perpetual and bitter denunciation flung on the men and the things of our time. He is inexhaustible in denouncing the lack of manliness and sincerity, the meanness and the slavishness, of the world which surrounds him. There is a word which is always recurring from his pen, as summing up the character of the age — the word "sham," an untranslatable expression, but one which designates at once false appearances, vain pretensions, lying conventions, and social hypocrisies. Carlyle has taken up a mission; he is a prophet, the prophet of sincerity. This sincerity or earnestness he would have applied everywhere; he makes it the law, the healthy and holy law, of art, of morals, of politics. The exaltation of force into something divine, whereof we spoke above, is nothing but a result of the need which the writer feels of going back in every case to the first and natural conditions. What is there, as a fact, more real than power? What more certain than that action which makes itself felt whether we will or no — than the personal authority, it may be of the man of genius, it may be of the sword?

Carlyle, however, never understood or tried to understand his time. He is like women and children who know no other form of expressing judgment except "I like it" or "I hate it." He is hurt in his sympathies (which are secret, and what is more very narrow), and he avenges himself by wrath or ridicule. Carlyle, who has been put forward as a sage, is the very reverse of one. "What is the good," as a witty woman once said, "of losing your temper with things in general, when you know that it produces not the slightest effect on them?" But Carlyle does not feel the inevitableness of the general transformation which we are witnessing, of that raising of the social level which indeed implies the lowering of the heights, which sends mediocrity to the surface, which hands over the world and the government of the world to everybody — that is to say, to somebody ignorant enough and vulgar enough — but which after all has the one pretty sufficient justification that it is fated. Let us grant that great art is no longer possible; that literature is condemned to decadence; that the time for fine things, things distinguished, exquisite things, is past beyond recall; that the guidance of society henceforward belongs to heads so coarse and to minds so uncultivated that our traditional sentiments feel a sort of consternation. Let us admit that we are on the way to an equality at once quite rational and hopelessly uninteresting. No doubt this is disagreeable

enough to the man whose roots, in virtue of his
early education, dive down to a different civilization. But is it not a little childish to celebrate the
obsequies of the past so noisily ? The wheel of
history has crushed many a past before.

One of the numerous minor services which the
Hegelian philosophy has done is to have suppressed
the distinction between matter and form. Every
matter has its special form, and every form sup-
poses its appropriate matter. But the two things
have never been in more obvious relation than in
the case of Carlyle's thought and his style. I am
unable when I read him to get rid of the idea that
he has a settled attitude — to put it more bluntly,
an affectation. There is something histrionic in
his incessant declamation against the cant of the
age. His vast mystical views on the unknown
that wraps us round, and the universe which lies
beyond our sight, on the reverential spirit in which
we must contemplate the problems of existence,
have to me (I hope his devotees will pardon me!)
an air of posing. If it is not the result of reflection and calculation, it at least looks like it. Now
it is exactly the same with the style in which these
thoughts are rendered. It is a dialect which the
writer has fashioned on purpose, and not without
knowing what he was about. For he owed a great
part of his success to it. Carlyle's vocabulary is
made up of long compounds in the German style,
of unusual forms, of comparatives and superlatives

of his own invention.   He rejoices in odd phrases,
in recurring epithets, in nicknames, in catchwords.
His phraseology is broken and hammered out; it
has been said to resemble *repoussé* metal-work.
He makes it, of set purpose, unmusical, unbalanced,
with sharp turns, with weak endings or mere lapses.
Add to this exclamations, interrogations, apostrophes to the characters, to the reader, to heaven and
earth, to things in general.   It is impossible to con-
vey an idea of the way in which our author abuses
the words God, Infinite, Eternity, Profundity.   It
is true that he freshens them up by putting them
in the plural, and saying "the Immensities," "the
Silences," "the Eternal Veracities."

Needless to say that this jumbled part of prophet
and buffoon, with its laborious eccentricities, produces the effect less of conviction and of something
natural than of a craving for attracting attention;
not to mention that this view has historical justification.   Carlyle did not originally write in the
manner of which I have just spoken.   His "Life
of Schiller" is ordinary English.   If his first
articles of literary criticism in 1827 and the years
following, perhaps, let us guess what is coming,
they are still not sharply parted off from common
speech.   "Sartor Resartus," which is nearly of the
same date, already affects oddity, but it may be
said that there it was dictated by the subject.   At
any rate, from that time forward the author takes
increasing delight in a manner which has the

double advantage of being easier than simplicity
and of tempting the curiosity of the public. As
we follow him, we can see him giving himself up
more and more to the style which he has created.
His "French Revolution," published in 1837, is
entirely cast in this mould. Unluckily it is the
nature of mannerism to fix and stereotype itself
always more and more, and it is not too much to say
that Carlyle's diction ended by becoming gibberish.

A less direct, but very curious, proof of the part
which we must acknowledge that purpose played in
forming Carlyle's manner is an article which he
contributed in 1827 to the "Edinburgh Review"
on Jean Paul Friedrich Richter. The article begins by a long and remarkable characterization of
the writer's genius; but the odd thing is that
one would swear Carlyle himself had sat for the
portrait. I regret that space does not allow me to
translate these pages. There is not a line which
would not apply to the English author — nay, there
is not a line in which he has not the air of having
tried to paint himself, or at least has not betrayed
the figure which he was ambitious of making in
the world of letters. The influence of Carlyle's
mannerism has been considerable. He has given
birth to a whole generation of writers, disdainful
of that manliness of style which consists in saying
things worth saying in the best way possible, and
set above all on the refinements of the virtuoso or
even the tricks of the charlatan. Some great tal-

ents in England have been ruined in this deplorable school. Mr. Ruskin ended like Carlyle himself by passing from the *recherché* to the *bizarre*, and from affectation to mere mystifying. Yet there are still some who feel themselves strong enough to be sincere and simple, and they are worth all the more for it. Mr. Matthew Arnold has, I should think, as many ideas in his head as Carlyle, and as much poetry in his soul as Mr. Ruskin, and yet he does not think himself obliged to speak like a mystagogue.

The philosophical influence of Carlyle has not been less than his literary influence, and it has been wholesomer. His name will remain in the history of English thought. He gave check to the supremacy of the commonplace. Just as, for all the faults of his style, he is an artist at bottom ; so, despite the too great pretentiousness of his formulæ, there is in him, if not a philosopher, at least a "midwife of minds." [1] He introduced thought to more than one of those truths which are lost under logical apparatus or hidden by social conventions. His declamations against jargon, pretension, and charlatanism may be tainted themselves with charlatanism and jargon. But all the same they helped to put sincerity back in the place of honor.

---

[1] [Socrates's well-known description of himself. It looks awkward in English, and despite the wrath of precisians, I think the adjective *maieutic* justifiable and even necessary. But, as M. Scherer renders it literally, so do I.— *Trans.*]

To sum up, if I had to characterize the moral and intellectual influence exercised by Carlyle, I should say that he seems to me to have, above all things, helped to loosen the fetters of positive creed in which thought was imprisoned among his countrymen. Carlyle was a mystic, and mysticism here, as elsewhere, discharged the function which belongs to it in the chain of systems : to wit, that of dissolving dogma under pretence of spiritualizing it, of shattering faith under pretence of enlarging it. When men heard Carlyle speak so much of divinity and eternity, of mystery and adoration, they hailed him as the preacher of a religion higher and wider than current belief. In vain did orthodoxy, more keen-sighted, point out the negations which lay hid under the writer's formulas. It is so pleasant to free oneself without appearing to break too sharply with consecrated words and institutions ! Since then speculation has made much way in England. The universal mysteries of our author have been exchanged for exact research, precise definitions, rigorous ascertainments. I do not know whether Carlyle was aware of it, but he lived long enough to see his influence exhausted, his teaching out of date. It is true that, as consolation, he could take himself to witness that he had served as the transition between the past and the present, and that this is in the long run the best glory to which a thinker can pretend here below.

February 1881.

XI

"ENDYMION"

"'ENDYMION,' by the author of 'Lothair.'"
Why of "Lothair"? I can understand why Lord
Beaconsfield did not choose to sign his novel either
by the name of Disraeli, which he does not now
bear, or by the newer name which he has not yet
made illustrious in letters. But I ask myself what
made him prefer "Lothair" among the memories of
his literary career. It would have been more natural to put his latest work under the patronage of
"Vivian Grey," his earliest, or that of "Coningsby,"
the prototype of the political novels wherein the
author has made a style of his own. Unless, indeed,
Lord Beaconsfield desired to point out a nearer re-
lationship, a special resemblance of kind, between
"Lothair" and "Endymion" — a resemblance
which is, I grant, striking, but which is not exactly
a recommendation for the newcomer.

Indeed, everything in the title-page of this novel
is a riddle. The name given to the chief personage
makes it impossible to help looking for a symbolic
sense in it, and yet nobody has yet been able to
discover an analogy between the career of Mr.
Endymion Ferrers and the love passages in the

cave of Latmos. The choice of the particular name is, then, a whim on the author's part, and a whim which looks like a trap for the reader. Nor is the motto of the book more appropriate. "Quidquid agunt homines" seems to promise a great composition in which all ranks were to mingle, all careers to cross, all the greatness and all the meanness, all the public efforts, the private intrigues, the diverse passions of which the human tragi-comedy is composed, to blend. The whole work of Balzac or of Dickens would not be too much to justify the quotation with which Lord Beaconsfield has adorned his novel's forefront. And yet even these great connoisseurs in reality have left many a gap in their galleries of society. As for "Endymion," it is simply a picture of political life in England — indeed only one corner of such a picture. Now, however great a place politics may hold in the life of nations, they are yet but one scene in the social drama, but a single episode in the medley of ambition and interests.

Since I am in the way of noting the weak sides of Lord Beaconsfield's book, I will at once point out another fault. A novel, when well done, is a biography. You are present at the development of a principal character which the revolutions of the story served to set in relief, which by turns dominates and submits to the course of things, and round which the other personages group themselves in order to contribute their contingent to that destiny the history of which is presented to interest us. Art, in this kind of writing, consists in putting as much diversity as is compatible with biographical unity in the devising of the facts and the tracing of the characters. The more varied and interesting the details are in themselves — thus showing the author's inventive resources and his exactness of observation — the more noteworthy the work will be ; but on one condition only, that these details shall be subordinate to the main end, which is, I repeat, the dramatic setting forth of a masterful personality. Now, the author of "Endymion" has neglected these conditions of his art. His hero is a rather insipid bundle of talents and virtues, the commonplace spoilt-child of a marvellous fortune. We are told what happens to him, but he is not made to live before us, nor is he shown to us acting upon others, counting for something in the direction of events. He has no power, he has not even a special physiognomy of his own. Endymion is nothing in the story but a thread somehow or other connecting together incidents which are themselves without any great romantic consequence, and personages whose traits are not more marked than his own.

"Endymion" belongs to the class of historical novels, and to a sub-variety of this class, that of the historico-political novel. It is clear that the attraction of this kind of fiction becomes lively enough when the work is written by a man who has

himself played a great part, and when the events
he tells of and the personages he introduces are
contemporary. Such is the case in "Endymion,"
the action of which passes between the death of
Canning and the Crimean war; and in the pages of
which we meet Sir Robert Peel, Lord Palmerston,
and Napoleon the Third. On the other hand, the
class has a drawback — the personages are too near
us for it to be permissible to keep their names, or
even to put them on the stage, in a strictly historical manner. It is clearly impossible to make dead
men like Lord Melbourne and Mr. Cobden, still
more living men like Prince Bismarck and Cardinal
Manning, act and talk with the freedom which
Walter Scott used in regard to Louis XI., to Mary
Stuart, and to Charles II. The novelist is obliged
to weaken their personality, to modify their character, to disfigure their physiognomy — in a word,
to falsify the history which frames the novel.
Lord Beaconsfield has got himself out of his difficulty by mingling traits, confusing characters,
creating personages who are at once real and ficti-
tious, historical and imaginary, who escape the
reader at the moment when he thinks he recognizes
them, and only excite his curiosity to baffle it
immediately afterwards. The pretender who afterwards became Emperor of the French is here a
handsome man, of a good figure, and witty. He
marries the widow of an English peer, and recov-
ers his dominions by a triumphant expedition. It

is difficult to imagine how irritating this trick becomes in the long run.

A man's talent — an orator's, for instance — is not always in the exact ratio of his personal value; and in the same way the interest excited by a book may be out of proportion to its intrinsic merit. Lord Beaconsfield's new novel is an instance of this. As a novel it is hardly distinguished from the run of those which the English press turns out every year. It permits itself to be, rather than insists on being, read. It amuses the reader without enthralling him. And yet it has been in everybody's hand, and for the moment has been the theme of everybody's talk. People were anxious to see the present state of the talent and the opinions of a man who has for so long a time both held the political stage and plied the pen of the novelist. They were curious once more to meet this puzzling personage on whose score public opinion has not yet made itself up. I venture to think that it is Lord Beaconsfield's personality which gives the interest to his books, and even to his policy. One cannot help, in the absorption of so remarkable a physiognomy, putting aside the question what both are really worth. With Lord Beaconsfield everything is in keeping; the novelist is part of the man, and the Prime Minister of the novelist. I can never read his books or see him at work on the world's stage without recalling the Mr. Disraeli of fifty years ago, as a contemporary

depicts him, dressed in velvet and satin, his wrists
encircled by ruffles, his hair cunningly curled, his
fingers loaded with rings, an ivory cane in his hand:
with all the exterior of a dandy — a dandy of
genius; a bundle of contradictions, ambition allied
to scepticism, determination hiding itself under
sallies and paradoxes. So much for his person:
his life has followed suit. A foreigner, a Jew, he
raised himself from an attorney's office to the peer-
age of England, and the headship of his country's
government. The character of his policy — full
of theatrical strokes, of new departures, whimsical
or bold as the case may be — is well known. In
everything that he has done, you feel the Oriental's taste for the brilliant, the adventurer's taste
for the turns of Fortune's wheel, the parvenu's
taste for pomp. But it is in his writings more
than anywhere else that he shows himself as he
is: because Lord Beaconsfield is at bottom an
artist first of all. His old dandyism was already
literary; and his modern policy is still romantic.
"Endymion" is in this respect really characteristic. The chief personages are all parvenus or
adventurers — the hero (to begin with him), as
well as his sister, Ferroll as well as Florestan,
Nigel Penruddock the future cardinal as well as
Imogene the future duchess, Job Thornberry the
manufacturer as well as Vigo the tailor. And
what is most remarkable of all is that these adventurous lives seem to have, at the bottom of them,

the love not so much of power as of the pomp that surrounds it. In "Endymion," as in "Lothair," the author takes pleasure in nothing so much as in the splendor of the life of Society: he rubs shoulders with none but ministers and ambassadors, dukes and duchesses; he dreams only of princely establishments, enchanted castles, magnificent horses, gold plate, sparkling crystal, porcelain beyond price. At every line one sees the Jew and the rings on his fingers. The talent of Lord Beaconsfield is, if I may use the expression, all on the street frontage. Do not ask him for heartfelt descriptions of nature, for profound analysis of motives, even for dramatic play of passion. Do not look in his books for any sincerity, any experience, any startling view, any philosophy of any kind. Be content with finding a certain vivacious wit, a kind of brio and "go," thanks to which the reader gets to the end of the three volumes without too much trouble. If the metal has not the resonance that one might wish for, we are obliged to confess that the tinsel is prettily worked, and does not fail to produce a certain effect of dazzling.

Lord Beaconsfield has velleities of creation, rather than the faculty of it. We see that at the outset of his novel he meant to sketch the epoch at which the story begins, the England of the first half of this century, in the infancy of railways, when Grosvenor Square was not even lighted by gas, and when the development of manufactures had not yet raised up, in the persons of the new rich men, a political influence rivalling that of the aristocracy. But it is all told rather than shown. What a difference, for instance, is there between this kind of statistical information and the description of England at exactly the same time by which George Eliot's "Felix Holt" opens. She, by patient study and by force of imagination, has evoked the past in a far more lively manner than the author of "Endymion," though he had the advantage of personal acquaintance with the times concerned.

Lord Beaconsfield is hardly more happy in the drawing of character. His personages lack originality, they are wanting in the real; they leave on us the kind of impression which we receive in passing through a drawing-room. We elbow men in full dress, we notice women richly costumed, we catch as we pass a few words on the events of the day; but we leave without having learnt anything of the world through which we have brushed. The men and women are strangers yet for us. We have been the audience at a play, and that is all. A more remarkable thing still is that Lord Beaconsfield's characters are not even very witty.[1] I must except some sallies of Waldershare's, some

[1] [It is odd that M. Scherer should have missed in the opening a phrase of political wit worthy of the most brilliant of his own countrymen. I remember that in reviewing it "the transient and embarrassed phantom of Lord Goderich" put me in good humor for the whole book. — *Trans.*]

amusing political paradoxes put in the mouth of a certain Bertie Tremaine. But the dialogue lacks the vivacity which we might have expected from a writer whose public speech is notable for its mordancy. And what happens when we get to sentimental scenes? There is a declaration in which the lover thus expresses himself: — "All seasons of the year would be a delight to me if I were only at your side. No; *I can no longer refrain from avowing my love. I am here only because I love you. I left Oxford and all its glories to have the happiness of your society now and then. My thoughts were not presumptuous — I thought this would suffice me. But I can no longer resist the prodigious charm, and I offer you my heart and my life." Elsewhere a lady, speaking of herself, says, "My pride, my intense pride, has never allowed me any slip of the heart."

The most interesting thing, as I have said, in the book is the author himself. It is always piquant to surprise the secrets of a man who has become part of history; and is not the publication of a book, especially of a novel, a fashion of surrendering oneself? The hero comes down from his pedestal, the orator from his tribune, and gives us the chance of catching him in the act, of taking his measure as best we can. Lord Beaconsfield could not write a political novel without betraying himself somewhere, without letting escape some of those words in which a career is summed up and

inner feelings are revealed. Endymion says somewhere, "Whether it is a question of temperament
or the result of the vicissitudes of my life, I have
a great power of waiting." He numbers among
the advantages of wealth to a politician that it
"gives him time to breathe and to expect." Elsewhere, again, we read that never a State perished
for lack of money, "nor a private man either, if he
had pluck." Do we not seem to hear Mr. Disraeli
speaking of his youth? But he will grow up, he
will become a statesman, and we shall recognize
him by other strokes. It is will that has made
him what he is, and so he believes in will above
everything. "Any man in the world can succeed
in doing what he has a mind to, if only he makes
up his mind to it." On the other hand, we find a
profound distrust of sentiment. "Sentiment without an object is sickness or drunkenness." He
has enemies, but what then? "I can't help it,
everybody is hated by somebody." Besides, he
loves fighting, and he sometimes thinks that, if he
has found so much pleasure in ministerial life, "it
is that it has been a constant fight for life." Certain reflections, even if they do not admit such
personal explanation, nevertheless exhibit the experience acquired in the practice of public affairs.
Such is the remark that judgment of character is
the capital element in the management of men and
things. Nor is exact information less important.
"As a general rule the man who succeeds best in

life is he who has the best information." "You will see that there is nothing more important in public life," says the Count of Ferroll, "than to know personally all those who direct the affairs of this world. Everything depends on the character of the individual, his ways of thought, his prejudices, his superstitions, his little foibles, his health. Politics without this advantage is a mere matter of stationery; pens and paper are in communication, not human beings."

If there is not exactly great novelty or depth in these sallies, they are certainly not without neatness. Sometimes, too, the point is whetted sharper: — "All men of intelligence are of the same religion," says Waldershare. "And what is that religion?" asked the Prince. "Men of intelligence never tell." [1]

Mr. Gladstone would not have permitted himself a gibe of this kind; but what a difference there is in everything between these two rivals, what a contrast in their characters, in their political careers, in their writings! Mr. Gladstone's nature is essentially moral; the categories to which he refers all things are those of good and evil. And his extreme seriousness, though it excludes extravagance, does not exclude enthusiasm. Mr. Gladstone brings the fervor of faith

---

[1] [It is very curious that M. Scherer should not have known that this is a borrowed jest, familiar long before the days of *Endymion*, and usually fathered on Chesterfield. — *Trans.*]

into every cause that he espouses. He is also
essentially a believer; he has the noble sides of
the character — its sincerity, its straightforwardness, its ardor. He has also its defects; his
gravity lacks humor, his solidity becomes stiffness,
his intelligence — gifted as it is with the most
varied aptitudes, served by prodigious activity
and capacity for work, able to descend from the
general direction of an empire to the technical
details of a bill or the complicated schedules of a
budget — his intelligence has more breadth than
suppleness. His reasonings are abstract because
he occupies himself rather with principles than
with facts; his judgments absolute because he
takes every truth at the same valuation — that of
an article of religion. This explains his tendency,
daily more pronounced, towards Radical ideas,
Radicalism being nothing but the application of
the absolute to politics. Unluckily politics are
the most relative things in the world, so that Radicalism is good for nothing but to bring about revolutions, and in ordinary times runs a perpetual
risk of letting institutions get ahead of moral and
social conditions. In his books Mr. Gladstone
shows himself the same man as in public affairs.
His solidity and sincerity are here translated into
conscientiousness of study and exactitude of erudition; but the lack of suppleness and of delicacy
betrays itself at the same time by his weakness in
criticism. Mr. Gladstone, in his craving for ready-

made theses, carries his submission of spirit into
the study of Homer as into the study of the Bible.
He has no more doubts about Homer and the siege
of Troy than about Moses and the passage of the
Red Sea. He even delights in combining the two
things in a single belief, in making Homeric mythology an echo of Christian revelation. Mr. Gladstone, rightly taken, is a survival of scholasticism.
He still belongs to those ages of human thought
when intellectual strength applied itself to data
furnished by tradition, when men discussed tenets
ad infinitum without dreaming of examining their
value, when the most keenly whetted subtlety kept
on good terms with a superstitious respect for
authority.

Take in every respect the exact opposite to Mr.
Gladstone's character, and you will have the character of Lord Beaconsfield. The latter's bottom is
scepticisn. He believes in success and that nothing succeeds like it, and he is consequently
inclined not to pry too narrowly into the ethics of
the means of succeeding. His worth is less than
his rival's, but his *savoir faire* is greater. He is
less austere but more genial; he has less substance, but more man-of-the-worldliness. Very inferior to Mr. Gladstone in studying the details of
a matter, he is not so in courage when a resolution
has to be taken, especially when there is something
adventurous about this resolution. I should not
venture to call Lord Beaconsfield the cleverer of

the two in the knowledge and the handling of men; for if Mr. Gladstone makes the mistake of believing them all as sincere and as impassioned as he is himself, Lord Beaconsfield deceives himself equally in supposing them to be his equals in freedom from prejudice. Sceptic as he is, and as I have called him, he is too prone to consult men's foibles rather than their virtues. In the same way, instead of going to the bottom of things, he contents himself with appearances and with the surface. Why, indeed, resolve problems, search questions out, if you can reach the end with a trumpet-blast or two and a *coup de théâtre?* The doubter becomes a manager willingly enough, and the manager easily has a dash of the charlatan. We saw in the history of the Berlin Congress, and in all the foreign policy of the late Cabinet, that Lord Beaconsfield thinks he has done enough if he has appealed to the imagination. I may add that he is just the same in his books: he shows in them as a writer brilliant, amusing, but superficial; he rouses the curiosity of the public for a fortnight, but he has not started a single profound sentiment or a single new idea. His last novel leaves the impression of talent which would be promising in a young man, but which in a veteran of literature denotes, on the contrary, the saddening close of a career that has been, on the whole, a failure.

Such are the two men who in turn attract the attention of the literary public by their writings

and that of Europe by their policy. To complete
their portraits I ought to be able to add a more
precise characterization of the eloquence of the
two orators than it would beseem a foreigner to
attempt. I have no doubt that there, too, one
would again discover traces of the fundamental
qualities I have pointed out: in Mr. Gladstone a
mixture of subtle dialectic and passionate conviction; in Lord Beaconsfield the sarcasm which
floors an adversary, and so saves the trouble of
refuting him, the smart saying which sounds like
an idea, the cleverness of a party chief more
busied about success than about truth. I ought,
too, to complete the parallel, to consider the two
antagonists as statesmen in their actual adminis-
tration of their country. But it is the event which
decides here — one cannot speak in full assurance
till facts have definitely pronounced. All that I
may say is that Lord Beaconsfield is to Lord Chat-
ham pretty much what Mr. Gladstone is to Pitt,
and the ancient European rôle of England to the
dwarfed and uncertain policy which now satisfies
that country's ambition.[1]

December 1880.

[1] [This is an odd antithesis, and I find it rather difficult to
work out its parts; but it is as M. Scherer wrote it. — *Trans.*]

XII

GEORGE ELIOT

THE name of George Eliot might serve as a measure of the distance which separates France from England. The fact that there is an English author whose life has been published in three volumes, and that this voluminous biography has been greedily read by all Englishmen, discussed and commented by all their newspapers, distracting their attention from painful political preoccupations; and the other fact that the very name of this writer, whom our neighbors regard with so much admiration, is hardly known among ourselves, and arouses neither memory nor interest — are not these things great matter for wonder?

And this wonder might even turn to vexation and incredulity if we were to add that this George Eliot, so utterly ignored in France, was one of the finest geniuses of our time, and that for the woman who adopted this pseudonym was reserved the honor of writing the most perfect novels as yet known.

Thus the life of George Eliot which Mr. Cross has just published, was a real event to our neighbors. But did it satisfy the expectation which it had aroused? Does it merit the interest with which it was received? I hardly know what to answer. If I myself set about the reading with a curiosity too greedy to find anything tedious in it, it has certainly, on the whole, left on me the impression that in these three volumes we must look rather for the materials of a book still to be written than for the book itself. The reasons lie in the plan followed by Mr. Cross — a new plan, but no doubt the only one which is seemly in the case of a husband who is sketching the life of his wife. Except a very few explanatory passages, the work is entirely composed of letters, written by George Eliot to her friends, and of fragments of a private journal in which she kept a record of incidents and of thoughts. From these manuscripts the editor has extracted the passages which seemed to him of such a nature as to be fitly set before the public eye. And as a fact these passages constitute a continuous history — the history of a very fine talent and a very beautiful soul.

We must then understand that this is neither a biography in the ordinary sense of the word — that is to say, the complete relation of an existence; nor a correspondence such as we possess many, and some of them precious — that is to say, letters printed as they were written and revealing the strong and weak sides of a character alike. Mr. Cross confines himself to letting the letters speak, and he takes good care not to give these

letters themselves as wholes. Indeed, he warns us
that he takes from them nothing that does not suit
his plan, and we may be sure beforehand that he
has not let slip any of those involuntary revela-
tions, of those blessed indiscretions, which rejoice
the reader and edify the psychologist. Yet from
this we must certainly not conclude that Mr.
Cross, despite his own reticences and those which
he has imposed on George Eliot, has published
anything but a book of the highest value. How
could it be otherwise when George Eliot holds the
pen and speaks to us of herself?

Mary Ann Evans was born in 1819. Her father,
a carpenter by trade, but of education superior to
his class, had made his way little by little and had
become the agent of a man of large property in
Warwickshire. He lived in the country, with an
establishment at once easy and rustic, in a part of
England which is not excessively picturesque.
Mary Ann had a brother three years older than
herself, with whom she played, and for whom she
felt the affection and the deference which she
afterwards described in some charming sonnets.
We cannot help recognizing in this passionate sub-
missiveness the need of affection and of support
which always distinguished George Eliot, and
which explains more than one incident of her life.
From the day when Isaac had a horse, his sister
could no longer follow him across country; besides, the time had come to send her to school.

She carried thither delicate health, a timid disposition, a vivacious intelligence, a passion for reading, a taste for taking trouble, and the gift of
making herself beloved. She found in return certain religious influences to which she abandoned
herself with the eagerness of a nature at once affectionate and idealist. Mary Ann became a model
of piety, and later when she had left school a
model of good works — starting prayer-meetings,
working for the poor, visiting the sick. Her biographer has preserved for us a certain number of
letters of this period of faith and fervor, and he
has done well precisely because of their insignificance — I had all but said of their platitudinous-
ness. It is not more interesting to see the girl
occupied in the spiritual combats wherein the soul
forms itself, pushing her conscientiousness to the
point of scruple and her sense of duty to the point
of asceticism, than it is curious to hear her talking
that conventional language of Protestant piety
which a witty lady once called "the *patois* of
Canaan." There is not a touch of genius to be met
with in these pages of devout exhortations — not
even, I am bound to say, an accent of personal
emotion. Here and there, on the other hand, are
symptoms which, in the eyes of an enlightened
spiritual director, would probably have justified
fears as to the lasting of this fine devotional ardor.
Mary Ann reads too much and too many kinds
of things. She has already learnt French, Ger-

man, and Italian, and she reads in all these languages — prose and verse, books of science and
books of fiction. She is ambitious and pained at
the thought that she will never do anything of
moment. Her mother is dead, and she has succeeded her in the cares of housekeeping; she
acquits herself brilliantly therein, but her thoughts
are at work while she is cooking or sewing, and
many questions begin to present themselves to her
mind. Worst of all, she brings to the considera-
tion of these questions a perfect sincerity and a
craving for complete satisfaction; whence it happens that doubts often occur to her. Let us add
that her nature is a rich, a mobile, and a complex
one, and that by lending itself in turn to every
aspect of things it is preparing her for the vexa-
tious discovery that our knowledge is relative.
Let her meet on her way some outspoken passage,
and in such dispositions it is impossible to foresee
how far her straightforwardness will lead her.
What is certain, on the other hand, is that this
beautiful soul will never rise up in offensive rebellion against the beliefs of her youth; that while
not affecting, as some do, to regret the faith she
no longer possesses, and while feeling the happiness
of being henceforward at unity with herself, she
will preserve a certain tenderness for the memory of old struggles, of simple enthusiasm.
George Eliot is an example of the religious sentiment as well of a tender conscience surviving a

theological shipwreck as complete as it is possible to imagine.

"All creatures about to moult, or to cast off an old skin, or enter on any new metamorphosis, have sickly feelings. It was so with me. But now I am set free from the irritating worn-out integument. I am entering on a new period of my life, which makes me look back on the past as something incredibly poor and contemptible. I am enjoying repose, strength, and ardor in a greater degree than I have ever known, and yet I never felt my own insignificance and imperfection so completely." Here there is nothing but the joy of the deliverance; soon, I repeat, she will show herself more tender towards her past.

Mary Ann had been helped in "casting her skin" not only by the books which had fallen into her hands, but by the acquaintance she had made with some freethinkers of both sexes in the town of Coventry, near which her father had retired. These consisted of a Mr. Bray, a ribbon manufacturer and a phrenologist, of his brother-in-law, Charles Hennell, the author of "Enquiries into the Origin of Christianity," and of the wives and sisters of these gentlemen, who all united honorable sentiments to a boldness of view then pretty rare in England. Miss Evans spent eight years of happiness in the society of these friends. She found in it what she so ardently desired — study in common, discussions which clear up and whet thought, and the satisfaction of that feminine craving for intimate intercourse which characterized a nature in other respects so virile, and which she recognized by comparing herself to the ivy. To balance this there was friction at home. Her old father — Tory in politics and orthodox in religion — was horrified to see his favorite daughter going astray. He became seriously angry when, in a first fit of heretical fervor, she left off going to church. There was a temporary rupture which Mary Ann contrived to heal by force of affectionate assiduity, yet without surrendering her liberty. I cannot help asking myself what the excellent old man must have thought when he learnt that his daughter was translating Strauss's "Life of Jesus." This was her literary *début*. She took two years over it, and acquitted herself of the task to the satisfaction of the author; but, though in undertaking the work she had obeyed her conviction that no kind of test ought to be shirked, she was still far from accepting all the critic's judgments. "It is all very well," says she, "when I think Strauss right; but I think he is often wrong — which is indeed inevitable when a man insists on following up a general idea in detail and making a complete theory of what is only one element of truth." To the very end of the task the translator remained thus divided between the attraction of an author whom she found "so clear and so full of ideas" and her dislike of the pitiless dissection which attacked the most beautiful legends, the most sacred memories. One of her friends tells how, when she came to the history of the Crucifixion, the young woman could only console herself for the want of sympathy in the treatment by looking at an ivory crucifix which hung over her desk. The story is slightly doubtful, but may be regarded as symbolizing a life in which intellectual honesty of the strictest kind never shut out religious sensibility.

The following passages will show at once the depth of the impression which certain readings made on Mary Ann's mind and the freedom of spirit with which she judged the writers who had moved her most. One of them appears to confirm an anecdote which I read two or three years ago in a volume of reminiscences on Emerson. He, during his visit to England in 1848, had met Miss Evans at Coventry, and had been struck by her conversation. "She has," he said, "a calm and serious mind." When he one day asked her suddenly what was the book she liked best, Mary Ann replied, without hesitation, Rousseau's "Confessions." Emerson could not hide his surprise, for it was the same with him. In his case we can understand it, but a woman — almost a girl? Mr. Cross's volumes supply the explanation which I confess I had thought was wanted.

I wish you thoroughly to understand that the writers who have most profoundly influenced me — who have rolled away the waters from their bed, raised new mountains and spread delicious valleys for me — are not in the least oracles to me. It is just possible that I may not embrace one of their opinions, — that I may wish my life to be shaped quite differently from theirs. For instance, it would signify nothing to me if a very wise person were to stun me with proofs that Rousseau's views of life, religion, and government are miserably erroneous, — that he was guilty of some of the worst *bassesses* that have degraded civilized man. I might admit all this : and it would be not the less true that Rousseau's genius has sent that electric thrill through my intellectual and moral frame which has awakened me to new perceptions, — which has made man and nature a fresh world of thought and feeling to me ; and this not by teaching me any new belief. It is simply that the rushing mighty wind of his inspiration has so quickened my faculties, that I have been able to shape more definitely for myself ideas which had previously dwelt as dim *Ahnungen* in my soul ; the fire of his genius has so fused together old thoughts and prejudices, that I have been ready to make new combinations.

Miss Evans's judgment of the author of the "Lettres d'un Voyageur," of "Lélia," and of "Jacques" is not less remarkable. She had just read the last-named novel.

I should never dream of going to her writings as a moral code or text-book. I don't care whether I agree with her about marriage or not — whether I think the design of her plot correct, or that she had no precise design at all, but began to write as the spirit moved her, and trusted to Providence for the catastrophe, which I think the more probable case. It is sufficient for me, as a reason for bowing before her in eternal gratitude to that "great power of God manifested in her," that I cannot read six pages of hers without feeling that it is given to her to delineate human passion and its results and (I must say, in spite of your judgment) some of the moral instincts and their tendencies, with such truthfulness, such nicety of discrimination, such tragic power, and withal, such loving, gentle humor, that one might live a century with nothing but one's own dull faculties, and not know so much as those six pages will suggest.

The same letter in which we read the apology of "Jacques" and of the "Confessions" ends by an expression of the happiness Mary Ann feels in possessing the "Imitation." She has just bought it in Latin, with old and characteristic woodcuts. "One breathes," she says, "a cool air as of cloisters in the book; it makes one long to be a saint for a few months. Verily its piety has its foundations in the depths of the divine human soul."

We should not have a complete idea of the workings of Miss Evans's mind — a mind at once virile and feminine — about this age of twenty-eight, when she was translating "Strauss," reading "Lélia," and being charmed with the "Imitation," if we did not take account of her enthusiasm for the French Revolution of 1848. She is very amusing about it. We are "the great nation." Away with those who cannot recognize what is noble and splendid without making reserves and insinuating doubts! She would willingly have given a year of her life to see the men of the barricades uncovering before the image of the Christ who first taught the world fraternity. The actions of Lamartine are worthy of a poet. In Louis Blanc Miss Evans reveres the man who wrote that sublime phrase, "the inequality of talents should result, not in the inequality of rewards, but in the inequality of duties." And Albert "the workman." What a pity one cannot procure his portrait! As for Louis Philippe, it will be time to pity him when there are no longer famished and ignorant millions on the earth. As for England, there is no hope of *her* having her revolution in her turn; troops in that country do not fraternize with citizens.

Three months pass; the days of June have come; and the sweet enthusiast can only sigh, "Paris! poor Paris! Alas! alas!" We are not likely to be wrong in thinking that the lesson was not lost on a nature in which reason trod very hard on the heels of impulse. Politics, indeed, have hardly any place in Mary Ann's letters. She took no interest in the play of the parliamentary machine, none in the strife of parties. Charlatanism and violence, the weapons of this strife, were repugnant to her. Her thoughts shot beyond them to the great social revolutions which her optimism could not help expecting. But even in this respect she had learnt to count less on the disorderly movements of the multitude than on slow moral reforms, on the advance of characters in seriousness and of souls in sympathy.

Miss Evans lost her father in the month of May 1849, after an illness in which she had nursed him with the most entire devotion. She found herself,

at the age of thirty, her own mistress, but home-
less and obliged to work for her living, for a small
annuity of about a hundred a year which came to
her could hardly have sufficed her wants. She did
not, however, at once make up her mind to anything; and either to give herself time for reflection, or to re-establish her health which had been
much shaken and always remained delicate, or perhaps from the necessity of economizing, she went to
pass the following summer and winter at Geneva.
There she boarded with a family of simple manners
and cultivated minds, where she found the calm of
which she had need. "I have become," she wrote,
"passionately attached to the mountains, to the
lake, to the streets of the town, even to my room,
and above all to my dear hosts. . . . Everything
here is so thoroughly in harmony with my moral
state that I might almost say I have never felt
more completely at home." She wants nothing
except a little more money, so as not to need to be
niggardly in fires, for the winter this year is unusu-
ally cold. And she adds: "I cannot think without trembling of returning to England. It is to
me the country of sadness, of boredom, of commonplace. It is true that it is also the country of my
duty and of my affections. The only ardent desire
I feel about the future is to find some feminine
task to discharge, some possibility of devoting myself to some one, and making them purely and
calmly happy." Observe this craving for an exist-

ence to share and to make happy.   Still no project
is as yet formed.   Miss Evans rests; that is to
say, she rests after her own fashion; takes a dose
of mathematics every day; "to prevent the brain
from softening," attends De la Rive's course of ex-
perimental physics, reads Voltaire.   She hesitates
about resuming a translation of Spinoza which she
had begun during her father's illness, and which
she finished later:· she feels clearly enough that
such books are untranslatable.   "Those who read
Spinoza in his own text find in his style the same
kind of interest which is found in the conversation
of a person of vast intelligence who has lived alone
and who expresses, drawing it from the bottom of
his heart, what others repeat by rote."

When she returned from Switzerland Miss Evans
passed several months with her friends at Rosehill,
near Coventry, staying from time to time in London, and at last, it would seem, occupied in earnest
at finding a career for herself.   It was now that
she wrote her first article for the "Westminster
Review," a periodical which, after having been the
representative of Bentham and of utilitarianism,
was in the way to become more especially the
organ of Positivism.   Miss Evans's article, which
had for its text a book of intellectual progress, was
characteristic, for although it held up the vanity of
the efforts made to retain the beliefs and the institutions of the past, it recognized the fact that these
forms were once living, that they presented sym-

bols which were appropriate to a certain period of development, and that they still remain fast bound to whatsoever is best in men. At Rosehill, too, Miss Evans made the acquaintance of the freethinking publisher Chapman, who was just about to buy the "Westminster Review," to renew its editorial staff, and to endeavor to increase its influence. He wanted an editor, or perhaps I should say a sub-editor, for this business, and he easily convinced himself that Mary Ann was just what he wanted. His offers were accepted — indeed, she went to board in his family — and for two years (1852 and 1853) she exercised the functions — unusual for a woman — of directress of an important periodical armed at all points of philosophy and sociology, and possessing considerable ability, but at once heavy and brilliant, doctrinaire and revolutionary, aggressive and starched.

Miss Evans had a good deal to do as editress-in-chief. She corrected the proofs, sometimes literally from morn to eve. Her table groaned under the weight of accumulating books. She was specially entrusted with the notices of new books, which still form one of the most interesting parts of the "Westminster," but which inflicted on our poor directress huge and hasty reading. "I have done nothing since Monday," she writes, "and now I must work, work, work." She did not contribute to Mr. Chapman's "Review" more than some ten substantive critical articles, and with one exception they all

date from later years, when she was freed from the
heavy work of proof revision and correspondence.
The exception I have mentioned has other and
special claims to interest, inasmuch as the article
treats of lady novelists. Naturally George Sand
holds the first place in it. "No man comes near
her for elegance and depth of sentiment." And of
her style: "The ideas shine through the diction as
light through an alabaster vase. Such is the rhyth-
mical melody of her phrase that Beethoven, one
would fain believe, would have written so if he had
expressed in words the musical passion which possessed him." We know from Mr. Cross's volumes
that Miss Evans was more struck by the faults
than by the beauties of "Jane Eyre," and the article of which we speak confirms the impression, but
the Germans come off worst — "the palm of ·bad
novel writing belongs to them."

The Chapmans' house was the meeting-place, not
merely of the staff of the "Westminster," of the
disciples of the Positivist school and of freethinkers, but generally speaking of the new literary
generation on its way to notoriety. All sorts of
society were received there, and soirées were given.
Mary Ann sometimes regretted the country and
would have liked to go to recruit by the seaside.
"But do not think," she says, "that I do not enjoy
my stay here. I like to see new faces, and I am
afraid after this the country might seem a little
monotonous." She made many acquaintances —

Carlyle, Miss Martineau, Grote, Mill, Huxley, Mazzini, Louis Blanc. She once received a two hours' call from Pierre Leroux, who had come to London with his wife and children on an errand of lecturing to keep off starvation. The talk was amusing. "He set before me all his ideas. He belongs neither to the school of Proudhon, who represents nothing but liberty; nor to that of Louis Blanc, who represents only equality; nor to that of Cabot, who represents fraternity. The system of Pierre Leroux is a synthesis of the three principles. He has found the bridge which is to unite self-love to the love of our neighbor. As for the origin of Christianity, he thinks Strauss insufficient because he has not succeeded in showing the identity of the teaching of Jesus with that of the Essenes. This is Leroux's pet notion. Essenism leads him to Egypt, Egypt to India, the cradle of all religions, &c. All this was delivered with amusing unction. He had already come to London once, when he was twenty-five, in search of work as a printer. Everybody was then in mourning for the Princess Charlotte. "And I," he cried, "happened to have an apple-green coat!"

Among the friends whom Miss Evans made in London there were two men who exercised a profound influence — the one on her thought, the other on her life. Herbert Spencer met her at the Chapmans' and at once became a friend of hers. He was about her age; he had just published his first great work on Social Statics. He had noticed the superiority of Mary Ann's intelligence, while she on her side delighted in intercourse with a man of so much learning and of undoubted speculative faculty. In the very abstract regions where they met the two thinkers had no need of paying a too servile respect to convention. "We agreed that there was no reason why we should not see each other as often as we liked," writes Miss Evans. "He is kind, he is delightful, and I always feel better after being with him." And in another letter, also of 1852: "The bright side of my life, after my affection for my old friends, is the new and delightfully calm friendship which I have found in Herbert Spencer. We see each other every day, and in everything we enjoy a delightful comradeship. If it were not for him my life would be singularly arid." A few months later Spencer had not become less dear, but another affection had been born of this one, and was about to take a far greater place in Mary Ann's destiny. She had already met George Lewes more than once in literary society, when Spencer brought him to see her one day in the winter of 1851. The acquaintance for a long time went no farther; the two met with pleasure, with interest, but nothing more. "We had a pleasant evening on Wednesday," says Mary Ann at the end of March 1853. "Lewes was as original and as amusing as ever." And a fortnight later: "Everybody here is very kind to me. Mr. Lewes

in particular is amiable and attentive, and has
quite won me over, though at first I was strongly
prejudiced against him. He is one of the small
number of persons in this world who are much
better than they seem. He is a man of heart and
conscience under a mask of coxcombry and *faconde*" [1] (the English word "flippancy" is untranslatable). As from prejudice she went to esteem,
so she did from acquaintance to intimacy. Lewes
was editor of a journal called the "Leader." But
he was lazy and Miss Evans corrected his proofs
for him, or he was ill and took a holiday, when she
acted as his substitute and worked double tides.
True, her pleasures disappeared with him; and
once when he had gone to recruit in the country
"No more operas and no more amusement for a
month to come," cries she. "Luckily I have no
time to regret him." Soon, other indications are
added. She cancels her engagements with Chapman; she speaks of travelling on the Continent.
In short the reader is only half surprised when in
July 1854 he finds her starting for Weimar with
Lewes, after announcing to her friends that she
considers herself, and wishes to be thenceforth considered, as his wife.

[1] [*Faconde* deserves almost the same description as "flippancy." But I should have thought it the equivalent, not so
much of this latter, as of " glibness," " gift of the gab."— *Trans.*]

II

We are now at the critical point of George Eliot's life, at a crisis the immediate effect of which was to throw her into an equivocal position and almost to make her a *déclassée*, but which was at the same time not without effect on her happiness and her literary career, inasmuch as it gave her a home life and a judicious adviser. The astonishment into which this step of hers threw those who had not of late years followed her career closely was boundless, and this astonishment survives in a sort for us at the present day. It would seem that few men were less suited than Lewes to captivate such a woman as Mary Ann. If his age was fairly matched with hers (he was two years older) his exterior was anything but attractive — unkempt hair and beard, his whole person neglected, and the air, if not exactly of a Bohemian, certainly of anything but a gentleman. Gifted with great curiosity of mind and with much facility, Lewes had learnt everything and tried every craft ; he had written novels, biographies, philosophical works, a play. He had been a journalist, a lecturer, even an actor. The only thing that he did not know how to do, said somebody, was to paint, and it would not have taken him more than a week to learn that. Thackeray asserted that he should not be surprised if he saw Lewes in Piccadilly astride on a white elephant. With this he had inexhaustible conversation,

great store of fact and anecdote, a knowledge alike
how to please and how to amuse, a good stock of
gayety despite his bad health, of probity despite his
vagabond life, and to crown all good humor and
that evenness of disposition which excuses so many
faults.   A singular contrast, on the whole, with a
timid and reserved woman eminently serious and
inspired with a particular aversion for that literary
species which is called the amateur!

But there was in the marriage[1] of which we
speak something more surprising than the hetero-
geneousness of the characters: there was the fact
that Lewes was already married, that his wife was
still alive, that he could offer Miss Evans nothing
better than a left-handed union, and that she was
about to change her name only to usurp that which
belonged to another.   Let us add, to cap the climax
of strangeness, that Miss Evans, in contracting this
union with Lewes does not seem to have yielded to
any irresistible attraction.   She was, it would
seem, if not a stranger to all passion, at least too
much under the control of reason and of reasoning
to be capable of a *coup de tête;* besides, she as well
as Lewes was of mature years.   We must therefore
content ourselves with supposing that with her
craving for intimate affection, with the happiness
she felt at being an object of devotion and of care,
touched also by the attentions and by the misfortunes

---

[1] [On the words "marriage," "husband," "Mrs. Lewes,"
&c. see note p.   *ante.— Trans.*]

of her friend, having recognized in him solid qualities
under a fantastic exterior, and promising herself to
complete the task of polishing and moralizing him,
Miss Evans thought she need not refuse herself
happiness, however unexpected and equivocal the
shape in which it presented itself. Besides, who
knows whether the effort which she made to conquer her hesitation did not help to strengthen her
to do so? She may have said to herself that she
was going to perform an act of self-sacrifice to
the man whose life she was about to repair
by risking her own, and an act of fidelity to her
own convictions by following them in despite of
the opinions of the world.

As for scruples, properly so called, for protests
of conscience, there could hardly be any in Miss
Evans. Lewes had been deserted by his wife; his
first marriage was virtually dissolved; and if it
could not be so legally, there was nothing in this,
as it were, accidental circumstance which could
touch the moral sense. It is true that the legal
impediment simultaneously made any religious celebration impossible, that the connection whereof
we speak was thus condemned to dispense with any
sanction whatever, to remain, so to speak, anony-
mous,[1] a mere matter of mutual consent. But after

---

[1] [In using the word *anonyme*, I think M. Scherer may have
thought of its use with *société*, which we only partially render
by identifying it with " limited liability." Strictly, it is a part-
nership where the partners are not known to be such by the
public. — *Trans.*]

all is not this the essence of marriage — is it not
even the canonical definition of it? The hesita-
tions which Miss Evans certainly had to surmount,
the doubts which she had to conquer, were of
another kind, and everything shows us that she
experienced these in all their force. She was going
to expose herself to unpleasant remarks, to offend
many of her friends, to put herself for life in a
false position. She was breaking social laws, the
importance of which she well knew, and she must
have felt that in breaking them she was setting a
deplorable example to others who neither had the
same excuses nor were held back on the downward
slope by the same principles. The notion that her
action might be interpreted as a whim, after the
fashion of George Sand, as an adhesion to the doctrine of free-love, must have been hideous to this
pure soul. If she disregarded it, it was because
she promised herself to refute by her life the criti-
cisms which her conduct was about to invite. This
promise, let us hasten to say, she kept, and with
the help of her literary glory she finally shut the
mouth of scandal. England, when she died, had
long excused or forgotten; but how much courage
must it not have needed to hold the lists to the
end!

In a letter written a year later, in explanation of
her conduct, Miss Evans thus expresses herself: —

If there is any one action or relation of my life which is
and always has been profoundly serious, it is my relation to

Mr. Lewes. It is, however, natural enough that you should mistake me in many ways, for not only are you unacquainted with Mr. Lewes's real character and the course of his actions, but also it is several years now since you and I were much together, and it is possible that the modifications my mind has undergone may be quite in the opposite direction of what you imagine. No one can be better aware than yourself that it is possible for two people to hold different opinions on momentous subjects with equal sincerity, and an equally earnest conviction that their respective opinions are alone the truly moral ones. If we differ on the subject of the marriage laws, I at least can believe of you that you cleave to what you believe to be good ; and I don't know of anything in the nature of your views that should prevent you from believing the same of me. *How far* we differ, I think we neither of us know, for I am ignorant of your precise views ; and apparently you attribute to me both feelings and opinions which are not mine. We cannot set each other quite right in this matter in letters, but one thing I can tell you in few words. Light and easily broken ties are what I neither desire theoretically nor could live for practically. Women who are satisfied with such ties do *not* act as I have done. That any unworldly, unsuperstitious person who is sufficiently acquainted with the realities of life can pronounce my relation to Mr. Lewes immoral, I can only understand by remembering how subtle and complex are the influences that mould opinion. But I *do* remember this : and I indulge in no arrogant or uncharitable thoughts about those who condemn us, even though we might have expected a somewhat different verdict. From the majority of persons, of course, we never looked for anything but condemnation. We are leading no life of self-indulgence, except indeed that, being happy in each other, we find everything easy. We are working hard to provide for others better than we provide for ourselves, and to fulfil every responsibility that lies upon us. Levity and pride would not be a sufficient basis for that.

And later in 1857 : —

> If I live five years longer, the positive result of my exist-
> ence on the side of truth and goodness will outweigh the
> small negative good that would have consisted in my not
> doing anything to shock others, and I can conceive no con-
> sequences that will make me repent the past.

Lord Acton, in a very remarkable article in the
"Nineteenth Century," thinks that George Eliot
was wrong when she thought she knew the price
she paid for her happiness with Lewes. What she
really sacrificed, according to him, was freedom of
speech, the first place among the women of her
time, and a tomb in Westminster Abbey.

I am surprised that no more attention has been
paid to the light which George Eliot's second marriage throws on her first. Less than eighteen months
after Lewes's death, and at the age of sixty, she
married a man, worthy of her in sentiment, as the
" Life " before us proves, but very much younger
than herself, so that she had not, indeed, a second
time to dare public opinion, but to astonish it afresh.
Once more George Eliot had been unable to refuse
herself the pleasures of life with another.

Let us lastly note, before quitting the subject, the
influence which was later exercised on her novels
by the crisis through which she had gone in uniting
herself to Lewes. So far from the false position in
which she had placed herself having for consequence
the lowering of the moral tone of her works, exactly
the contrary happened. One might almost say that

she became constantly more eager to set duty above
passion and to recall to notice the danger of entering into conflict with public order, were it only of
a conventional kind. And in the same way, as far
as she is personally concerned, there is not a situation or even a word in her writings which can be
interpreted as an apology for her own conduct.
We feel that she pays special attention to this —
that she has a punctilio about it.

Lewes and Miss Evans disappeared after announcing their connection. They set out for Germany towards the end of July 1854, gave three
months to Weimar, and spent the winter in Berlin.
The choice of these two towns was not a matter of
liking nor yet one of caprice. In one Lewes hoped
to collect impressions and materials for a "Life of
Goethe," and in the other he was sure to find help
for the physiological studies to which he was beginning to turn his attention. The stay at Weimar
was very agreeable — famous men, easy intimacies,
plenty of good music, and above all great literary
memories. It was not without emotion that our
traveller visited the houses of the two famous poets.
"Among such memorials," she wrote, "one breathes
deeply and the tears rush to one's eyes." She
learned with regret that no portrait of Schiller is
like him. Rauch said that he had a wretched fore-
head, and Tieck, the sculptor, declared that his
whole person made one think of a camel. The
Leweses heard much Wagner at Weimar, but with-

out succeeding in relishing him. On the other hand, they made great friends with Liszt, who conducted the orchestra at the Opera, and whose talk was as amusing as his play was extraordinary. He told them that when he met Madame d'Agoult after the publication of "Nélida," he asked her, "Why were you so unkind to that poor Lehmann?"[1]

Berlin seemed to our travellers cold and prosaic after Weimar. They set to work again, Lewes finishing his biography and his friend writing articles for the "Westminster" or continuing her translation of Spinoza's "Ethics," not to mention a mass of reading, especially in German. She particularly relished Lessing — her dear Lessing, as she calls him. Goethe does not always charm her : she is chiefly amused at the want of point in the "Xenien"; the "Wanderjahre" draw from her the cry, "à mourir d'ennui."[2] Among the acquaintances she made in Berlin, the sculptor Rauch seemed to her in all the respects the most distinguished, and Gruppe the oddest. Gruppe ought to have suited Lewes, for, if he was not a Jack of all trades, he had tried every kind of literature : he left lyrics, five epics, a play, works in literary history and criticism, learned studies of

[1] Lehmann, the representative of Liszt himself, who had been on the most intimate terms with the author. George Eliot thought the remark "felicitous and characteristic." This was charitable. — *Trans.*]

[2] [The French is George Eliot's. — *Trans.*]

antiquity, and books of philosophy. He was university professor to boot, and an enthusiastic boar-
hunter. Mary Ann describes him clothed in a
dressing-gown which had once been a winter great-
coat,[1] his velvet cap on his gray hair, reading
aloud his own works with enthusiasm, but simple
and kind-hearted, and (oddly enough), despite his
prodigious fertility, rather slow of apprehension
and delighting in poor plays on words. "*Apropos*
of jokes," she adds, "we noticed that during the
whole seven months of our stay in Germany, we
never heard one witticism or even one felicitous
idea or expression from a German."

After German heaviness came French feather-
headedness. The travellers met, in a Berlin *salon*
a countryman of ours, who marvelled at the talent
with which Meyerbeer in the "Huguenots" had
grasped the spirit of the epoch of Charles the
Ninth. "Read the chronicles!" cried he. "What!
Froissart's?" slipped in a malicious voice. "Yes,
something of that kind, or else the chronicles of
Brantôme, of Mérimée, and you will find that Meyerbeer has expressed all that perfectly — at least,
I think so." "But perhaps, monsieur, it is your
own genius which put these ideas into the music?"
Whereat the agreeable rattle modestly disclaimed.
Varnhagen, to whose house the Leweses constantly
went, continually recurred to the antipathy with
which Carlyle had inspired him when, after long

[1] [She only says that she "fancies" it had. — *Trans.*]

correspondence, they came to meet. Varnhagen, though not without admiration for some of the English humorist's work, had been shocked by his taste for despotism and by his rough, paradoxical talk in general. Yet we have a neat saying of his.[1] At a dinner given to him in Berlin the talk was of Goethe, and some of the guests affected to deplore that the great poet had so little religion.[2] During this talk Carlyle was visibly uneasy, fumbling with his dinner-napkin. At last he broke out thus, "Gentlemen, do you know the story of the man who railed at the sun because it would not light his cigar ? "

Mrs. Lewes's final judgment at her departure does honor to her impartiality. She had become very weary of the heavy finery, the noise, the indiscriminate smoking.[3] "But, after all," she says, "Germany is no bad place to live in, and the Germans, to counterbalance their want of taste and politeness, are at least free from the bigotry and exclusiveness " of the English.

On their return to England the couple set to work seriously on the life which they had deliberately foreseen and chosen. They hired at Richmond, near London, a modest house [4] where the drawing-

---

[1] [Not from Varnhagen. — *Trans.*]

[2] [In original " evangelical sentiment," which is not quite the same. — *Trans.*]

[3] [It is fair to say that George Eliot limits this to German *inns.* — *Trans.*]

[4] [Lodgings rather. — *Trans.*]

room was the only study, and this had to do for both of them. Lewes had to provide for the needs of his first wife, now fallen very low, as well as for the education of his three boys at school. This made a good many mouths for which to find meat, and that, too, with no very profitable craft. Mary Ann had published the translation of Feuerbach's "Wesen des Christenthums" before her departure for Germany, but she could not expect much profit from a book which was already rather out of date, and in any case ill-adjusted to the intellectual meridian of Great Britain. The translation of Spinoza which she had finished at Berlin was still less promising, and, indeed, has never been printed. So she went back to periodical literature. Her health, unluckily, was weak, and caused frequent interruptions, but to make up for this she enjoyed domestic happiness and the success of the union she had contracted. She feels, she says, her esteem and affection for Lewes increase every day. "I am very happy," she wrote after three years' experience, "happy with the greatest happiness that life can give, the complete sympathy and affection of a man whose mind stimulates mine and keeps up in me a wholesome activity." But it was not only activity, it was talent as well which developed itself in our author through this beneficent contact. Like most strong and deep natures, Mrs. Lewes arrived but late at the consciousness and the exercise of her gifts. She was thirty-six years old when

her "Westminster" articles began to rise from the
level (high enough, to be sure) which they had
hitherto kept, and to attract attention more vividly.
Lewes used to say that it was in reading one of these
pieces, a biting satire on the apocalyptic dreams of
a popular preacher,[1] that he first gained insight into
his wife's genius. Two other fine articles — one
on Young of the "Nights," the other on Heine and
German wit — must have strengthened this impression. Moreover, as it happened, Mrs. Lewes was
at this very moment entering on a path in which
she was to give rise to far different astonishment.

The history of her *début* in novel-writing is
memorable enough for us to hear the telling of it
by herself : —

September 1856 made a new era in my life, for it was
then I began to write fiction. It had always been a vague
dream of mine that some time or other I might write a
novel; and my shadowy conception of what the novel was
to be, varied, of course, from one epoch of my life to another. But I never went further towards the actual writing
of the novel than an introductory chapter describing a Staf-
fordshire village and the life of the neighboring farm-houses ;
and as the years passed on I lost any hope that I should
ever be able to write a novel, just as I desponded about
everything else in my future life. I always thought I was
deficient in dramatic power, both of construction and dialogue, but I felt I should be at my ease in the descriptive
parts of a novel. My "introductory chapter" was pure
description, though there were good materials in it for

[1] [Poor Dr. Cumming, if not witty, yet a great whetstone of
wit. – *Trans.*]

dramatic presentation. It happened to be among the papers
I had with me in Germany, and one evening at Berlin
something led me to read it to George. He was struck with
it as a bit of concrete description, and it suggested to him
the possibility of my being able to write a novel, though he
distrusted — indeed disbelieved in — my possession of any
dramatic power. Still, he began to think that I might as
well try some time what I could do in fiction; and by-and-by,
when we came back to England, and I had greater success
than he ever expected in other kinds of writing, his impression that it was worth while to see how far my mental power
would go, towards the production of a novel, was strength.
ened. He began to say very positively, "You must try and
write a story," and when we were at Tenby he urged me
to begin at once. I deferred it, however, after my usual
fashion, with work that does not present itself as an absolute duty. But one morning as I was thinking what should
be the subject of my first story, my thoughts merged themselves into a dreamy doze, and I imagined myself writing a
story, of which the title was "The Sad Fortunes of the Rev-
erend Amos Barton." I was soon wide awake again and
told G. He said, "Oh, what a capital title!" and from that
time I had settled in my mind that this should be my first
story. George used to say, "It may be a failure — it may
be that you are unable to write fiction. Or perhaps it may
be just good enough to warrant you trying again." Again,
"You may write a *chef-d'œuvre* at once — there's no telling."
But his prevalent impression was, that though I could
hardly write a *poor* novel, my effort would want the highest
quality of fiction — dramatic presentation. He used to say,
"You have wit, description, and philosophy — those go a
good way towards the production of a novel. It is worth
while for you to try the experiment."

We determined that if my story turned out good enough,
we would send it to Blackwood.

When she returned to Richmond Mrs. Lewes set to work, and at the end of a week was able to read the first part of "Amos Barton" to her husband. Lewes's fears were at once dispelled.

The scene at Cross Farm, he said, satisfied him that I had the very element he had been doubtful about — it was clear I could write good dialogue. There still remained the question whether I could command any pathos; and that was to be decided by the mode in which I treated Milly's death. One night G. went to town on purpose to leave me a quiet evening for writing it. I wrote the chapter from the news brought by the shepherd to Mrs. Hackit, to the moment when Amos is dragged from the bedside, and I read it to G. when he came home. We both cried over it, and then he came up to me and kissed me, saying, "I think your pathos is better than your fun." [1]

The tale finished, the next thing was to get it published without, of course, betraying the author's sex and name. Anonymity was sure to add the attraction of curiosity to the merit of the story, and, besides, Mrs. Lewes's position made secrecy desirable. Her husband undertook the transaction. He sent the MS. of "Amos Barton" to Blackwood as the work of one of his friends, and making no secret of the admiration with which the story had

[1] [According to a practice of M. Scherer's, which I have before referred to, this passage, though given in the first person and in inverted commas, is much shortened and paraphrased, probably because the original contains references to the actual story, which French readers might not understand. It seemed better to restore the actual text. — *Trans.*]

inspired him. Others were to follow under the general title of "Scenes of Clerical Life," a phrase which at once warns us of the difficulty of translating into French writings such as those of George Eliot, inasmuch as the very words "church" and "clergy" have for us a sense quite opposite to that which they carry with them in a country where ministers of religion have the right to feel and to suffer, to love and to marry, like other men. Blackwood at once recognized the worth of the story sent him. "It is long," said he, "since I read anything so novel, so amusing, and at the same time so pathetic." The first part of "Amos" appeared in his magazine for January 1857, and success encouraging the author, she produced two other stories, after which the whole was reprinted in volume form under the name of George Eliot. For Mrs. Lewes, wishing still to preserve her *incognito*, thought she had better adopt a pseudonym. The secret was kept to admiration, and it was many months before Blackwood himself knew with whom he was dealing. The author's most intimate friends of her own sex (with the exception of one who guessed at first sight) felt the deepest astonishment when they learnt the truth. As for the public, conjecture ran riot, and still went astray when another work, "Adam Bede," had already followed the "Scenes." In particular, endless discussions were held on the sex of the new author. In France M. Montégut made a long examination of the question,

weighed the *pros* and *cons.*, and finally inclined to
the masculine. "In fact," said he, "the author
seems to have something of both sexes ; and as only
ecclesiastics, by a special favor of circumstances,
enjoy this epicene privilege, we shall take it on
ourselves to say that we think the author a minister of the Established Church." An English journal (the "Saturday Review"[1]) was still minuter
in its conclusions, and decided that the name of
George Eliot must hide some scholarly clergyman,
who had taken his degree at Cambridge, who lived
or had passed the greater part of his life in the
country, who was the father of a numerous family,
of pronounced High Church tendencies, and very
fond of children, the Greek tragedians, and dogs.
The care with which George Eliot kept her secret
for two years and more had unexpected consequences. An inhabitant of Nuneaton, where Mary
Ann had been at school, availing himself of the
local memories which had slipped into the tales,
gave it to be understood that he was the author,
and so interested the neighborhood in his poverty
and hidden genius that a subscription was got up
for him.

Dickens was keener-sighted than most critics.
Having received a copy of the "Scenes," he
thanked the unknown author in a letter breathing

---

[1] [I have looked up this article with some interest. The intention is pretty evidently ironical. — *Trans.*]

the frankest admiration, but not hiding the conclusion to which his literary tact [1] had led him.

TAVISTOCK HOUSE, LONDON,
Monday, 17th Jan. 1858.

My Dear Sir, — I have been so strongly affected by the
two first tales in the book you have had the kindness to
send me, through Messrs. Blackwood, that I hope you will
excuse my writing to you to express my admiration of their
extraordinary merit.   The exquisite truth and delicacy, both
of the humor and the pathos of these stories, I have never
seen the like of ; and they have impressed me in a manner
that I should find it very difficult to describe to you, if I had
the impertinence to try.

In addressing these few words of thankfulness to the
creator of the Sad Fortunes of the Rev. Amos Barton, and
the sad love story of Mr. Gilfil, I am (I presume) bound to
adopt the name that it pleases that excellent writer to
assume.   I can suggest no better one : but I should have
been strongly disposed, if I had been left to my own devices,
to address the said writer as a woman.   I have observed
what seemed to me such womanly touches in those moving
fictions, that the assurance on the title-page is insufficient to
satisfy me even now.   If they originated with no woman, I
believe that no man ever before had the art of making himself mentally so like a woman since the world began.

You will not suppose that I have any vulgar wish to
fathom your secret.   I mention the point as one of great
interest to me — not of mere curiosity.   If it should ever
suit your convenience and inclination to show me the face
of the man, or woman, who has written so charmingly, it
will be a very memorable occasion to me.   If otherwise, I

[1] [Perhaps it would be more correct to say " his experience as
an editor." — *Trans.*]

shall always hold that impalpable personage in loving attachment and respect, and shall yield myself up to all future
utterances from the same source, with a perfect confidence
in their making me wiser and better.

Your obliged and faithful servant and admirer,
CHARLES DICKENS.

George Eliot, Esq.

Having come to the consciousness of her genius,
having received an unanimous vote of encourage-
ment, and having, at the same time, hit upon a vein
of literary production which promised to bring her
modest home into easy circumstances, George Eliot
began work on a larger scale almost before she
had finished the novel, " Scenes of Clerical Life."
"Adam Bede" was already begun by the end of
1857 : its second volume was written at Munich
and at Dresden. The Leweses were passionately
fond of travelling, and the sale of the previous
book had been sufficiently profitable, the reception
given to these stories by the public sufficiently
promising for the future, to let them give themselves the pleasure of making acquaintance with
new countries. Besides, they resolved to work and
kept their resolve. "Munich," she writes, "swarms
with professors of all sorts, all *gründlich*, of course,
and one or two of them great. There is no one we
are more charmed with than Liebig." Bodenstedt
made our travellers think of their friend Gruppe,
at Berlin, by the multitude of his acquirements and
the variety of his productions. In fact, Bodenstedt

was a traveller, a journalist, a professor, and the
manager of a theatre. He translated from Persian,
from Russian, and from English; he wrote a great
work on the peoples of the Caucasus; he paid
special attention to Shakespeare. He was the
author of plays, of novels, of a volume of verses
which went through nearly a hundred editions, and
he crowned the whole by a history of his own life.
"Enormously instructed after the fashion of the
Germans," writes George Eliot, "and not at all
stupid with it." The translator of the "Leben
Jesu" had the pleasure of meeting Strauss at
Munich, and was very agreeably impressed by him.
"He speaks with very choice words, like a man
strictly truthful in the use of language." George
Eliot loved the arts, music most of all, but painting
also, and she naturally bestowed part of her time
on the galleries. She had little admiration for the
modern German school. "Kaulbach's great compositions are huge charades." "His 'Destruction
of Jerusalem' is a regular child's puzzle of symbol-
ism."

He is certainly a man of great faculty, but is, I imagine,
carried out of his true path by the ambition to produce
" Weltgeschichtliche Bilder," which the German critics
may go into raptures about. His "Battle of the Huns,"
which is the most impressive of all his great pictures, was
the first of the series. He painted it simply under the
inspiration of the grand myth about the spirits of the dead
warriors rising and carrying on the battle in the air.
Straightway the German critics began to smoke furiously

that vile tobacco which they call *ästhetik*, declared it a
"Weltgeschichtliches Bild," and ever since Kaulbach has
been concocting these pictures in which, instead of taking
a single moment of reality and trusting to the infinite sym-
bolism that belongs to all nature, he attempts to give you
at one view a succession of events — each represented by
some group which may mean "Whichever you please, my
little dear."

Our author might have added that it is the same
with the other arts ; that the Germans, loving them
only in an intellectual manner, insist on thrusting
scientific elements into them; that even poetry
pleases Germans better when they find in it matter
for comment and interpretation. The worship
paid to Goethe by his countrymen is due less to
his really perfect works, to his really immortal
creations, than to the endless field which he has
opened to the pedantry of scholiasts. Is there a
single German *savant* who is not more attracted by
the second "Faust" than by the first ?

At Dresden our travellers resolved to make no
acquaintances, and to work with no other distrac-
tion than the picture-gallery, the open-air concerts,
and excursions on foot. "We have been as happy
as princes — are not, George writing at the far
corner of the great *salon*, I at my *Schrank* [desk]
in my own private room with closed doors. Here
I wrote the latter half of the second volume of
'Adam Bede' in the long mornings that our early
hours, rising at six o'clock, procure us." The

third volume was written in England, after returning from the journey, and straight off: this was
the author's way, as I remember hearing her say
herself. As soon as ever she had a thorough grasp
of her subject, or rather it of her, she did her writing with great speed. The first volume of "Adam
Bede" was hardly revised at all; and her husband's
advice, to which George Eliot always attached
great value, was occupied with nothing but verbal
alterations. The MS. of the book bears a dedica-
tion which attests not merely the gratitude due
for useful collaboration. "To my dear husband,
George Henry Lewes, I give the MS. of a work
which would never have been written but for the
happiness which his love has conferred on my
life." She did the same with all her books, and
inscribed on the autograph of each of them the
touching expression of her gratitude and her
tenderness for the companion of her life.

George Eliot's readers are, I believe, agreed that
the "Scenes of Clerical Life" contain the germs of
the beauties of all the author's later works; but
"Adam Bede" is a real novel, and in this more
extended form it fulfilled and surpassed the expectation which the author's early work had excited.
Moreover, it is to the second attempt that it is
usual to remand new-comers in letters to convince
one's self that the first success has been something
more than a lucky accident. In this case no doubt
was possible, and men had an indisputable power

before them. It was not easy to know which to
admire most—the pathetic interest of Hetty Sor-
rel's fortunes or the rustic salt of the sallies of
Mrs. Poyser, one of those creations which, from
the first moment, take their place in the literature
of a nation. It was but a few weeks after the
appearance of "Adam Bede" that a speaker in
the House of Commons quoted one of the genial
farmer's wife's sayings like a man who was sure
that his hearers would understand him. The noise
which George Eliot's name made echoed even in
France. M. Montégut spoke of "Adam Bede" to
the readers of the "Revue des deux Mondes," and in
this article, which George Eliot thought the best
of all that had been devoted to her novel, our colleague made no secret of his enthusiasm. "Oh!
what delightful and refined reading," said he, referring to the "Scenes of Clerical Life." "One's soul
was filled with it as with a perfume of sweetness
and piety; one was not seduced into admiration,
one was taken by storm; it was not merely moving, it was affecting." Then, passing to "Adam
Bede," and after extolling the combined delicacy
and precision of the observation, the often exquisite style, the sympathetic, and, so to say, luminous
impartiality which sheds itself on all the occupants
of the stage, he said: "Twelve hundred pages
occupied in telling of the seduction of a girl at a
farm by a youthful squire, the ill luck in love and
the happiness in marriage of a poor country car-

penter! 'tis much, you will say. Well, I can assure
you that when I had read them I wanted more.
What the author offers us is a huge nosegay of
wild flowers, full of wealth in scent and color, one
of those nosegays that we have often brought home
in youth after a country excursion and delighted in
preserving for several days after in a large vase as
a souvenir of a few hours of reckless activity —
thorny branches of wild eglantine torn from the
living hedges, flowering brambles, great tufts of
lilac, hand-broken from the favorite tree of spring,
huge bearded grasses, rushes in golden bloom."

I am the more glad to recall M. Montégut's study
that it remained pretty much without a companion,
in French criticism. It is with few exceptions[1]
the only piece of cordial praise that this illustrious
lady has received in our country. Most of the
judgments of her works which at long intervals
have appeared in our reviews have shown either
the disdain of a jaded taste, or (which is worse)
the reluctance of envy, especially feminine envy, to
recognize a superiority by the side of which, it is
true, the commonplaces of the day seem more commonplace than ever.

Dickens was again one of the first to express his

---

[1] [Among the exceptions, of course, are the two earlier articles
of M. Scherer's own, which appear in this book. I do not know
whose was the " feminine " jealousy glanced at below. The above
sample of M. Montégut is a good deal more flowery than is his
wont. — *Trans.*]

admiration. The reading of "Adam Bede," he wrote to the author, was an event in his life. Herbert Spencer was enthusiastic, declaring that he felt a better man for having read the book; but George Eliot's head was not turned. "I sing my Magnificat under my breath," she said, "and I feel great delight, deep and silent. But few writers, I think, have known less than I have of the transports and the feelings of triumph which they describe as the result of success." It was from this time that she contracted the repugnance to speaking and hearing speak about her books which became a note of her literary life, and which had already made her intrust Lewes with the duty of intercepting reviews in newspapers, whether laudatory or the reverse. "If people were to hum their remarks or their comments round me, I should lose the calm mind and the honest labor without which nothing good and wholesome can be written. To talk about my works is to me as though I were to talk of my private thoughts or my religion." Moreover she felt the obligations of success, and was nervous about a new novel just begun. "'Adam's' good fortune," she said to her publisher, "makes me write more anxiously than ever. I fancy it is a kind of feeling of responsibility joined to a good deal of pride."

We need not follow out the history of George Eliot's works. Quite contrary to the ordinary fate of the works of a writer who has at once gained

the public vote, and to the fate of novelists more
especially, because they draw more and more
deeply on their fund of experience and observation — the public at each new book of George
Eliot's, even while regretting, so to say, its infi-
delity to the earlier ones, could not keep proclaim-
ing the superiority of the new-comer. " The Mill
on the Floss," which appeared in 1860, might be
looked upon as the author's master-piece if " Middlemarch," ten years later, had not contested that
title with it, and if there had not appeared in the
interval " Silas Marner," an admirable rustic idyl,
and the historical romance of " Romola," which
was destined to show George Eliot equal to herself
in all the styles she tried. Even " Deronda," her
last story, spoilt as it is by inexplicable preoccupations, includes passages equal in power to anything that the author has done.

The scene of " Romola " is the Florence of the
fifteenth century, and the plan of it came to George
Eliot in the course of an Italian journey, " one of
those journeys which seem to divide one's life in
half, so many new ideas do they suggest, so many
new sources of interest do they open to the mind."
Having fixed on her scheme, she returned to Florence, visiting the old streets, rummaging ancient
books, seeking to impregnate herself with the
spirit of the venerable city. But she was still far
from her goal. When, on her return home, she at
last set to her work, she saw all its difficulties rising

before her. Would not her genius desert her when she left the familiar scenes of rustic life in the England of to-day for foreign countries and past ages ? Would she succeed in reviving in their true physiognomy the town, the epoch, and the figure of Savonarola? She despaired more than once, gave up her task, then took to it again, plunged (conscientiously as she did everything) into historical studies, and brought forth in sorrow a kind of moral tragedy which even the reader cannot behold without emotion. It seemed as if a weight were crushing her down. Each phrase, she said, had been written in her heart's blood. "I began the novel a young woman," she added; "I was an old one when I finished it." Yet it had only taken her eighteen months to write. Either owing to the pains she had taken in the writing of it, or to the moral importance which she attached to the drawing of the characters whereof she composed her picture, George Eliot seems to have had for "Romola" a partiality which I find some difficulty in sharing.

I only mention the two volumes of George Eliot's poetry for the sake of not omitting them ; because, fine as some passages are in their pathos or in their wit, and deeply interesting as they all are regarded as experiments, these poems add nothing to the author's reputation save by completing the proof of the variety of her gifts.

An author's works, it has often been said, are

the true events of his life. Putting aside the
books I have just named, there is nothing to note
in George Eliot's later years except a continually
increasing fame, the respect which a blameless life
won her, affluence which became riches, frequent
travels both abroad and in England; and lastly,
what is not given necessarily either by glory or by
fortune, a happiness of which she herself said in a
letter, "Altogether we are dangerously happy." It
seemed to her that she had a ransom to pay to fate,
and she well knew also that old age, sooner or
later, takes on itself the duty of levying this tax
by parting those who love. Lewes died in 1878.
As we have already remarked, she married again
less than eighteen months later, her husband being
a man who was much younger than herself, but
whose affection had touched her, and the delicacy
of whose sentiments made him worthy of her. The
happiness she found in this new union was of no
long duration, and she died within the year from
the result of a chill. She was sixty-one, but had
as yet shown none of the infirmities of age. She
loved life, she had said to one of her friends a
little before; she was full of plans, and then the
world was so interesting.

The engraved portrait which Mr. Cross has placed
as a frontispiece to his wife's biography is as like
as the reproduction of a singularly expressive face
can be. George Eliot's features, a little heavy and
strongly marked in their frame of abundant hair,

expressed a soul which is in command of itself, a
great intelligence which has remained kindly.
One felt in them the union of timidity, which is
driven back into itself, with an affectionate need
of sympathy. The entire personality was gentle,
distinguished, suited to gain confidence and inspire
respect.

The moral unity of George Eliot's character is not
easy to fix. Not that I take her literally when she
calls herself a chameleon, and says she is in danger
of losing her personality. My difficulty comes from
her very depth. What we see in George Eliot's
maturity is a great and beautiful soul, clear and
calm, which has known or guessed, felt or anticipated, the feeling of everything. But at what price
has she bought this dominion of reason over passion, this ascendency of reflection over spontaneity?
Is it not probable that the "Life" was not allowed
to tell us everything? Is it not permissible to believe that the history of Maggie in "The Mill on
the Floss" was an inspiration of memory? And
is it not natural to suppose that personal experience
counted for something in the final self-possession,
and in such an intimate knowledge of life?

In studying such a character as that of George
Eliot the danger is lest we should mistake this acquired empire over impulse for a natural want of
warmth. Indeed, more people than one have been
the dupes of this mistake, and have wondered at the
absence of fire and "go" in the letters which have

been given to us. This was to forget the conditions
of Mr. Cross's publication, but it was also to misjudge the intellectual and moral history of George
Eliot. She had known what impetuosity is. "I
love," she wrote at thirty, "souls which hurry
towards their end, carried on the springtide of sentiment, and not harassed by perpetual negations."
Twenty years later, and we find her fearing to
come to a conclusion too quickly, and to show herself more positive than inner light allows. "I
dread all positive assertion on matters of great importance, through fear of committing myself by my
own words, and of degenerating into a mere echo of
myself. A horrible destiny, yet one of which, it
must be confessed, many and great men have been
the victims." Here we have the two things, the
carrying away and the reaction. Serenity spreads
itself over this life, but the hidden emotion, the
throb below, do not fail to betray themselves still.
A book, the sight of a picture, will often bring
tears to her eyes. Or it may be gaiety which breaks
out; for, grave as we fancy her, she was none the
less capable, her biographer tells us, of the frankest
hilarity, of joyous, catching, irresistible laughter.

Literary predilections are telltales of character,
and for this reason we may collect George Eliot's.
She calls Milton her demigod, and we see in this a
soul inclined towards things serious and sublime.
In the same way, Wordsworth ranks high in her
affections. Yet this does not prevent her from

adoring Molière, "our great favorite," she writes. "We are not reading him just now, but we are constantly talking of him. The 'Misanthrope' seems to me the greatest and most complete production of its kind in existence." On the other hand, she holds Byron "the most vulgar-minded genius who has ever produced a great effect in literature." Nor let us forget her admiration for the works of Comte, which was sincere, though the expression of it was perhaps exaggerated by the desire of pleasing her friends Mr. Congreve and Mr. Harrison, who evidently wished to make a convert of her. In writing to others, she confessed that Positivism seemed to her narrow and exclusive; while, as for the religion which was grafted on Comte's philosophy, she subscribed to the scheme, but avoided becoming a member.

We have already seen that one distinguishing point of George Eliot's mind was a very rare combination of intellectual boldness and religious sensibility. She was absolutely honest in examination, and to her all questions were open questions. "You ask if I am ready to allow myself to be convinced. Most certainly; I admit discussion on every matter except dinner and debts. I hold that the first must be eaten and the second must be paid: these are my only prejudices." But this rationalizing temperament did not exclude a certain mysticism of the kind which, according to herself, belongs to all poetic souls, "the delight with which the soul bathes in emotions exceeding the precision of thought."

She felt sympathy for all the great historical religions, especially Judaism and Christianity, as monuments of struggles similar to our own. If she had followed her inclination she would often have gone into those religious assemblies, the essence of which is the recognition of a spiritual law, appealing to our voluntary obedience and ready to deliver us from the tyranny of capricious impulses and untamed passions. It is true that when she has got as far as this rationalism reappears and resumes the upper hand. What is it that these believers who meet to worship God worship under that name? What but the loftiest possible conception of good? So far is it, according to our author, from being true that morality derives from religion, that the religious idea *par excellence*, the idea of God, merely personifies the moral idea of some nation or some time. This is why theology transforms itself, why religions succeed each other in proportion as humanity perfects itself. And this perfectibility of religions is a thesis big with consequences. For if we give to the notion of the Supreme Being a connotation so variable and so extensive as that of moral emotion, we come to the identification of God with humanity, to making piety consist in reflecting tenderly on the mystery of mortal fate, to reducing the science of life to two elements only, commiseration for the fate of other men, and for ourselves, "that consent to the inevitable which submits to it without bitterness and is called resignation."

Unsubstantial as George Eliot's religion may seem, nothing made further breach in it. She remained persuaded that if human actions do not escape the universal chain of cause and effect, this character of necessity does not affect their moral quality, does not diminish their ugliness or their beauty, and consequently cannot weaken our motives for preferring one to another. Besides, one last link continued to attach George Eliot to mystical tradition, and to that idealist and romantic period of humanity which contemporary naturalism is at work to destroy. She had read Darwin's works with interest; but she does not seem to have grasped or to have accepted their whole bearing. She saw in them only the idea of evolution. "Now," says she, "this theory, like all the other explanations of the way in which things have come into existence, affects me little as compared with the mystery which is at the bottom of existence itself." And so behind the fact she looks for something else than the fact; she raises the questions which cannot be answered; she is of those who, as Schiller says,[1] want to know why ten is not twelve.

George Eliot cannot be ranked among modern adepts in pessimism. She does not look on life as bad in itself — she is only, as it were, oppressed with the difficulties of the struggle, with the uglinesses and the sufferings of humanity. She was disposed to believe with the ancients that those are

[1] *Die Weltweisen.*

happiest who die young ; and, as we have just seen, she brought herself to place the highest virtue in resignation, or, as she also calls it, "the courage which can do without narcotics, the fortitude which supports evils with full consciousness of them, and with eyes wide open." This want of trust in human destiny is such that George Eliot will not yield to the ideas of social progress which have seized so tyrannously on the modern spirit; she is too thoroughly persuaded that happiness is above all a moral state to expect much of institutions; and improvement seems to her likely to be less the necessary effect of intellectual culture than the fruit of a slow contagion of good.

If I insist on the kind of pitifulness with which George Eliot considers our earthly state, it is because this disposition is what in reality constitutes the main principle of her art. All great wit draws inspiration from some philosophy or other, and the philosophy of George Eliot is a gently sad one. There reigns in it what Wordsworth, in a beautiful line, calls

The still, sad music of humanity,

the melancholy note which human destiny gives out. She does not aspire to paint irreproachable characters, but characters in which good and evil are mixed, which call for indulgence, for which we feel attachment even while we condemn them. To speak more correctly, she does not aspire to anything; she does not pursue any end; she is too great an artist for that. With her serious and moral nature she ran the risk of becoming a moralizer; with her sympathy for the faults and the foibles of her kind, inclination must have carried her towards the didactic. But she knows the danger, and remains on her guard against it. If art, she thinks, has its lessons, they are the lessons of life itself, which art reproduces in its truth and its complexity. "When it ceases to be purely æsthetic, when it tries to prove instead of painting, it becomes the most disgusting of all teachings." And in a remarkable letter written to the painter Burne-Jones: —

Don't you agree with me that much superfluous stuff is written on all sides about purpose in art? A nasty mind makes nasty art, whether for art or any other sake; and a meagre mind will bring forth what is meagre. And some effect in determining other minds there must be, according to the degree of nobleness or meanness in the selection made by the artist's soul.

It was not with her ethics that George Eliot wrote her novels, it was with her psychology; and in this lies the secret of her power. This woman, who lived an exemplary life in a narrow world, had entered into all things, had felt all things. Nothing astonished her, accustomed as she was to read her own heart, and gifted with the faculty of observation, which helps one to read the hearts of others. She is at home with the most secret and the subtlest entanglements of motives. She knows that "a na-

ture incapable by virtue of its whole moral consti-
tution of committing a crime may yet experience
criminal motives." I find this striking expression
from her pen: "In the most absolute confidence of
man and wife there is always a residue of secrecy,
an unsuspected lower depth: it may be of the worst,
it may be, on the other hand, of the loftiest and
most disinterested." George Eliot possesses the
clairvoyance which divines the interior play of passion, the experience which knows that the human
being is capable of all contradictions, the indulgence which tolerates because it understands; and
lastly, the gift of measure and the taste for truth
which prevent an author from rushing into ex-
tremes, from idealizing either the beautiful or the
ugly, from making figures which are heroes or mon-
sters in block. If we add to psychological divina-
tion the faculty of creating living characters, we
shall have George Eliot's novel. When she was
still very young — in 1848 — she defined the talent
of which she was later to give such memorable
examples. "Artistic power," she said, "seems to
me to resemble dramatic power; it is the intuition
of the different states of which the human mind
is capable of taking, accompanied by the faculty
of reproducing them with a certain intensity of
expression."

The dramatic art in George Eliot's works comes
from her living conception of personages. The
strength with which the moral coherence of the

beings she has called into existence and the conduct of a story determined by the development of these characters impose themselves on her is so great that she forfeits the freedom with which authors usually control their work. She was unable to make any change in it. The intuition to which she sought to give body and life took such complete possession of her that she seemed to become a mere instrument and to obey a superior force. There is in "Middlemarch" a famous scene — an explanation between two women — which forms one of the turning points of the novel. George Eliot used to tell how the scene was done. She knew that the two characters must meet sooner or later, and that there would then be an explosion; but she had avoided thinking of it up to the moment when she had to bring them face to face. And then, giving herself up to the inspiration of the moment, she wrote the narrative as we have it now, without a change, without a cancel, in an extraordinary state of agitation, and, as it were, entirely dominated by the sentiments which she had to express. Her pen galloped, not as a result of haste or desire to have done, but because the hand which held it obeyed an emotion. "Writing," said George Eliot, "is to me a kind of religion, and I cannot trace a word unless it comes from within." Yet she did not wish to hold herself out as a pattern, for she added, "But I think that the best books in existence have all been written simply to make money."

The truth is that the inspiration under the sway of which George Eliot worked must not be confused with the purely subjective and personal ardor of the novelist who lends to his characters the passions which he himself feels. She was rather of the opinion of Diderot, who asserted that the great actor remains master of himself, and calculates by reflection the manner in which he ought to read a character or a situation.[1] The emotion which she felt when writing was that of the very personages whom she put on the stage, and into whom she transformed herself. Her soul was engaged in the game; she palpitated, yet not on her own account, if I may say so; she palpitated in harmony with the diverse sentiments which the situation brought about. The author, by dint of her psychological penetration and her power of sympathy, identified herself by turns with the most diverse situations, with the most contrary passions. And it is in this sense only — it is because she thus blended herself with her creations, and devoted all the warmth of her nature to their complete realization, that she may be said to have written with her soul.

It seems to me that we have now before us almost all the elements of George Eliot's talent — conscientious research and mature reflection in the preparation of work; the depth of moral intuition which creates true and coherent character; the interest of an action which starts from these pri-

---

[1] [In his famous *Paradoxe sur le Comédien.* — *Trans.*]

mary conceptions; the dramatic force which results from the combined suppleness and vivacity
of sentiment with which the author takes up the
part of her different characters; and, lastly, the
sincerity of an artist passionately in love with
truth. But I am wrong, for, indeed, to make this
analysis complete, we must add dramatic incident,
picturesque description, and those two great faculties which seem mutually exclusive, and which are
here at once combined and carried to an extraordinary pitch of power — the pathos which draws
tears from the driest eyes, and the most abundant,
the most amusing, the most original comedy.

It is a union of these two conditions of art, the
fusion of the elements in the flame of the sacred
fire, which assures to George Eliot so high a place
as a novelist, and among the highest class of novelists.   There are illustrious types in the telling of
tales, such as Defoe, Alexandre Dumas, and Dickens; in the painting of manners, such as Balzac
and Thackeray; in the eloquent delineation of passions, such as Rousseau and George Sand; while
there has been founded in our days, not without
some success, a new school, which subordinates
everything else to elaborate skill of description.
But is it not true that the highest power in any art
is that which creates personages so lively, true,
and individual that we carry away with us an indel-
ible memory of them just as if we had met them
in the paths of daily life?   Is it not true that here

lies the chief gift of superior genius, the most substantial enrichment of a literature? I only know one of the novelist's gifts which is wanting to George Eliot. You must not look in her pages for the troubles, the excitements, the disorders of love. She could neither have written the "Nouvelle Héloïse" nor "Dominique." A woman cannot sketch a man's passions, because she cannot feel them; and as for painting those of her own sex, she would have to begin by unsexing herself to dare to take the public into confidence as to the last secrets of the feminine heart. Women may write novels — novels better than those of men, but not the same. Genius in their hands meets with, "Thus far and no farther."

A good deal has been said about realism in connection with George Eliot's novels. Indeed, M. Montégut's article, which has been referred to above, bore as its general title "On the Realist Novel in England." And it is true enough that our author's talent is distinguished by a certain fancy for painting common life, even commonplace life, and by the truth with which the details of this painting are followed out. "The Mill on the Floss" could, in this respect, but strengthen the impressions which "Adam Bede" had left. "Romola," on the other hand, and "Middlemarch" are there to show that the author was not absolutely condemned to the minutiæ of Dutch painting. Besides it is but an awkward word, this term of realism, which gives those who use it the air of setting against each other things which are different, but not contrary — the admiration inspired by the beautiful and the interest aroused by the true. The beautiful is nature selected, magnified, generalized; the true is the same nature seen as close as possible, with every feature of its physiognomy, every detail of character, revealed by an observation which has set its heart on being exact. Hence the human mind has two simultaneous and legitimate enjoyments — the delight which the soul feels in suppressing time, extending space, opening glimpses of the infinite, and the kind of fascination which is exercised on us by nature, thanks to her unexpectedness, her sovereignty, her very unreason, the impossibility which we feel in the attempt to bring her all under the law of our thoughts. There is nothing here that is great or small, beautiful or ugly. It is the fact *qua* fact which disturbs or attracts us, and we are grateful to the artist who, by dint of his truthfulness, acquaints us with new aspects of things.

George Eliot's style is not irreproachable. It becomes, as has been observed, artificial by dint of wish to avoid the commonplace, and stiff by dint of condensation of thought. Happily she has divided herself in her novels, keeping clearness in her narrative and naturalness in her dialogue, and reserving loaded phrase and abstract terminology for her reflections. The faults of her didactic style are, as it were, aggravated and crowded together in the last work she published, certain "Characters," after the fashion of Theophrastus and La Bruyère, a volume without grace and without taste, absolutely out of place in the total of her work. The finest and most perfect genius not only ·has its limits, but its hidden vices; the purest metal has its alloy. "Felix Holt" is weak, the Jewish story in "Daniel Deronda" spoilt a novel which gave promise of yielding to none of its forerunners, and "Theophrastus Such" is simply unreadable. Everything else, novel or short story, is a pure masterpiece, and, as is proper to masterpieces, leaves nothing to desire, and nothing to regret. The name of Shakespeare has sometimes been uttered in speaking of George Eliot, an hyperbole which ceases to be shocking if we limit the terms of comparison to the creation of characters. But I had rather indorse, though here also with the necessary distinctions, the judgment of Lord Acton, that George Eliot is the most considerable literary personality that has appeared since the death of Goethe.

March 1885.